The
Colonization
of Literacy
Education

Studies in the
Postmodern Theory of Education

Joe L. Kincheloe and Shirley R. Steinberg
General Editors

Vol. 266

PETER LANG
New York • Washington, D.C./Baltimore • Bern
Frankfurt am Main • Berlin • Brussels • Vienna • Oxford

Julie L. Pennington

The Colonization of Literacy Education

A Story of Reading in One Elementary School

PETER LANG
New York • Washington, D.C./Baltimore • Bern
Frankfurt am Main • Berlin • Brussels • Vienna • Oxford

Library of Congress Cataloging-in-Publication Data

Pennington, Julie L.
The colonization of literacy education: a story of reading in one elementary school /
Julie L. Pennington.
p. cm. — (Counterpoints; v. 266)
Includes bibliographical references.
1. Reading (Elementary)—Social aspects—Texas—Austin—Case studies.
2. Mexican Americans—Education—Texas—Austin—Case studies.
3. Reading teachers—Texas—Austin—Attitudes—Case studies.
4. Elena Elementary School (Austin, Tex.)—Case studies.
I. Title. II. Series: Counterpoints (New York, N.Y.); v. 226.
LB1573.P536   372.4—dc22   2004014125
ISBN 0-8204-6925-4
ISSN 1058-1634

Bibliographic information published by **Die Deutsche Bibliothek**.
Die Deutsche Bibliothek lists this publication in the "Deutsche
Nationalbibliografie"; detailed bibliographic data is available
on the Internet at http://dnb.ddb.de/.

Cover design by Joni Holst

© 2004 Peter Lang Publishing, Inc., New York
275 Seventh Avenue, 28th Floor, New York, NY 10001
www.peterlangusa.com

Printed in the United States of America

CONTENTS

ACKNOWLEDGMENTS

Everything is made possible only through trying, and this book would never have been attempted without the many people who encouraged me to try. They touched my life and are threaded throughout every page. I have had several families throughout the years, and the convergence of all of them within the text was never clearer to me than when I wrote the final chapter late one night.

I would like to thank my family. My father Edward, who thinks I can do anything, and encouraged me—a very mediocre student—to try graduate school in the first place; my mother Mary, who taught me always to speak my mind; my sister Sandy, who listened to my various ramblings and actually read drafts while juggling a family and a new job; and my nephew David, who baked cookies with me when things got tough.

This book was also made possible because of friendships that molded me in ways I could never fully express. To my friends Barbara and Laura, who gave me the idea to become a teacher in the first place I say thank you. I also must thank Rachel for encouraging me to apply to graduate school and being a pillar of strength for me. I also have to thank Marg, Sherry, and Kathryn for all of the late-night conversations, the editing of papers, and the unwavering support that continues today.

My acknowledgments would not be complete without thanking my university family—the professors who challenged, guided, and gave me a chance throughout my almost 20-year career at the University of Texas, Austin. I thank Judith Lindfors, the first professor I encountered as an undergraduate who held my attention through her compelling research; James Hoffman, who encouraged me in my early years as a graduate student; Jo Worthy, who brought research directly into my teaching; Lisa Goldstein, who introduced to me writing with my heart; Henry Trueba, who brought his ferocious intellect to my coursework and challenged my development; Douglas Foley, who encouraged me to follow my experiences at Elena; and James Scheurich, who irrevocably altered my views of the world, my research, and myself. And finally Colleen Fairbanks, the chair of my dissertation committee and my mentor, who encouraged me and supported me not only through her active involvement in my study and academic life but also through her daily examples of commitment to writing and scholarship. None of this work would be possible without her.

To my new family at the University of Nevada, Reno, I say thank you. Over a thousand miles from my beloved Texas, I feel at home. Cindy, Diane, Shane, and Donald welcomed me with open arms and allowed this Texan to speak openly, and for that I am grateful. I thank my WIRED writing group, Kathy, Tammy, Ann, Kim, Lynda, Bob, Elavie, Elza, Rod, and Shanon for providing a forum for all of us junior faculty to indulge in chocolate while changing the world through our discourses put to paper.

Finally, I thank the children, the parents, and the teachers of Elena Elementary. From the moment I arrived there in 1987 to the day I left in 2002, I was blessed with the opportunity to work in an environment dedicated to children. Spending my years as a teacher in such a school has been everything to me, and I know that the lessons I learned at Elena will remain. That all children can learn and all teachers can teach is what I take from my years there.

I would like to thank The Guilford Press for their permission to use Pennington, J. L. (2003). Teaching interrupted: High stakes testing in an inner city elementary school. In Boyd, F.B., Brock, C.H., & Rozendal, M.S. Eds. *Multicultural and multilingual literacy and language practices: Constructing contexts for empowerment.* New York: Guilford Publications.

·1·

THE FIGURED WORLDS OF
SCHOOLS AND STANDARDS
THE FIGURED WORLD OF
ELENA ELEMENTARY

*Elena students will be empowered with the confidence, knowledge and cultural pride
to succeed in their academic, personal and social lives.*

This mission statement for Elena Elementary was created by teachers in the early 1990s to guide and direct the education and development of the children who attended the school. The notion of confidence and cultural pride in all aspects of the children's lives was a consistent focus of the staff at Elena when I arrived in 1987. By 2001, the goals of the campus remained the same on paper, but there were significant changes in the philosophy of the teachers and administrators. My intent is to explore the literacy definitions and goals of the educators at Elena. In order to paint a picture of the complexity of literacy education at Elena, I will contextualize the literacy views of the teachers through comparisons to the views of administrators in the school district and the policies of the state of Texas. I will also reference the practices of literacy instruction in 2001 to the literacy practices and policies the school enacted throughout the early 1990s.

Elena was located in a Latina community located on the east side of Austin, Texas. It is where I student taught in 1987. It is where I still taught fourteen years later. The city was somewhat segregated, and the east side consisted of inner-city neighborhoods separated from the rest of the city by an interstate highway.

This is a part of East Austin that most outsiders don't know . . . this is a unique place, a mishmash of dumpy houses with littered yards and historic homes and beautifully landscaped bungalows with La Virgen de Guadalupe fountains in the front yards. It's one big neighborhood that houses two communities. The Mexicanos, or the immigrants from Mexico, and the American-born Latinos—Mexicans call them Chicanos—respectfully stay out of each other's way . . . It's been that way since the 1940's. (Gandara, 2000, p. A14)

There was a strength and pride in the community of Elena that included frequent interaction between the teachers and the neighborhood. Many children who attended elementary school there were the children of former students, and from the moment you walked onto campus you could see that the school reflected the community that sustained it. Spanish was frequently heard in the halls, and all of the bulletin boards were in Spanish and English. Most of the artwork displayed in the school mirrored the art in the community. The year I arrived, 1987, the school building began to crumble, and I witnessed the fast and effective workings of the community and teachers as they approached the school board to fight together for a new building for the children. Eight years later, the children of Elena attended school in a beautiful mission-style facility decorated with colorful ceramic tiles of student artwork, a courtyard complete with benches, a peace garden, and various other gardening projects. From the first moment I entered, I knew this was a loved school and a haven for teachers and children. The laughter of children, teachers, and parents echoed throughout the day, and community holidays such as Día de los Muertos and Cinco de Mayo were celebrated regularly.

The Student Population of Elena Elementary

Elena Elementary served pre-kindergarten through sixth grade children. Elena's attendance area had recently shifted to include children bused in from a school across the river, altering the population somewhat. For the most part, however, the school served neighborhood children within walking distance of the grounds. The socio-economic status of the families varied; many of the children received free or reduced lunch services, and Elena received Title I funding. Eighty-one percent of the families were classified as economically disadvantaged. In 2001, the school had approximately 631 students and had recently completed a five-year implementation of a Dual Language program that ensured all children received both English and Spanish instruction and focused on graduating biliterate sixth graders. Bilingual education had a strong history at Elena, since 38 percent of the children of Elena were classified as limited English-proficient. Ninety-three percent of the students were Latina.

TABLE 1. Student Population by Ethnicity

Ethnicity of Students	Elena	Texas State Average
African American	3%	14%
American Indian	1%	0%
Asian	1%	3%
Hispanic	93%	41%
White	2%	42%

Although Elena's students were of primary importance, this study focused tightly on the educators of Elena Elementary. Teachers, administrators, and policy makers controlled the lives of the children within the school's walls. Understanding the breadth, depth, and the power of how literacy is defined requires delving into the knowledge and beliefs of those defining and structuring the children's literacy experiences.

Four Walls and a Teacher:
The Figured World of the Teachers at Elena

[Katia, a fourth-grade teacher at Elena:] Challenging—to me [the students] are very challenging. I had to get this mentality in my head, my husband helped me with that, because I spent many sleepless nights at the beginning [of the year]. You can only control what happens in those four walls. Anything that happens outside of that, you have absolutely no control of it. You have to deal with it and just forget about it. You can only control and make a difference inside those four walls.

Illustrating ways in which a collision between the world of one elementary school and the world of state standards subjugated one beneath the other requires an understanding of the figured worlds of each. Just as the teachers of Elena held particular views and ways of interpreting and understanding the world of the school, policy makers also participated in a figured world of their own. Holland and her colleagues use anthropological, psychological, and social science theory to explain the complexity of the idea of identities within the self (Holland et al., 1998). Theoretically, she and her colleagues combine research from Vygotsky, Bakhtin, and others to frame a typology for identity within what they name "figured worlds." I propose to use their notion of figured worlds to frame the intersection between the worlds of policy and one elementary school in Texas. According to Holland et al. (1998), figured worlds is a complicated but noteworthy view of relating the interactions and meanings of individuals within communities.

By "figured world" then, we mean a socially and culturally constructed realm of interpretation in which particular characters and actors are recognized, significance is assigned to certain acts, and particular outcomes are valued over others . . . The production and reproduction of figured worlds involves both abstraction of significant regularities from everyday life into expectations about how particular types of events unfold and interpretations of the everyday according to these distillations of past experiences. (p. 53)

Although I refer to Elena as a clearly defined figured world at times, I will also bring in views outside the four walls of Elena to illustrate how the influence of the figured worlds of the city, state, and nation affected the teachers' views and daily lives within the four walls of the school. Holland et al. (1998) describe a few basic premises of figured worlds that are applicable in viewing teachers at Elena as they related to the policies of the state of Texas:

- "Figured worlds *happen,* as social process and in historical time" (p. 55).
- "The very multiplicity and partiality of [figured worlds] . . . hedge the interpretations of action" (p. 56).
- "Figured worlds are encountered in day-to-day social activity" (p. 56).
- Figured worlds can be viewed as "communities of practice" that utilize the idea of "situated learning," whereby identities become outcomes of taking part in activities structured by the figured worlds (p. 56).
- Figured worlds are subject to what Bourdieu (in Holland et al., 1998) defines as a field, "a separate social universe having its own laws of functioning independent of those of politics and the economy" (p. 58).
- "Figured worlds rely on artifacts" (p. 60). "To attend to the materiality of cultural artifacts is also to recognize the force of their use in practices—practices responsive to changing historical circumstances" (p. 63).
- Figured worlds can use artifacts as "tools of liberation" to affect the environment, others, and ourselves (p. 63).

Overall, Holland et al. (1998) suggest that figured worlds are communities in various shapes and forms that provide some predictable order to the human behavior within them. Therefore, the figured world of Elena was encased within the four walls of the school: the community of the school, the heartbeats of those who walk within its walls, the teachers and how they continually construct visions of their roles, and the character of their students. All teachers were individuals, but there was an overriding sense of a larger shared identity: to some degree, all who walked inside the school possessed similar traits. They were a culture unto themselves, in a way, and being a part of the culture of Elena affected their identities as teachers. Holland et al.'s (1998) assumptions can be applied to teachers at Elena to describe the figured worlds of a school where socially constructed fields are school practices and artifacts such as assessments and textbooks had the power to change the direction of teaching and ultimately teachers and children. I will continually refer to the figured world of Elena as a way to explore more specific areas throughout the study. One aspect of the figured world of Elena was teacher population; the teacher population at Elena in the spring of 2001 is shown in Table 2.

Those who taught at Elena viewed the school from individual perspectives and yet adhered to a few common ideas about navigating the teaching environment. Holland et al. (1998) propose that identities may result from participating in activities experienced by the inhabitants of the figured world. "Identity is a concept that figuratively combines the intimate or personal world with the collective space of cultural forms and social relations . . . Identities are lived in and through activity and so must be conceptualized as they develop in social practice" (p. 5). One shared view among the teachers was the notion of commitment and dedication. They acknowledged that this was not an easy school to teach in, and teaching took more effort and knowledge than other schools.

[Caroline, a fifth-grade teacher:] The teachers at this school like myself . . . don't necessarily have a husband that goes out and supports us. This is not something that we do just to do something—[it is not] our charity case. This is something that we do because we're dedicated . . . We are concerned with what's going on. I think that there are a lot of teachers [in other schools]. . .They weren't concerned with what was going on and all the different [district] regulations and all the different things that were happening to teachers that I didn't necessarily feel were fair or the things that were happening in the classrooms that didn't seem particularly fair. What difference does it make to them? It's over at the end of the day when they go home at 3 o'clock.

[Dolores, a third-grade teacher:] It's so different [at Elena] and my family is [always asking] why are you so tired? You know they know other teachers and they don't look like you. [laughs] They don't sound like you. Why are you so tired?

TABLE 2. Teacher Population by Ethnicity

Ethnicity of the Teachers	Elena	State Average
African American	0%	9%
American Indian	0%	0%
Asian	2%	1%
Hispanic	50%	17%
White	48%	73%

There's a big difference. I don't think they—I don't know if people realize it. But, I did want out this year. Part of it was the stress of Elena, it is hard. A lot of it is TAAS [Texas Assessment of Academic Skills] stress . . . who wants to be a good TAAS teacher? I want to be a good teacher. Let me be a good teacher. I'll be happy.

Along with the idea that teaching at Elena required dedication, the teachers also related their thoughts about the importance of being educated themselves. This illustrated Holland et al.'s (1998) idea of figured worlds as "communities of practice" that utilize the idea of "situated learning," whereby identities become the outcomes of taking part in activities structured by the figured worlds. Since the teachers at Elena had a history of extensive literacy training, they shared a common knowledge base and were organized around the literacy training philosophies and formed a type of "situated learning." They were members of a specific "community of practice." As a campus, the school was ahead of most of the school district's training and held elevated standards for teacher knowledge and student success. This resulted in highly educated teachers, and this affected their descriptions of their views of teaching there. One teacher, Dolores, summed up her feelings about her literacy knowledge during our first interview by stating, "I already know that my answers are right." Penny, a reading specialist/special education teacher, shared her feelings that Elena provided a very strong, supportive base for her as a teacher:

My belief is that your school is only as strong as the people that are in it and if we're not strong, if we're not together, if we're up in arms you might as well forget doing home visits or literacy night . . . Now with my masters [degree] I could easily go other places. I can't leave what I've built here because building it was so hard. [Teaching here] never seemed hard to me. I've been very supported with friends and faculty [and] I can go and say, let's work together on it . . . I feel like an effective teacher here. I feel like I've been very effective with my students. I wonder if we'd be ineffective in a White school. I go to St. Bart's and I don't know what to do. I'm having the worst luck with some of these kids because I'm [wondering], why are you here? You're fine. You're an at-risk reader and you're reading this? Or you're going into fourth grade and reading [at an eighth-grade level] right now? I don't even know what to tell you.

Penny's thoughts revealed her ideas that Elena was difficult, but she was up to the task. She was highly invested in the school and the children. Penny also explained that her perceptions of the children at other schools such as St. Bart's, a local private school, were that children at those schools thought to be in need of reading interventions were really not in need at all. Her experiences with schools outside of Elena left her feeling that those children did not need help when compared to the children at Elena. Many teachers shared the view that Elena required more teaching knowledge, and most teachers felt that Elena teachers met that requirement and were highly dedicated and educated. Caroline thought that Elena was difficult and not "an easy ride." She compared Elena to her experience as a student and felt that Elena teachers were much more prepared to meet the needs of the students than her teachers had been.

> [Caroline:] The teachers I know are very well read. First of all, they're very aware of what's going on around them not just in their environment but in their world. They keep up with current events, they visit places, they travel, and they experience things. They're not just . . . the coaches at my school who taught me social studies that were stuck with who's going to play football tonight and who is going to win the game. This isn't the type of school you would go to if you want an easy ride. If you want to have an easy go at it and want all of your kids passing the TAAS test then go work at a school where the kids are doing that already. These aren't those kids so you have to be more involved in it then.

Caroline explained the need for teachers at Elena to be more involved in the children's education than teachers at other schools might be. Holland et al.'s (1998) concept of "situated learning" as a component of the figured world of Elena can be applied to how the literacy and bilingual knowledge of the teachers affected their identities and goals as teachers there. "Situated learning" in communities of figured worlds can have an effect on the identities of those taking part in the activities organized within the figured world by influencing their beliefs through practices. The trainings and focus in the hiring of teachers at Elena historically centered around a specific view of literacy and bilingual education, which subsequently moved the teachers' and administrators' goals and attitudes in directions congruent with the view of reading instruction encased within high expectations and a knowledge of English Language Learners. As a "community of practice" (Holland et al., 1998), Elena had a commitment to specific ideas. These ideas are evident in Illeana's (an administrator) description of what administrators looked for as they screened prospective teachers. During interviews, they took time to find out if applicants were well versed in the types of literacy practices the Elena community of teachers valued. There was a definite search for candidates who would fit into the teaching community with its high expectations.

> [Illeana:] When we interview, some of the questions we do ask are: Are you willing to get your English as a Second Language certification? We don't say you have to, but are you willing to do it if hired? Would you be willing? We at least get a commitment. We also ask about guided reading. Tell us what you know about guided reading and we really try to expand on that so that they understand

what they are getting into. We also ask about assessment. Do you know how to do a running record? So we are real specific about the reading portion. Some are, some aren't. I'm surprised that some have never heard of Reading Recovery. Part of that is also our job as administrators. When people come in, we need to really make sure that they understand that they have to have high expectations that the kids can do it. The high expectation is not going to do it—you also have to give the support and the guidance it takes. I think when we interview, that's what we try to get to. What does the teacher really believe and sometimes it's hard to get a genuine answer.

No matter the difficulties expressed, all of the participating teachers felt the same way when "push came to shove." "Elena is where my heart is," stated Dolores as we ended our last interview. She had acknowledged the challenges of teaching there, but she felt that in the end it was worth it. Every teacher I spoke to felt drawn to teach at Elena, and all expressed great love for the children, while at the same time referring consistently to difficulties they encountered.

A total of eight teachers participated in the study. Six were currently teaching in the classroom, and two were in administrative positions. Four of the teachers were Latina, and the other four were White. They ranged in experience from twenty years to two years. Two of the participants had taught at Elena for over fourteen years, and two had taught there for only two years. Six of the teachers were parents themselves. Five of the participants had either degrees in literacy at the master's level or extensive training outside of the district in literacy and were classified as literacy specialists by the district.[1]

I began with the view that the teachers at Elena were members of a "figured world," constructed by the common experiences of teaching at Elena. Holland et al.'s (1998) definitions of a socio-cultural view of identity is used to examine teachers' formation of their teaching identities, their navigation of their teaching lives, and their construction of the children by way of their own identities and their subjection to policy mandates. Beginning there, I will continue to deconstruct and open up the teachers' multiple identities to reveal how deconstruction can allow us to see, within the figured world of Elena, how teachers construct the children they teach.

Teacher Identities within Figured Worlds

Seemingly contradictory to the design of figured worlds is the concept of multiple and individual identities. Even as teachers reside in the common worlds of schools, which rely on synchronized movements for smooth travel, their identities within the figured worlds remain to varying degrees elusive and unbounded. Individuals may still hold unique positions and adapt according to contextual factors. Blumenthal (1999) writes of how individuals consist of multiple identities. She states: "As we relate to different people, we collect identities" (p. 383). Teachers' identities are complex in that they are situated in schools but formed in many ways outside the walls of the classroom. Blumenthal (1999) asks about the possibility of groups of people sharing a common identity and finds this form of essentializing individuals into groups impossible. Thus she formulates an alternative view:

> To characterize shared identities as inhabiting the Self. I do not inhabit an identity, but an identity inhabits me. Viewing identity in this way, we could say that the community that shares an identity is a collective consciousness, in a sense, and inquire about contradictions within and across the conceptualizations of identity within the community as if it were a single individual. (p. 389)

Therefore, as teachers remained bound to the common identity they shared as teachers at Elena, they also contradicted and created new individual interpretations of their own teacher identities. In other words, to a degree, teachers vacillated between their identities as teachers, parents, members of various social classes, and ethnic groups. Clandinin and Connelly (1995b) pay heed to teachers' "landscapes" of life. They describe how teachers' knowledge is mediated by their life both inside and outside of the classroom. They recognize that teachers' experiences in the classroom are affected by their lives outside of the classroom. Most teacher research has tended to look at how teaching is enacted within the classroom walls (Cochran-Smith & Lytle, 1993). Clandinin and Connelly (1995b) illustrate how teachers journey between both worlds, bringing and allowing what they deem to be the relevant aspects of their identities to light in each world.

While the concept of figured worlds allowed me to identify common traits and themes across the staff, I also used identity theory to view teachers as individuals constructed by their lives outside of the figured world of schools. Regardless of the positioning of all of the participants as teachers, their conversations with me revealed the complex nature of how their identities shaped their views of the children and families of Elena.

> People tell others who they are, but even more important, they tell themselves and then try to act as though they are who they say they are. These self-understandings, especially those with strong emotional resonance for the teller, are what we refer to as identities. (Holland et al., 1998, p. 3)

The teachers' identities became a compelling means of mediating their understanding of their teaching and their constructions of the children of Elena. Each teacher at Elena played various roles and utilized various aspects of their lives in order to do so. This underlying sense of self, both conscious and unconscious, served to guide the teachers' perceptions of their mission as teachers in relation to the children's needs. In the late 1980s to the late 1990s, the teachers of Elena identified with the children and articulated the possibilities of fulfilling the school's mission of seeking to ensure that all of the children would be successful through becoming "empowered with the confidence, knowledge, and cultural pride to succeed in their academic, personal, and social lives." By 2001, the community of educators at Elena had altered their perceptions of the children; the influence of figured worlds outside of Elena could be seen in the teachers' views of the children.

Outsiders' Conceptions of the Children at Elena as At-Risk

Just as Holland et al. (1998) posit that figured worlds are communities in various shapes and forms that provide some predictable order to the human behavior within them, there is the implied notion that not all figured worlds are the same. While Elena's community held to its mission, outside views from other populations filtered in at several junctures. The first formal incident occurred in 1994. Because of the school district's definitions of what constitutes an "at-risk" school, Elena had always been a "watched" school. Almost all schools that existed on the east side of the city were subject to similar classifications. Elena was considered a high poverty school, a "minority" school with a 93 percent Latina population, which meant that Elena received assistance from the school district and the state because of this status. Elena's children and their parents had a long history of being labeled "at-risk" by those outside of the community:

> According to the *Austin American-Statesman* in late January and early February of 1994, the Austin Independent School District—attempting to comply with state regulations that require parents be notified if they have an at-risk student—sent home 33,450 notices informing parents their children were prime dropout candidates (Lott, 1994a). The 33,000-plus notices, which were sent to 17,000 elementary and 16,450 secondary school students, comprised 46 percent of the total 72,000 AISD [Austin Independent School District] student enrollment . . . [O]n February 10, 1994, a group of parents of Elena Elementary School (approximately a 95 percent Mexican American school) organized and held a meeting at a community center in East Austin. (Valencia & Solorzana, 1997, p. 198)

Almost all Elena parents received letters from school district officials notifying them that their children were classified as at-risk by the state government. The primary indicator was the classification of the students as being Spanish-speaking. Parents and teachers quickly rallied and held a meeting with district officials. The result of this meeting was an apology from the superintendent and an assurance not to repeat the mistake of classifying students according to such criteria. The parents and teachers had gathered together to denounce the school district's view of their children as dropout candidates. The community and the teachers fought for the right to view the children through their potential rather than their deficits. Most of the discourse involving the community of Elena that came from outside of the school and the community was filled with the idea that these children were not going to be successful in school. Yet inside the school's walls there was a unique standard of expectation that every child at Elena was capable of learning. The educators of Elena fought the deficit classifications of their students, at times risking their jobs as they reproached upper-level administrators. During the first few years I taught at Elena, I began to understand the "bunker" mentality of the teachers as they strove to hold on to the school's notion that "all children could learn" and "all teachers could teach." As the state government expanded its efforts in 1996 to continue to improve education, teachers witnessed the student population of Elena described and addressed more specifically every day. By 2001, the federal government's view of Elena's children read as follows:

- Hispanic children often don't attend school until they reach mandatory school age.
- They have the highest dropout rates of any group in the country—more than 27 percent of Hispanic students drop out.
- On the 2000 National Assessment of Educational Progress reading assessment, 40 percent of white fourth-graders scored at or above proficient, compared to only 16 percent of their Hispanic peers.
- In math, Hispanic achievement also lagged: 35 percent of white fourth-graders scored at or above proficient. Just 10 percent of Hispanics scored as high achievers.
- The racial achievement gap is real.
- Just 13 percent of Hispanic students get a college education.
  (http://www.nochildlftbehind.gov/start/facts/achievement_hisp.html)

These descriptors of Hispanic students were relevant to this study and to the school because of the ways in which the teachers, the state, and the federal government classified the children of Elena and targeted them when policy decisions were made. Throughout the study, I will share the views both of teachers in the school and entities outside of the school in order to show how these two sets of views eventually meshed into one clearly articulated philosophy about the literacy of the children.

The state of Texas had become subject to the 1996 Reading Initiative designed under the George W. Bush administration. The battle cry in 1996 began the push by policy makers to ensure that every child would be able to pass a reading exam by third grade. Met with little resistance, the reformation of literacy definitions, literacy instruction, and literacy assessment was overwhelming and complete by 2001.[2] The story of Elena Elementary begins here, at the end of the Texas Reading Initiative implementation and the beginning of the No Child Left Behind Act. Presenting the figured world of literacy policy, as framed within the Texas Reading Initiative and the No Child Left Behind Act, requires attention to the situated events and beliefs that provided foundations for the call of leaving no child behind. Charles Miller, the chairman of Governor Bush's Business Council, stated at the 1996 presummit meeting:

> I don't want to exaggerate, but I believe the Governor's Reading Initiative could be one of the most important steps towards improving Texas education that we've ever taken. However, it's going to take continued and sustained effort by a large part of the community in Texas to succeed. You could say we're in the beginning skirmishes of a major battle . . . (Taylor, 1998, p. 63)

The battle for guaranteeing that every child read by third grade was proclaimed throughout the state, and Elena Elementary participated in illustrating how setting standards for schools, teachers, and children is a double-edged sword.

Creating a World of Standards

> While race, gender, and class regularities are key to the social construction of the problem group, governmentality plays a critical role in the public identification of the group. The describing, numbering, and naming processes of governmentality (which includes policy processes) provide a description of the problem group that can be infinitely circulated in both academic media and the public media . . . the problem group is made "real." Consequently, the doctors of social diseases, professionals of all sorts including educators, social workers, health workers, and psychologists, are all called forth to treat the problem group with the chosen policy intervention. These professionals then use their "knowledge" (knowledge that is congruent with and reproductive of the social order) to adjust or transform the social group . . . The public performance of the treatment of the problem group by the professionals, even if it fails, as it typically does, satisfies society that it is doing its best. (Scheurich & Young, 1997, p. 108)

The responsibility of policy makers: identify and target the problem group within the context of an epidemic, provide a diagnosis and a cure, and circulate the results in such a fashion as to ensure that only the best efforts are applied to remedy the situation. Such is the case within the figured world of standards in schools. The policy world can be viewed as its own "community of practice" (Holland et al., 1998), removed from real classrooms and yet highly involved in issues directly related to the daily lives of teachers and children. Within this "community of practice," Holland et al.'s (1998) idea of situated knowledge rings true. Policy designers are not research experts or educational practitioners; they are in the business of setting forth assessments, declarations, and answers. Simplicity and measurable results are the "artifacts" of their figured world and the tools with which they "liberate" and affect the environment. In the case of schools, children and public opinion provide the environment and test scores the artifacts that guide decisions. There is a long history of setting standards for schools and defining what it means to educate a nation's children. Yet never before has policy so clearly set the standard before children, parents, and educators.

Dewey (1990), Bobbit (1918), Bruner (1959) and others in education have all sought to seek standards and pedagogical recommendations for schools. Yet the luxury for educational theorists lies in their ability to embrace complexity and ambiguity as they adjust their understanding of the varying needs children bring to classrooms. Today, educational theorists and practitioners can be outsiders in a figured world "whereby identities become outcomes" (Holland et al., p. 58). Policy makers are product-focused and have little use for the intricacies of more intellectual pursuits. The world of educational standards has gained momentum in the past twenty years. *A Nation at Risk* (1983) can be portrayed as the defining moment in the current standards movement, what Holland et al. (1998) might describe as "a cultural artifact" with the strength to develop "practices responsive to changing historical circumstances" (p. 63).

The release in 1983 of *A Nation at Risk* set the tone for what was to become the Texas Reading Initiative, the Reading Excellence Act, and ultimately the No Child Left Behind Act. *A Nation at Risk* (1983) provided what Scheurich & Young (1997) called "the description of the problem group that can be infinitely circulated in both academic media and the public media" (p. 108). The problem group set aside in *A Nation at Risk* was the educational system and its lack of attention to the dire needs of the country as a whole.

Our Nation is at risk. Our once unchallenged preeminence in commerce, industry, science, and technological innovation is being overtaken by competitors throughout the world. This report is concerned with only one of the many causes and dimensions of the problem, but it is the one that undergirds [sic] American prosperity, security, and civility. We report to the American people that while we can take justifiable pride in what our schools and colleges have historically accomplished and contributed to the United States and the well-being of its people, the educational foundations of our society are presently being eroded by a rising tide of mediocrity that threatens our very future as a Nation and a people. (1983, p. 1)

The language and ideology embedded in *A Nation at Risk* was a call to arms; the country was in danger and in need of reform. As Berliner & Biddle (1995) assert, "In many ways this report was the 'mother of all critiques' of American education . . . never before had criticism of education appeared" that

- was sponsored by a secretary of education in our national government;
- was prepared by such a prestigious committee;
- was endorsed by a president of the United States;
- made such explicit charges about a supposed recent, tragic decline of American education—charges said to be confirmed by both longitudinal and comparative studies;
- asserted that because of this putative decline of education the nation was losing its leadership in industry, science, and innovation;
- assigned blame for said decline to inadequacies in teaching programs and inept educators; and
- packaged its messages in such flamboyant prose (p. 139).

The National Commission on Excellence in Education's *A Nation at Risk* was powerful in the figured world of policy makers as it set up a challenge to improve the educational system, a challenge embedded within language closely tied to the patriotic duties of the citizenry, a challenge that could not go unattended.

The best term to characterize it may simply be the honorable word "patriotism." Citizens know intuitively what some of the best economists have shown in their research that education is one of the chief engines of a society's material well-being. They know, too, that education is the common bond of a pluralistic society and helps tie us to other cultures around the globe. Citizens also know in their bones that the safety of the United States depends principally on the wit, skill, and spirit of a self-confident people, today and tomorrow. (*A Nation at Risk*, 1993, p. 3)

The wave of reform led by *A Nation at Risk* in 1983 has held true to its push for change in the United States' educational system. The clear-cut identification of the cause, the educational system, and the request for higher standards and measurement through standardized testing remains threaded throughout the years 1983 to 2003. Chester Finn (1991) in *A Nation Still at Risk* described the perpetual need for an "alignment between the personnel needs of a changing economy and the typical products of our schools" (p. 18). Tying school success to patriotism, economic achievement, and the success of a modern democratic nation has been a running theme in the figured world of policy makers as they engage in the service of their country. The literacy of the nation has played a prominent role in the continuing call to arms of the standards movement.

Literacy and Testing for All

> Some 23 million American adults are functionally illiterate by the simplest tests of everyday reading, writing, and comprehension. (*A Nation at Risk*, 1983, p. 8)

While *A Nation at Risk* (1983) focused on the nation as a whole and touched many subject areas, the call for a literate citizenry was clear. The notion of literacy existing in a state of crisis is not new to educational circles or to the public at large. Reading education has a strong history of flowing in and out of a cyclical pattern. Nila Banton Smith described the United States' historical relationship with reading in 1965:

> The story of American reading instruction is a fascinating one to pursue . . . [I]t is a story which reflects the changing religious, economic, and political institutions of a growing and progressive country. It is a story shot through with glimpses of advancing psychologies, of broadening and more inclusive philosophies, of ever-increasing attempts to apply science to education. This evolutionary progress in reading has been marked by a series of emphases, each of which has been so fundamental in nature as to have controlled, to a large extent, both the method and the content of reading instruction . . . (1965, p. 1)

Smith's historical overview of reading instruction in America is revived in the standards movement of the twenty-first century. In the past, reading instruction had focused on nationalistic-moralistic concerns in the late eighteenth century, intelligent citizenship in the years beginning around 1840, reading as a cultural asset in the 1880s, and the first foray into the scientific investigation of reading in the early 1900s (1965). Although these periods in history are not classified as crises, they all came to be defined through national trends and mirror the ways in which the reading situation of today has grown to alter the future and history of reading instruction and research. Aligned with Smith's (1965) observation that many areas and movements serve to influence methods of reading instruction, Rudolf Flesch (1955) moved reading pedagogy into the public realm.

> The teaching of reading—all over the United States, in all the schools, in all the textbooks—is totally wrong and flies in the face of all logic and common sense. Johnny couldn't read until half a year ago for the simple reason that nobody ever showed him how. Johnny's only problem was that he was unfortunately exposed to an ordinary American school . . . Do you know that the teaching of reading never was a problem anywhere in the world until the United States switched to the present method around 1925? (p. 2)

Why Johnny Can't Read: And What You Can Do About It (Flesch, 1955) began a public dialogue about reading instruction through a letter to a parent. Scheurich & Young's (1997) notion of the problem group requiring circulation in the academic and public media applies here as well. Flesch's critique and subsequent recommendations for a specific type of reading instruction preceded what is known as "The Great Debate," the dispute regarding the need for decoding skills versus a focus on meaningful text. "The Great Debate" was an exploration of how to teach reading in the primary grades by Jean Chall (1967). Chall summarized research and investigated the ways in which children learn to read and came to the conclusion that while beginning readers need instruction with both a code emphasis and attention to meaning, upper elementary students do not benefit from decoding instruction. This specific delineation of reading methods into dichotomies of practice illustrates a dialogue that continues today, but the great debate is also characterized by the research struggle in the 1980s and 1990s among reading researchers over how best to teach reading to young children (Adams, 1990). Phonics versus other more holistic methods of instruction became a battleground, and ultimately the reading research community found that many methods of instruction including phonics should be applied in classroom settings (Adams, 1990). While the figured world of policy took note of the larger picture of a reading crisis, and the research community honed in on specific methods and theories of learning, a new wave of reform began to center around the reading achievement of the nation's children. A call for standards was heard, and then policy turned its attention toward reading pedagogy and accountability through assessment to ensure that all children would become literate.

"A significant majority of educational reform initiatives over the past dozen years have aimed to hold schools more accountable. But this desire actually began to surface in most developed countries in the 1960s, acquiring significant new energy during the mid to late 1980s" (Leithwood & Earl, 2000, p. 1).

From the 1980s until today, the standards movement in literacy can be viewed through the statements in the current No Child Left Behind Act. In the figured world of policy, the reading researchers, the teachers, and often the parents are not participants. The buildup of a strong spotlight on literacy instruction for young children encased in a standards movement focused on searching for answers through specific teaching methods, and specific measures aligned the figured world of policy and streamlined the agenda of the Texas Reading Initiative, the federal Reading Excellence Act, and, finally, the No Child Left Behind Act. These three legislative initiatives operate under the same premise, that every child will be reading by third grade. Holding to the 1994 perceived lowering of fourth-grade student reading performance on the National Assessment of Education Progress (NAEP), the Texas Reading Initiative, the Reading Excellence Act, and the No Child Left Behind Act slowly sculpted reading instruction and assessment. The powerful combination of a perceived reading crisis in the country and the rise of Governor George W. Bush's educational policy in Texas laid the groundwork for the community of policy makers shaping education today. In 2001, the ideology of reading standards embraced by the state had moved to the national level and moved literacy education into a high-profile political arena.

> Improving the reading skills of children is a top national and state priority. The President, the First Lady, the Secretary of Education, governors, business leaders, elected officials, citizens, community organizations, parents, and teachers are deeply committed to doing whatever it takes to ensure that every child can read. In the past few years, science has provided tremendous insight into exactly how children learn to read, and related research has identified the most essential components of reading instruction. (No Child Left Behind Website, 2002)

Reading methodology was a cornerstone of the Texas Reading Initiative, and only a select few methods for reading instruction were recommended by the state. Many researchers outside of the reading community were used as experts.[3] Taylor (1998) describes the research community's atmosphere in Texas at that time:

> Let me be even more explicit about what had happened within the scientific community that studies reading. There is no doubt that a small cadre of researchers, many of whom are in the payment of basal publishing companies and who are working closely with state governments, have conducted a campaign for public opinion in which the information provided to the public has been manipulated to such an extent that it is nothing more than spin doctoring. (Taylor, 1998, p. 128)

It should be noted that a parallel community existed alongside policy makers and educational practitioners during these movements. The reading research community lived within its own figured world, and though not the primary focus of this study, they go on record in many instances as disagreeing that a reading crisis exists. Berliner & Biddle (1995) examined the myths surrounding the push for standards that followed each crisis call, stating that "these charges have often been picked up and endlessly elaborated on in the media."

> Since the early 1980s, Americans have been subjected to a massive campaign of criticism directed at their public schools and colleges . . . [I]f we go by the evidence, despite greatly expanded student enrollment, the average American high school and college student is now doing as well as, or better than, that student did in previous years. (Berliner & Biddle, 1995, p. 64)

Allington (2002) concurs, explaining that the National Assessment of Educational Progress (NAEP) test scores have not declined. The NAEP, a national reading assessment given to students since 1969, is known as the "Nation's Report Card" and is the basis for the policy world's assessment of reading achievement. "The National Assessment of Educational Progress (NAEP) data indicate that reading achievement has remained relatively stable for thirty years . . . In fact, the reading achievement of fourth-grade students has inched up on each assessment since 1988" (Allington, 2002, p. 7). Yet by 2001, policy makers held onto statements such as this:

> Our students are not reading nearly well enough. As mentioned earlier, results of the most recent National Assessment of Educational Progress on reading showed that only 32 percent of the nation's fourth-graders performed at or above the proficient achievement level, thus demonstrating solid academic performance. And, while scores for the highest-performing students have improved over time, those of America's lowest-performing students have declined. (National Assessment of Educational Progress 2001)

Although there are many voices in the area of literacy acquisition, instruction, and standards, this story of Elena Elementary takes place during a time when literacy was a focus of policy makers in Texas and the country. The Texas Reading Initiative, the Reading Excellence Act, and the beginnings of the No Child Left Behind Act all served to create a context for Elena Elementary. Regardless of literacy researchers' views, the policy world of standards moved forward with great efficacy and resolve. The antidote for the illiteracy epidemic was to measure reading standards through testing. Using the NAEP as the principal artifact for changing and liberating the environment (Holland et al., 1998), policy makers moved toward the idea that increased accountability through testing was the only road to success.

> Testing is not new: The federal government has required testing since the first federal education programs began. Accountability is not new: Schools have always been accountable to parents and taxpayers. Even federalized accountability, in the sense of reporting progress toward meeting specified goals, is not really new: Federally funded education programs have for almost thirty years set and required schools to meet outcome targets or lose the funding. Working to close the rich/poor achievement gap is not new: That was the specific purpose of the original Elementary and Secondary Education Act of 1966. The *new, new* education bill (and accompanying federal plan) is actually the *same old, same old* when it comes to the basic design. What has changed with the new law is the locus of decision making, especially decisions about curriculum. (Allington, 2002, p. 240)

Figured worlds "happen, as social processes and in historical time" (Holland et al., 1998, p. 55). Policy makers were a part of a community attending to what they perceived as a great crisis. Their interpretation of events, artifacts, and actions was mediated through the filters of their community. They possessed a "situated learning" (Holland et al., 1998) that relied on their base of personal knowledge and those outsiders they perceived to be experts in the area they intended to reform. "These professionals then use their knowledge (knowledge that is congruent with and protective of the social order) to adjust or transform the social group" (Scheurich & Young, 1997, p. 108). Therefore, the figured worlds of Elena Elementary and the policy makers of Texas met at the point of transformation. Policy identified the children of Elena as a target group in need of literacy, and the teachers of Elena identified the children of Elena as in need of literacy. Each community held similar goals, yet the collision of the two worlds exposed substantial differences as to how literacy was defined, acquired, and measured.

When Two Worlds Collide

The figured worlds of policy and Elena can be characterized by Guerra's (1998) metaphors of literacy. These metaphors will be used to frame the literacy definitions of the teachers, the school district, the state, and the nation throughout the study. The complicated views of literacy by all of these entities are not to be simplified by the metaphors, but contrasted to each other in order to reveal their similarities and differences as they affected the teachers' views. The language and practice of the standards movement in literacy and the beliefs and instructional practices of the teachers of Elena can be viewed through Guerra's (1998) metaphors of literacy as institution and literacy as entity.

Literacy as Institution

[These notions] position literacy as an institutional artifact that circulates throughout the society-at-large in both positive and negative terms. The capitalist-oriented approaches [in this metaphor] recommend literacy as a currency that makes it possible for members of the society to buy their way to success. (Guerra, 1998, p. 55)

[These] recommendations that literacy be conceptualized as a body of information that any member of our society must know and be able to manipulate [are clear in this idea of literacy] . . . The view that students have to operate within existing institutional constraints in order to demonstrate their literacy survives as a cornerstone of this position . . . [as is the idea that] learners have to be provided with the necessary scaffolding and are judged on their ability to meet certain institutional expectations. (Guerra, 1998, p. 56)

The No Child Left Behind Act is closely related to the 1996 Texas Reading Initiative and the tenets of literacy as institution (Guerra, 1998) in that the primary role of schools was to educate children for successful participation in a capitalist society, as mentioned in *A Nation at Risk* (1983). The narrowing of teaching methodologies and the use of testing to set the institutional expectations demonstrate the stance of policy's figured world as clearly geared toward narrowing the view of literacy to fit it within an institutional design. Literacy as entity (Guerra, 1998) expands on the institutional ideals and ties literacy to the broader issues of the nation.

Literacy as Entity

The mutual goal of isolated individuals and integrated institutions is to find ways that will enable the society to function most efficiently for its own sake and, one hopes for the good of all. In such an idealized state, of course, issues of poverty and injustice do not exist or are simply ignored. Because of the objectified nature of this construct, equality of opportunity and outcome is also assumed. While this ideological perspective is on the wane and had been broadly criticized within the academy, many of the assumptions underlying it still operate tacitly in notions about how literacy is conceived and how it is institutionally possible to help people become literate. (Guerra, 1998, p. 52)

In Texas, the reform movement was a top-down systematic movement to restructure reading standards and education, what Scheurich and Young (1997) describe as "The traditional model of educational administration, functionalism, [concentrating] power in the educational expert" (p. 24). The world of policy views literacy in ways that are simple and effective. "The rationale for literacy education, just like the general rationales for aid to the poor is clear—increased funding for literacy programs, particularly those aimed at the poor, will reduce the long-term costs of social services, increase per capita productivity, and better lives" (Shannon, 1996, p. 442). Literacy was to be delivered to the group in need, with the inspiration described by Guerra (1998) as "for the good of all." Ideas of socio-economic status were erased, and the institutions of schools, supported by the government and assessed through testing, were prepared to dispense literacy to all children. The policy makers entrusted the experts to find the correct "scientific" way to teach reading and rounded the turn mentioned in 1965 by Smith as she referenced the first wave of scientific focus in the early 1900s.

The philosophy of the Texas reading goals is congruent with the national policy of the No Child Left Behind Act. Yet the teachers of Elena resided in a figured world replete with notions of literacy very different from policy makers. Educators at Elena Elementary were well versed in literacy theories and methods, and were deeply steeped in the daily lives of children learning to read. Their construction of literacy is best portrayed in Guerra's (1998) literacy as practice.

Literacy as Practice

Literacy is a socially constructed and highly contextualized activity. Literacy is no longer considered a singular, monolithic, or universal entity; instead, scholars who take a practice-oriented perspective contend that there are many literacies in any society serving multiple and culturally specific purposes. (Guerra, 1998, p. 57)

An individual's literacies vary according to the personal and social circumstances of his or her life, so everyone is considered literate in certain situations and not in others. The goal, from this perspective, is not to master a particular form of literacy, but to develop one's ability to engage in a variety of social practices that require us to operate in a plethora of settings and genres to fulfill different needs and goals . . . [I]t becomes our responsibility to identify and understand the varied ways in which different groups of people make use of literacy in their lives and to assist everyone in becoming more adept at making use of whatever literacies they deem important in their present and future lives. (Guerra, 1998, p. 58)

Elena's educators believed that literacy was diverse and individual. The community of Elena Elementary was bilingual, and the notion of multiple literacies extended beyond simply reading text. The teachers' knowledge of teaching reading was extensive, and their ability to seek out multiple ways to teach children to read kept in mind the unique nature of each child.

With the overriding idea that policy makers entered into discussing and planning reading instruction with an orientation toward literacy as institution and entity (Guerra, 1998), and that the educators of Elena held views of literacy as practice (Guerra, 1998), it should come as no surprise that when these two figured worlds collided, one view of literacy would prevail. "A major shift in education is under way in America—from a tradition of local control of schools for the federalization of the educational system, with decisions about teaching and learning more often being made by legislators or bureaucrats in faraway offices" (Allington, 2002, p. 240). The teachers at Elena had little power to circumvent the literacy policy of Texas as it moved into the school. The transformative nature of reform set goals. "We have to reorient. We have to help reorient a large number of educators who are poorly informed about reading skills development" (Charles Miller at the 1996 Texas Governor's Business meeting; in Taylor, 1998, p. 83). Any knowledge the teachers possessed was negated by the idea that teachers in Texas knew little about teaching. Policy makers set about to remedy the situation, and the story of Elena demonstrates the outcome.

If "no child is to be left behind" does that imply that they will ever get ahead? Although a noble and worthy call, the policy when enacted clearly defines literacy as a simplified product to be delivered to a specific market.

The button said "All children can learn." In 1987, I was required to wear the button every day I walked the halls of Elena Elementary. Fourteen years have passed since that first day of my student teaching. Now no one wears buttons. In this study, I took the goals of Texas government and the goals of the teachers at one school and sought to find out where they met and where they diverged. I found, to my surprise, that in the end, both groups wanted the same thing, and the students were meeting the goals of both teachers and policy makers. I found that the task of teaching reading at Elena was becoming a shrinking, simplistic list of skills effortlessly provided by the state and quietly being accepted by the teachers. The incantation of "every child reading by the end of third grade" became the mantra for a colonized, functional literacy model of instruction.

The figured world of standards is replete with the idea that Latina children of color are in danger of being left behind because of an absence of effective reading instruction. The idea that the literacy education of the children of one elementary school in Texas was colonized by the literacy definitions of policy makers and eventually teachers in control of the curriculum will be illustrated throughout this book. Street's (1995) view of colonization relies on three conditions: (1) literacy is defined as a monolithic idea transmitted into communities with little concern for preexisting local literacies; (2) literacy is an ideological notion enacted through power relationships and encased within the cultural practices of the governing culture dispensing the literacy education; and (3) literacy is viewed as necessary to the community it colonizes, a community judged by outsiders to be illiterate.

The chapters herein are organized around the sequence of the teachers' stories of teaching at Elena elementary. Chapters 2 and 3 outline the teachers' ideal definitions of literacy and their more pragmatic teaching methods and assessment measures related to the children's literacy instruction. Chapter 3 specifically marks a turning point in the study as it describes how the teachers' literacy instruction was interrupted by the required state assessments and consequently altered by policy mandates. Chapter 4 follows the side effects of the state policy enforcements on Elena and how the teachers' literacy ideas were transformed by the impact of policies directed at the school. Chapter 5 explores the relationship between the school and the community and how the teachers' interactions with parents influenced their literacy expectations for the children. In Chapter 6, the overall conclusions shared throughout the teachers' stories are framed within Street's (1995) view of the colonization of literacy, and Chapter 7 contextualizes the study in the broader perspective of the possibilities of literacy for all. Each chapter can be viewed with an eye toward how the teachers, the district, and the state viewed the community of Elena as illiterate and in need of a specific type of literacy that should be delivered through the institution of the school. The book concludes with an examination of how ensuring that all children become literate might affect the functioning of the world. I hope to tell a story of teachers and children at a school tightly focused on doing the right thing—teaching children to read. But I also want to complicate that simple argument constantly. As I turned to invite discussions about the children, I began with one very simple question: How do you teach a child to read?

·2·

LITERACY AT ELENA

Literacy definitions at Elena in this chapter are depicted by the teachers as aligned with Guerra's (1998) metaphor of literacy as practice wherein "literacy is a socially constructed and highly contextualized activity. Literacy is no longer considered a singular, monolithic, or universal entity; instead . . . there are many literacies in any society serving multiple and culturally specific purposes" (Guerra, 1998, p. 57). Teachers at Elena recognized that students brought knowledge from their community, and the teachers expressed literacy goals for the students that reflected the tenets Guerra (1998) outlined in his literacy as practice metaphor:

> [A]n individual's literacies vary according to the personal and social circumstances of his or her life, so everyone is considered literate in certain situations and not in others. The goal, from this perspective, is not to master a particular form of literacy, but to develop one's ability to engage in a variety of social practices that require us to operate in a plethora of settings and genres to fulfill different needs and goals. (p. 57)

This chapter follows the conversations with teachers and how they described their ideal literate student and their desire to develop a love of reading and a critical, useful stance for the literacy development of the children. Dolores, a third-grade teacher, summarized the literacy focus of the teachers as she described what she would expect from an ideal student:

> [My ideal third grader] is able to summarize and retell a story with a spark in her eye. She's not robotic. I don't know why that spark has to be there for me, but it has to—it has to. She is able to share and discuss and either agree or disagree with other students. And she can pull a lot out of a book. It reaches inside of her. This year I've been really blessed. I'm very blessed and I'm about to burst into

tears because it doesn't happen often, but there are several students who are touched by books.

Dolores hoped that her students would love reading and be able to discuss critically and evaluate what they read. As she spoke, her thoughts were positive about her students, but she reflected that she did not usually have many students she believed were capable of meeting her literacy expectations. Dolores describes what literacy instruction was to the eight participants I interviewed. They all shared her emphasis on developing a love of books with students and nurturing their ability to discuss and debate the books they read. This goal was a large factor in the teachers' constructions of the children. Teachers repeatedly referred to the children as not being highly literate, and this encouraged the campus to search for additional training. As mentioned in Chapter 1, just as the school district, the state, and the federal government had characterized the Latina students at Elena as being in danger of dropping out of school, as the teachers spoke, there were recurring references to the children as not being able to meet the literacy goals of the teachers. When viewed through the construct of "literacy as practice," the belief teachers held was that many of the students of Elena were not capable of meeting higher-level literacy goals. This belief reflected their ideas that literacy within the walls of the school was aligned with "literacy as practice" as far as how various genres of literacy could be approached and literacy activities could be socially constructed and facilitated, but the idea of literacy as more culturally diverse and particular to the community outside of Elena's walls was not explored by the teachers at the time of the study.

An Historical Look at Literacy at Elena

Literacy at Elena had been a specific focus since 1991. My first year at Elena, 1987, found the school in a position of being a few years into a "priority school" model adopted by the school district to address the issue of segregation. The district decided to cease busing students and returned to a neighborhood schools model. Schools on the east side of town, mostly Title I schools, were set up with specific support structures. Each priority school was given a full-time counselor, a full-time parent training specialist, and class sizes were set at fifteen students per class. This additional support structure for Elena was associated with the Title I view that extra funding and resources should target schools with low socio-economic status and significant numbers of children of color. The teachers relied upon the state-adopted textbooks to teach literacy. This particular textbook adoption reflected the trends in reading education at the time. The teachers I worked with used its phonics-based model of teaching sounds, spelling patterns, and vocabulary prior to introducing the story for the week. Spelling books adopted by the state were used, and writing instruction was relegated to the English book text which was dependent on grammar instruction. In 1989, after one year of teaching in California, I returned to Elena. The teachers were still using the same reading, writing, and spelling textbooks to teach, and there was a cohesive view of how to teach reading and a similar knowledge base within the grade-level teams. This approach to reading instruction can be placed within two of Guerra's (1998) metaphors of literacy. In 1998, to some degree, "Literacy as Entity" could be applied to Elena Elementary using the ideas that literacy was "the mutual goal of isolated individuals and integrated institutions [and seeks] to find ways that will enable the society to function most efficiently for its own sake and, one hopes for the good of all" (p. 52). The teachers at Elena were efficient in their teaching of literacy and followed the teacher directions in the textbooks well with little thought to other methods for teaching reading. "Literacy as Institution" also applies to the status of literacy education at Elena in 1987. The idea that literacy education could "be conceptualized as a body of information that any member of our society must know and be able to manipulate" (Guerra, 1998, p. 56) was a part of the philosophy that teachers followed as they taught the children the specific skills listed by the state with minimal alterations. This view was coupled with the teachers' ". . . view that students have to operate within existing institutional constraints in order to demonstrate their literacy survives as a cornerstone of this position . . . [L]earners have to be provided with the necessary scaffolding and are judged on their ability to meet certain institutional expectations" (Guerra, 1998, p. 56). Teachers relied on the state and textbook criteria for measuring literacy and generally did not go beyond the scope and sequence of the curriculum.

In 1991, several events led to new definitions of reading education at Elena. New theories of literacy education began to trickle down to teachers in Texas. The state had a new Commissioner of Education, and site-based decision making allowed schools to be more autonomous. My experiences teaching in California in 1988 were unique in that I had been taught and mentored in a specific theory of literacy education loosely referred to as Whole Language. After returning to Texas in 1989, I was alone in my exposure to Whole Language ideas, but within a few years the same principles appeared in various places such as staff development presentations, teacher books, and eventually state-adopted textbooks. Several teachers on campus began to read books on the topic, and the region service center ran workshops aimed at presenting new teaching philosophies and methods to teachers. Most of the trainings and workshops were not based on the instructional methods advocated in the textbooks but on recent studies conducted by reading researchers. For the first time in my history at Elena, teachers were being encouraged to take control of the teaching materials and make educated, well-informed decisions about how to teach children to read. Site-based decision making allowed the campus to choose how to spend funds, and Elena made several decisions related to literacy instruction during the years 1991 to 2000. We had excellent trainers who began as teachers and who are now in top-level positions with the school district. Natalie, our literacy curriculum specialist, relates the ways that Elena was ahead of the district and utilized literacy experts to develop a campus literacy focus:

> The school is more powerful. I feel like it almost came from the bottom up because I feel like as teachers we saw a need for a change in reading instruction. We needed leveled books, we needed those people (trainers). They ended up in positions in the district in the language arts department. They came from being classroom teachers and they moved up to be the head of language arts. I just think it was Reading Recovery teachers and teachers who were getting more training in reading and said we need something different and that finally filtered through to the top.

Natalie describes how many teacher educators at Elena went on to create the district's trainings. Elena teachers' knowledge was ahead of the district initiatives. On many occasions teachers attended trainings by literacy educators outside of the district before the ideas were filtered down to the other schools. The campus spent money on training the staff in literacy education, and this brought a new need for materials. In 1993, Natalie and I wrote a grant asking for money to purchase additional material to start a literacy bookroom. This afforded us the opportunity to choose the books our students read rather than relying solely on the state textbooks. Elements of the new teaching ideas focused on teaching novels and using as much real literature as possible in teaching reading. Students were encouraged to read and discuss the books, taking instruction a step further than the textbook model had previously suggested. The textbook materials required a substantial commitment to a design of instruction where students read new vocabulary and learned letter sounds and spelling patterns prior to reading a story. The students then answered questions about the story. The years I taught first grade with these materials, reading one story could take up to three days because of the instructional activities required.

The Whole Language method shifted the focus of instruction to the story and encouraged teachers to allow students to read as much as possible. The skills of spelling, phonics, and story structure were embedded within the lessons and not necessarily seen as separate sequential steps predetermined by teacher editions. Teachers were instructed to evaluate their students daily and make instructional decisions based on how their students were performing. The state required that each teacher teach the state-mandated essential elements of reading and writing, including specific skills such as stating the main idea, spelling words appropriate to their grade level, and writing with specific grammatical clarity. Teachers were able to teach with any philosophy or materials and still meet the state requirements. All students were assessed with a minimum state skills test called the Texas Examination and Assessment of Minimal Skills (TEAMS) and a nationally normed skills test, the Iowa Test of Basic Skills (ITBS). The campus administration did not mandate a specific teaching style or materials. Teachers at Elena were required to turn in lesson plans and mark each essential element covered. Teachers were accountable to the administration of the school and were expected to teach all students. Our campus held the belief that all children could learn. On my first day on the job I met with my new principal, who told me the campus philosophy and gave me the button that stated "All children can learn." This philosophy permeated every decision at Elena. We were highly discouraged from retaining students or referring students to special education. In my fourteen years at Elena I only referred one child to special education. We began with the idea that small classes allowed teachers to reach all of their students and meet their needs within the classroom. As a campus, we met the standards of the TEAMS test, and we were considered a successful staff.

We had a commitment to reach out to the community. We were required to meet all of our parents by making home visits twice a year. The first visit was conducted during the first month of school and was designed as a "meet and greet" type of interaction. This permitted teachers and parents to develop a relationship for the year to come. We then met the family at the child's home again early in the second semester to share information about the child's progress. These visits helped us as teachers to see the families in their own homes, learn about their lives, and get to know them. Home visits allowed our teachers to be close to the parents, and they worked with the community on several occasions.

One example of how we worked with and for the parents occurred my first year at Elena. Our building was in continual need of repair. We had to move the library downstairs because inspectors told us that the floor could not support the weight of the books, and plumbing problems were common. The teachers and parents gathered together and approached the school board to request a new school. We all worked together to no avail, until one day the ceiling caved in on a lower-floor classroom.

The parents and teachers also fought the historical society when it wanted to preserve the old building. We claimed we needed the land to build a larger play area and school for the children. Two years later, we moved into a brand-new school. Parents and teachers fought to secure a new principal, and they rebuked the district for sending letters to all the parents of Elena children indicating the at-risk status of the children who spoke Spanish as a first language. A coalition of teachers, parents, and community leaders formed a task force to turn the tide of the Title I classification that assumed all Spanish-speaking children were at risk.

Through such efforts, the figured world of Elena had a history of a staff deeply involved in the community. Most of the teachers were Latina and took great care to include the culture of the students in the literacy program design. This was evident in curriculum planning and keeping a close, family-type relationship with the parents of their students. Elena, from 1989 to the mid 1990s, embodied an understanding of its culture. The Latina culture was a strong presence within the school's walls. This awareness and understanding of the children's culture was due to two factors: (1) teachers' close relationships with the parents of the children in their classrooms, and (2) the strength of our Latina teachers and their influence on the rest of the staff. Therefore, our literacy focus was influenced by the cultural literacy of the context of the teaching and learning experiences that occurred within the four walls of Elena's classrooms. The closer the teachers came to knowing the community, the more they moved from the ideas of "Literacy as Entity" and "Literacy as Institution" to the view of "Literacy as Practice" where "literacy is a socially constructed and highly contextualized activity. Literacy is no longer considered a singular, monolithic, or universal entity; instead, scholars who take a practice-oriented perspective contend that there are many literacies in any society serving multiple and culturally specific purposes" (Guerra, 1998, p. 57).

To state that literacy is a cultural act of transmission requires exploration of literacy outside of our own culture. Street (1995) argues that many times the literacy of societies is measured by Western standards, while ignoring the diverse and at times culturally specific forms of literacy that evolve in local contexts. At Elena, teachers took care to know students' strengths and to be aware of the knowledge the families and students brought to the school. Elena's attention to language issues, the cultural content of our lessons, and even our celebrations of holidays such as Diez y Seis, Día de los Muertas, and Cinco de Mayo, tied our literacy instruction into a cultural, social way of meeting the goal of having all children enjoy and understand the world around them through reading and writing. Literacy was not relegated to the former monolithic view typical of simply reading and writing guided by Texas textbooks.

Teachers read stories from the culture our students brought to school, and the students wrote about their own lives. Graff (1995) names areas of literacy such as "alphabetic, visual and artistic, spatial and graphic, mathematical, symbolic, technological, and mechanical" (p. 64). He stresses the common emphasis on the alphabetic form of literacy by schools, but I would add that to ignore and misunderstand the literacies individuals bring to schools is to discount the relevance of the connections between cultures that the conception of literacy's broader definitions allows. Therefore, at Elena, literacy was more than reading and writing in the classroom. Literacy encompassed understanding the community's literacies, its songs, stories, and traditions that the children brought to school and that the teachers built on to foster literacy. It is important to recognize that not all societies feel the school is the vehicle for learning. Scribner and Cole (1978) pursued the idea of how literacy was connected to schooling by studying the Vai culture in West Africa. This community did not "school" themselves in literacy practices. They were literate and used literacy continuously, but without formal instruction. Based on this work, Scribner and Cole opened up the definition of literacy to

> finding out what people in various communities and walks of life do with literacy
> . . . to help us understand the differences between school-based literacy practices
> and literacy practices unrelated to schooling as well as their possibly different
> implications for intellectual outcomes. (p. 459)

Elena strove to meet this challenge of bridging the worlds between home- and school-based practices. Scribner and Cole (1984) also claim that literacy is a social practice, related to the social practices of its context. They state that we tend to view literacy as an individual accomplishment when in reality literacy is "a *social* achievement . . . Literacy is an outcome of cultural transmission" (p. 72). In the early 1990s Elena teachers and administrators embraced the culture of the students and allowed literacy instruction to do the same. Along with this socio-constructivist view, they add that definitions of literacy are subject to historical change and must be interpreted as such. Scribner and Cole's call for social analysis of the contexts of literacy is powerful and echoed by Graff (1995) as he states the importance of

> . . . reconstructing the contexts of reading and writing: how, when, where, why,
> and to whom literacy was transmitted; the meanings that were assigned to it;
> the uses to which it was put; the demands placed on literate abilities; the de-
> grees to which those demands were met; the changing extent of social restrict-
> edness in the distribution and diffusion of literacy and the real and symbolic
> differences that emanated from the social conditions of literacy among the
> population. (p. 11)

Elena teachers were aware of the contexts of the children's homes and the context of the school. They made it their priority to build links between the two to make the students successful. The children were encouraged to be bilingually proficient in speaking, reading, and writing. At the time I was hired, every teacher at Elena was either a certified English as a Second Language (ESL) teacher or a certified bilingual teacher. Contingent upon being hired, I was required to complete twelve hours of university coursework in ESL and second-language acquisition. Supporting the language development of the students was a priority. Each child received instruction in their native language, and Spanish-speaking children learned to read in Spanish first. Once they were fluent readers in Spanish, they were transitioned to English, usually by third grade. By 1994, Elena had moved into a multi-age format, a year-round schedule, and we received federal support to implement a five-year Dual Language grant. All of the programs were brought onto the campus by teachers and approved through the Campus Leadership Team (CLT). The CLT committee was made up of elected teachers from the staff, administrators, one community representative, and one parent. Under the State's Site Based Decision Making model, teachers became a part of all decisions on campus, from budget allocations to hiring to curriculum design. We adopted a Quality Schools (Glasser, 1992) design and targeted literacy as an area for development. Therefore, literacy education at Elena was led by the teachers and influenced by the teaching ideas of Whole Language, a focus on dual language instruction, and a commitment to maintaining ties to the families. The staff was creative and willing to try such configurations as multi-age classrooms to increase the positive atmosphere and enhance the learning of the children.

Teacher Training: The Shaping of a School-Wide Definition of Literacy

During my tenure at Elena, there was a philosophy of eclecticism. Teachers did not adhere to one program. Teachers took control of the materials and made informed, professional decisions about the instruction of their students. And they did so with minimal involvement from the state or district, but with a great deal of support from our local administrators. Dolores provided another reminder of the expertise in literacy education the Elena teachers possessed when she contrasted the teaching methods she observed at a private school versus the methods used at Elena. She thought that the teachers at Elena had a higher level of training than teachers at the private school, and although Elena teachers were supported well, she saw a continued need for literacy education for the staff.

[Dolores:] When I taught in the private school sector, [the teachers] had very little training: almost nil. It was amazing some of the practices that took place. People were paying big bucks for it and children were learning from children. And in that kind of setting, that's okay—that's fine when other children have that kind of knowledge to share. It's not a problem. When you come into a different setting, you have to find books that will help you meet the needs of your students. I would have to agree that Elena teachers are very very well trained, they seek training, training is brought to them and recommended. There is a lot of support [at Elena]. Well, support as far as training. Support as far as answers? God, I wish. We've had a lot, but sometimes it still doesn't feel like enough.

Dolores also reiterated the sense that teachers needed more support at Elena. As I conversed with the teachers, I heard echoes of past years at Elena, echoes of newspaper articles, school board meetings, and echoes of research in reading. Elena continually received the same message, in words that vary but ideas that meshed: urban children of color struggle with reading. Teachers of those children cannot walk into the classroom expecting certain events to occur. Elena teachers were told they were not like the "other" schools for fourteen years. Most teachers never argued it, disputed it, or challenged the notion that the children at Elena were in need. The teachers talked about it, the community talked about it, and the state and federal government legislated it. We were a Title I school because of our high number of ESL and bilingual students, most of whom the government classified as "at-risk" youth— thus the letters Elena parents received indicating their children were at risk of failure. In the past, teachers and parents fought the constant rhetoric defining the students as less able to succeed, but by 2001 there was little attention paid to the messages about the children. The state's Title I definition of at-risk youth applied to many of the students at Elena.

"At-risk youth" is defined under Title I, Part D:

Answer: The term "at-risk youth" means school-aged youth who are at risk of academic failure, have drug or alcohol problems, are pregnant or are parents, have come into contact with the juvenile justice system in the past, are at least one year behind the expected grade level for the age of the youth, have limited English proficiency, are gang members, have dropped out of school in the past, or have high absenteeism rates at school. (Texas Education Agency Website, 2002)

Just by virtue of their language dominance, most of the students at Elena carried this label. Elena's answer to the obvious call to assist the struggling readers was simple. Teachers learned how to teach reading. Administrators allocated money for books and workshops for teachers. As the administrator Illeana stated, "there was no training by the state . . . [I]t was our own local campus doing the training." And as Dolores put it, "Where did I go for help? Training on my own, just going out and finding out what is it that I can do. There's no one answer because every child has been different as far as what their needs are." Elena had a knack for pushing the education of its teachers. Our attention to literacy was partly due to the pervasive Title I designation and the view of our children as needing additional assistance. But the campus did not wait for training to come; teachers sought it out.

> [Natalie:] [During our] history, we've changed so dramatically from what teachers were really expected to do, we work miracles as far as I'm concerned. I think we do a better job of teaching kids to read than we did a long time ago. I know from ten years ago, I am a much better reading teacher than I was. I think it's more to do with the training I've received.

Fourteen years ago there was a focus on multiple literacies and the cultural aspect of literacy at Elena. The community was important as evidenced by a campus push to maintain a strong bilingual program. Literacy was a broad idea, as teachers found possibilities for the children of Elena. The cultural history at Elena was one of searching for ways to follow the child. The curriculum views were similar to what Dewey (1900) might label educative experiences. Children were placed at the center of the curriculum, and though they did not necessarily determine the content, the idea that activities and experiences must have meaning for the child was taken into account. Dewey was child-focused as were the teachers at Elena, yet Freire (1970) goes past focusing on the child to promoting the idea that education should be a vehicle for transformation. Just as the teachers were more aware that the children needed more aid, they in turn were led to seek assistance for their teaching. The more knowledge the teachers received, the more powerful they became.

Freire (1970) understood the concept of the power and politics of literacy well. Freire's goal, in his view of literacy education, was to avoid what he termed "banking education," where the students were receptacles of knowledge. Freire advocated "problem-posing education," which allowed for critical thinking as literacy was acquired and led to educational reform. This idea could be applied to the teachers at Elena. The perceived "problem" at Elena was educating children of color. Therefore, teachers became highly educated in reading instruction. They thought articulately and altered the landscape of the figured world of literacy at Elena. Teachers changed the way they taught:

> [Illeana:] I've seen a lot of progress in how reading is taught here. I think a lot of it has to do with some of the workshops we've had and the purchasing of the material. Getting the literacy library set up and really working on how to use those

books in guided reading, but then again the workshops were voluntary. Whoever wanted to attend did. We had a great turnout, we really did well. I guess you could mandate something, but if it's after hours we can't. I guess we could put it as part of the growth plan, whether they do it here or do it elsewhere, as long as they do it.

At the time of the interviews, most teachers were voluntarily trained in a number of reading methods, depending upon which wave of staff development had washed over them. Most trainings were optional yet well attended. Trainings tied to the Dual Language grant were required. Upon my arrival fourteen years ago, literacy instruction was traditional and skills-oriented. Teachers had ability-based reading groups and moved through the state-provided reading basal series while aligning their methods with the various state-mandated skills. There were few, if any, outside resources or materials sought. We believed all children could learn and all teachers could teach. There was a sense of pride and a desire to rise to the challenges of educating all of the children to be bilingual and literate according to the ideals of the school. All teachers were teaching ESL or Spanish in order to meet the needs of our Latina population. Children came first. Our trainings were responsive to what we had determined through our Quality Schools (Glasser, 1991) review to be important. Quality Schools was used by Elena to identify areas of need and inquiry and address those issues. Literacy was chosen by the teachers at that time as an area to be researched and improved upon. The staff had formed a literacy inquiry committee focused on literacy and proposed funding for specific trainings and materials.

Through the years, Elena followed national trends, and teachers received training in the Whole Language approach sweeping the nation. This training focused on opening up the previously teacher-scripted model of reading instruction—dependent on teacher editions—to include a more theoretically grounded, independent style of teaching—dependent on the education of teachers. Teachers attended trainings such as Frameworks and Early Literacy Inservice Course (ELIC), which opened up literacy instruction in ways that were friendly to diverse student needs. These two trainings addressed teachers through an educative model. Rather than train them in a predetermined program of instruction with a set scope and sequence of skills, Frameworks and ELIC were dependent on teacher empowerment through knowledge. Teachers explored research on how children learned language and became more adept at meeting the children's needs through assessment and techniques designed to enhance literacy. Our teachers and administrators developed close relationships with the regional service center trainer, and we paid to have many trainings at our own campus and at our own expense. These trainings were a mixture of the mandatory and the voluntary. Intensive trainings such as Frameworks and ELIC were voluntary and required a commitment from each teacher to remain after school once a week for a semester. They read professional books, wrote papers, and made changes in their teaching approaches. Other trainings supportive of the basic tenets of the ideas espoused by the Frameworks and ELIC were small, specific, and were provided for the whole staff on required staff development days. Therefore, all of the teachers had the same information but different degrees of exposure and expertise. As the Dual Language grant was approved, we all received mandatory training in Montessori language and math methodology and intensive training in second-language acquisition. The grant lasted five years, and we were frequently audited and supervised by personnel hired to facilitate and support the teachers' use of the additional methods.

Guided reading became a popular method of teaching reading, and the trainings were attended by many staff members and both administrators. Guided reading has many incarnations, but it generally can be defined as any moment in teaching when a teacher is guiding a child through a text that is on an instructional level, a text they cannot read alone but is easy enough for them to navigate with minimal assistance (Clay, 1991). This process provides an opportunity for the teacher to see what strategies the child uses and what can be done to expand his or her repertoire of methods to access text. We found a bilingual former classroom teacher, Andrea, employed as a reading specialist and a trainer for a publishing company. She led our campus trainings and greatly affected our literacy program through her participation in meetings and her individual mentoring of specific teachers. She was later promoted to district supervisor. Most of the primary informants were highly trained and educated by her in reading and were naturally reflective and explorative of their own teaching practices. Since this period at Elena was also characterized by a time in which schools in Texas, including Elena, were operating with more local control under a site-based, decision-making model, teachers had more input as to the types of staff development, teaching methods, and measurement tools they used.

In 2001, teachers at Elena found themselves swinging back with the pendulum to more traditional, skills-based, compressed literacy practices, again supported by the state. The district has in recent years advocated a program entitled Balanced Literacy, to promote a middle-ground view of how to teach reading. Balanced literacy professional development advocated teaching with a specific focus on skills and literacy with authentic and informal assessment measures used to guide teaching decisions. The intertwining of philosophy, practice, theory, curriculum, and public policy in literacy education is intricate, and I will continue to revisit these relationships in the next three chapters.

Teachers' Definitions of Literacy

> [Bob, a sixth-grade teacher:] [Literate people] read something and discuss it or fit it into their life. [And wonder] did that change my opinion? Real literacy, that's 100 percent.

Bob's definition alludes to the metaphor of literacy as "Literacy as Self" where "meaning is embedded in the mind or being of the individual and reflects the unique circumstances that he occupies" (Guerra, 1998, p. 53). Bob talked about the importance of students being able to take what they had read into their lives and think about how what they read might affect their lives. Scribner and Cole's (1984) notion of literacy as power can also be seen in Bob's desire to have students use literacy to form, confirm, or alter their opinions about the world around them. Scribner and Cole (1984) promote the idea that literacy is a moving social force that includes critical thought and reflection. Literacy is viewed as advancement within a community. This idea exposes the true force, limitations, and possibilities behind the idea of a literate nation. Do we want citizens to read—or to read and think? They cite the use of literacy in developing countries and countries involved in social change as examples of the perception that literacy is power, ". . . that literacy per se mobilizes people for action to change their social reality" (p. 76). Literacy as power does indeed go beyond reading and writing. It is a vehicle for enhancing and changing lives for both the teachers and their students. Devin, a second-grade teacher, expressed her wishes for her students to love reading and to make connections between their reading and their lives:

> My dream child can read . . . They can talk to you about that story. They can somehow connect it to something else, whether it's something real or any other story. They can write about it; when they write about it they make connections in their writing to other things. They want to keep reading once they finish something . . . they want to keep reading. They are interested in something. I know a lot of my kids got into authors. That's one of the things I did differently between first and second grade . . . kids were able to talk to the librarian about authors . . . that's the ideal second grader. They become interested in what they are reading or who they are reading.

Devin felt it was crucial that students remain interested and self-motivated to read and use reading in their lives. Caroline, a fifth-grade teacher, also expressed her definitions of literacy as moving away from the simple act of reading words on a page to the idea that a literate student was one who was educated beyond the performance of skills to the actual use of those skills.

[Caroline:] Literacy, you automatically think of reading and writing, but I think it goes way beyond. What makes a literate person? Someone who is educated not just in reading and writing, but also in socializing and knows what to do in certain situations and makes good choices. I think it does go beyond reading and writing.

For these teachers, literacy involved reading the world and "the word" through personal, cultural experiences (Freire, 1987). In fact, all of the teachers interviewed responded with definitions of literacy that fit the notion of literacy as power. Language's meanings and movement into symbolic text representation are culturally signed and delivered. Paulo Freire (1970) illustrates a definition of socially constructed literacy from which I will draw. He speaks of his world and how he was able to read it through himself, his family, and his life experiences.

> . . . the world of my first reading. The texts, the words, the letters of that context were incarnated in a series of things, objects, and signs. In perceiving these I experienced myself, and the more I experienced myself, the more my perceptual capacity increased. I learned to understand things, objects, and signs through using their relationship to my older brothers and sisters and my parents. (p. 22)

Freire's conception of literacy as a part of his very being mirrors what Vygotsky's theory of learning invokes and runs parallel to the teachers' claims to want their students to make deep, meaningful connections to what and who they read. Scholars describe Vygotsky's interpretation of learning as connected to the historical context of culture (Blanck, 1990; Cole & Engestrom, 1993; Vygotsky, 1978; Wertsch, 1985). Language is described as the key tool in the transformation of the physical and social reality in which we live. This socio-cultural view of learning places an emphasis on culture and how language is used to make meaning—meaning that exists within cultural contexts, not abstract worlds of black text on white pages. If reading and writing are interpreted through the vision of Vygotsky, we can see that they are more than exercises with books and pen and paper. Teachers at Elena understood this conception of literacy. Devin illustrates her goals for the children to read and become as literate as possible, and she shares her feeling that the students at Elena did not necessarily possess those skills:

> When you're building on literacy you are building a joy of just reading first and foremost. Literacy is not just the joy of reading but the joy of it includes everything. It doesn't only include the reading part and reading instruction. I think a lot of times what happens is we get so involved in reading instruction that we don't spend enough time on building that foundation . . . I wish that our kids had

that. I wish our kids had that because that's exactly what literacy is. You learn so much from [reading] you learn about life in general or you learn ideas.

Devin wanted her students to apply the knowledge gained from reading to their lives rather than just reading for the sake of reading, which she referred to above as "reading instruction." The idea that developing their love of reading would result in the children going beyond what simple reading instruction required was important to Devin. She did not mention the role of culture specifically but implied that in order for the children to learn about their lives or gather new information they must begin with a desire to read.

Language acts are embedded within our culture as it is transmitted to us through our families, communities, and eventually schools (Heath, 1983). Therefore, literacy in one culture may not be the same across cultures. This means that to go beyond reading and writing as discrete skills we must look at broader ideas of literacy. Elena teachers expressed a collectively strong desire to instill more expansive ideas of literacy in the students, and thus the figured world of literacy at Elena typifies what Holland et al. (1998) would depict as one way "figured worlds happen, as social process and in historical time." At this specific point in time, during the study, Elena teachers were an educated group of teachers teaching "literacy" to what many outsiders such as the state described as a struggling population of students. Yet literacy has been presented in many educational and political venues as simply "reading." The complex notion of literacy is often overlooked as an overriding factor in the goal of reading education. Reading and literacy are sometimes seen as interchangeable terms, and defining the parameters of literacy versus reading requires attending to differences in the use of the terms. By almost anyone's definition, a literate child is one who can visibly read and write. Teachers discussing children's literacy often spoke of children in terms of whether they were reading on grade level or not. Parents recognized quickly that a child could read a specific book. Reading and writing were easily described behaviorally by the state's objectives for each grade. Standardized tests and informal reading and writing tests supplied reading and writing information and quickly placed a grade-level measure on a child after hearing them read a passage once and answer questions. Computer programs provided efficient five-minute tests to determine reading ability. The ease with which reading and writing were measured and discussed betrayed the deeper, more encompassing nature of what possibilities expanding the notion of literacy could bring. Teachers, parents, and policy makers felt quite comfortable discussing literacy as they viewed it within an either/or construct.

These simplified versions of literacy accomplishments are insufficient. I would argue that at Elena, teachers understood literacy in its broader meanings:

as more than just the ability to read text off of a page or answer questions on a test. Cultural factors in literacy definitions were not in the fore as they were in the early 1990s, but teachers during the spring of 2001 were attempting to define literacy as a higher-level thinking activity somewhat socially interconnected. As a fourteen-year member of the figured world of literacy at Elena, I spoke to the teachers about how they would describe a literate child. They all mentioned their ideal. As they did, they went far beyond the perfunctory definitions of literacy as reading and writing.

Literacy Instruction at Elena

[Penny, a special education teacher:] When I see three kids who don't normally get along well together, on their bellies, on a bean bag, going "Look at that picture. You read one page, I'll read the next," and acting it out on their own. I'm like . . . there you go. That's all I want. That's what I want, enjoyment for them. When they [say], "Look Ms. Baxter, I don't understand, if he's doing this, why can't he do that?" Questioning what the author wrote, that's it, that right there.

Literacy instruction in the figured world of Elena had a common belief— enjoy reading, think about what was read, and question it. The intensive training teachers received created a knowledge base that can be compared to the artifacts label Holland et al. (1998) uses. She proposes that artifacts are used by those inhabiting a specific figured world as "tools of liberation" to affect the environment, others, and ourselves. These tools of liberation at Elena were the instructional methods the teachers began to use and the trainings that encouraged a common "community of practice" that utilized the idea of "situated learning." Many of the teachers had attended the same types of training, and they all shared similar goals as stated by Dolores:

I'm trying to help my students [become] lifelong readers, that's my goal. I hope I entice them to love reading . . . modeling reading, providing them with ideas as far as what books they can read, providing quality literature in the classroom. Using strategies and techniques that Andrea has taught to help children get through literature that they enjoy. Guided reading groups have really helped this year. It has helped me better understand what my students' strengths and needs are and where I need to go with my instruction. Just being able to understand what their weaknesses are and [knowing] these are the students struggling in this area. Knowing where I need to go next, so I can help them build. Hopefully, I'm spending more time with students reading rather than busy work. That's what my goal has been.

Because of their high level of training and education, many teachers exerted power over the curriculum to meet these aims. Their training was used to form or reinforce their beliefs about how children learned and how literacy should be taught. The extensive atmosphere of literacy training at Elena in the early-to-mid 1990s served to establish a definite community of thought regarding literacy instruction. Teacher expertise was valued. Teachers possessed a common language regarding literacy instruction and shared collective ideas and practices. Understanding how beliefs and knowledge are related becomes crucial to appreciating how literacy instruction was defined and enacted at Elena, just as the belief that all children could learn was emphasized. Over the years beliefs about literacy instruction began to become tightly defined. Understanding the relationships between belief and knowledge enhances the explanation of the literacy positioning of the teachers at Elena.

> [Beliefs are formed] with material drawn from experience or cultural sources . . . [B]elief systems, unlike knowledge systems, do not require general or group consensus regarding the validity and appropriateness of their beliefs. Individual beliefs do not even require internal consistency within the belief system. This nonconsensuality implies that belief systems are by their very nature disputable, more inflexible, and less dynamic than knowledge systems . . . [B]eliefs are more influential than knowledge in determining how individuals organize and define tasks and problems and are stronger predictors of behavior. (Pajares, 1992, p. 311)

Understanding the relationship between knowledge and beliefs is crucial to comprehending how teachers at Elena interpreted information and how they incorporated their interpretations into their teaching. By 2001, many teachers in the study still held on to the notion that teaching reading was more than following a list of reading behaviors. They looked to the affective nature of reading and stressed the importance of educating students to use literacy in thoughtful ways in their daily lives. These beliefs were powerful and remained evident in many conversations as the teachers spoke about the goals they had for the children. If Freire (1987) supposes that we read our world through our experiences, and Vygotsky (1978) exposes learning as a cultural event, then our beliefs about our world must influence our learning and perceptions whether we are teachers or children. Beliefs and knowledge are two separate organizing categories used to navigate our decisions. Teachers may know what they believe and may not believe what they know. An ongoing example of this is evident in the majority of the comments made by the teachers as they described the abilities of the children of Elena. Although the teachers were educated about the potential for all children to become literate, the teachers' overriding beliefs that the children of Elena were not truly capable of being successful illustrate the ways that belief can shape or alter specific "factual" knowledge. Interviews, and many quotes used throughout the study, were laced with a language of doubt about the abilities of the children of Elena to meet the literacy goals of the teachers. In order to place the seemingly contradictory views of the teachers within a workable frame, I will introduce the notion of the interrelatedness of beliefs and knowledge. The high level of knowledge about literacy instruction held by the teachers was subjected to their beliefs about the children's abilities, and these themes will be threaded throughout the piece.

Beliefs and Knowledge in Literacy Definitions

For example, my beliefs transcended most information I gathered as a teacher at Elena and as a researcher. My beliefs assist me in placing new knowledge within the frames I designed, frames I used to view the world as I wanted to see it. I watched my own "mental gymnastic" performances while my beliefs about children were challenged by new information, as my identity as a teacher at Elena was formed so early on in my career. I was extremely adept at navigating around new information and molding it to fit within or against what I already believed—not what I knew. My indoctrination to the Elena philosophy of "all children can learn" still guides my categorization of knowledge. My experiences at Elena and my university experiences have shaped and reshaped my beliefs to a very large degree. The teachers at Elena were subjected to the information they received in their teacher education programs, as parents themselves, through trainings, continuing education, or simply each other. One administrator describes how a grade-level team's beliefs and teaching methods eventually rubbed off on a colleague and subsequently altered her teaching style.

> [Illeana:] I'll give you a good example of the power of the team. There is a grade level where there was a teacher that's been here for a while and she was still pretty traditional. Now she's with two other very powerful people. She's picked up a whole lot. Sonja [the principal] and I were just discussing [teacher] evaluations. I did [this teacher's] evaluation. [Sonja asked] are you sure this is how [her] rating is? And I said definitely and I explained to her I saw this and this and this. It was a lot of the new phonemic awareness, the making words, the guided reading, the really knowing where your child is at as an individual. I know it is coming because of the team. You walk into all four rooms and they all have the literacy based centers, not any more of the worksheets where you go and sit at your desk while I teach reading. You're learning something about words as I'm teaching reading. I think the power of the team is that you have to empower those teams to do that.

Teaching children did not occur in a vacuum. If we think of knowledge as any type of factual information provided, we can see how it was used in education. This one traditional teacher was influenced by her co-workers and the environment enough to alter her teaching. Knowledge was valued by teachers, administrators, and policy makers. They all clamored to know what research said about how to teach reading. Teachers were subject to their knowledge of learning theory, their knowledge of teaching techniques, their knowledge about their abilities as teachers, and their knowledge about children. Knowledge and education were ideas that went hand in hand comfortably in the world of education—but beliefs? What Pandora's Box does discussion about beliefs within education open? The reality was that not only do teachers rely on knowledge handed to them by research or district mandates; they also rely on personal experience and each other, but it was personal beliefs that acted as the filter. Natalie shared her thoughts about the role of beliefs in teaching:

> You have your world view and you have your beliefs and your knowledge. I do believe your world view can be changed by education and by experience. I don't believe that maybe some people are so locked into it. It takes a lot of educational experience to ever change their beliefs, but I feel like in my case, I've had views or beliefs that have been changed by what I've learned and by experience. Like the one I was talking about earlier, about language. Before the course I took, I had the belief system that someone who spoke with a Black dialect or some sort of slang was somehow lower, somehow less educated, just not as good. They don't speak as well as me. That's how I had attached a hierarchy of what was right, better or worse. After that course, I changed my view. It's not a matter of this is the best and this is not. There isn't a ranking, all of it is equal. The languages are equal but the culture imposes a standard that the people are going to be judged by. I realize how my judgment of that was really invalid.

Natalie was able to move outside of her beliefs about language in the context of her coursework. She valued the knowledge and was able to fit the new information about dialect into the belief structure in ways that permitted her to alter her views of the appropriateness of dialect in language evaluation.

Research on beliefs and knowledge leaves room for the possibility of change and is explained by the literature review by Pajares (1992). Pajares reviewed literature on the contrast between beliefs and knowledge. His summary found that deep-seated beliefs thrive independent of new knowledge. Nespor (as cited in Pajares, 1992) "suggested that beliefs have stronger affective and evaluative components than knowledge and that affect typically operates independently of the cognition associated with knowledge" (p. 309). The overriding power in beliefs even in the face of contradictory knowledge has influential repercussions when applied to teaching. Specifically, teachers will maintain their beliefs despite new or contradictory information. Nespor (as cited in Pajares, 1992) also describes the voracity with which teachers may hold onto beliefs by illustrating that they are stored in episodic memory rather than being mapped out semantically. Therefore beliefs are tied more to emotional connections than they are to logical meaning structures.

Subsequently, the beliefs of teachers are woven within and throughout their teaching practices, shaped by their experiences outside the school context, and strengthened by the affective effect they exert. One teacher demonstrated her beliefs about literacy and how she dealt with explaining her approach to teaching reading to her evaluator. They did not have the same belief about the same knowledge. The dispute was centered around the popular reading method called guided reading. The administrator had one definition of the teaching method and the teacher another.

[Katia, a fourth-grade teacher:] Ms. Garcia and I had a disagreement about guided reading. I feel I am [right]. Her vision of guided reading is traditional, which is: you pick up groups of kids, and that is guided reading. But I told her I do guided reading all day. To me, guided reading is not just picking up a group of kids and having them all reading on the same book. It was a big disagreement and she didn't give me my exceeding expectations scores in that section because of that. She said, "You need to start guided reading groups," and I thought, "That's not guided reading, Ms. Garcia. Guided reading is everything I do in my classroom." I have independent reading going on, I guide the kids, if they want to choose books that are really low level I'm going to let them go below level just to get [fluency] but you know what? I have control over that. I'm impacting them and then [they work on] critical thinking and that to me is connecting with the writing. The writing and the reading are connected and the critical thinking. The university helped me a lot, Ramsey's class, and the fact that we do book talks but those are out of independent reading books. And she said, "Well, how do you get them to critically think?" And I said, "Well, we do our whole class together. We may do one book . . ." I told her I integrated! I did tell her, "I'm not doing guided reading the way you want me to do it. I'm doing guided reading the way it's supposed to be done." I took Andrea's workshop, but I also took guided reading experience from Dr. Ramsey [a university professor]. It's not just Andrea's style, it's not just picking up a group. Her argument was, "Well, you need to implement guided reading next year". . . I talked until I was blue in the face.

Once the door to the classroom was closed, every teacher knew they had a fairly large amount of leeway to implement curriculum and instructional strategies as they saw fit. The more knowledgeable the teacher, the more they could manipulate the materials and methods to meet the beliefs they had about the needs of the children. In this example, Katia and the principal never reached an agreement on the definition of guided reading. Their knowledge base about guided reading was the same, but Katia's beliefs were different. Guided reading is defined as literally guiding a child's reading as they read a book. The administrator and teacher understood the basic concepts, but they possessed different beliefs as to how that concept was to be implemented. They were operating from different fields of beliefs about the concept of guided reading. This was due to their knowledge base, experience, and positioning. Katia and the principal were confident in their belief about guided reading instruction, and neither one was willing to change their beliefs.

Teacher beliefs were relevant to my view of teacher perceptions of children and literacy education because they were the foundation from which all teachers began. Teacher knowledge is defined in many ways (Clandinin & Connelly, 1995a; Cochran-Smith & Lytle, 1993; Hamachek, 1999). For the purposes of discussion in this area, I am limiting my use of the term to the ways teachers' knowledge was viewed by them in relation to how they perceive children and their teaching. As evidenced above, the beliefs teachers hold influence their teaching decisions. Even in the face of new information presented at faculty meetings, staff development workshops, and interpersonal conversations, teachers may hold tightly to their own personal viewpoints. Therefore, a large portion of my inquiry rested on the idea that whatever beliefs the teachers at Elena held, they guided the instruction and the progress of the children. I conclude with a synthesis of findings on beliefs as presented by Pajares (1992):

- Beliefs are formed early and through cultural transmission.
- Beliefs are relatively immune to new knowledge as they strongly influence perception, but they can be an unreliable guide to the nature of reality.
- The belief system has an adaptive function in helping individuals define and understand the world and themselves.
- Knowledge and beliefs are inextricably intertwined, but the potent affective, evaluative, and episodic nature of beliefs makes them a filter through which new phenomena are interpreted.
- Thought processes may well be precursors to and creators of belief, but the filtering effect of belief structures ultimately screens, redefines, distorts, or reshapes subsequent thinking.
- The earlier a belief is incorporated into the belief structure, the more difficult it is to alter. Newly acquired beliefs are most vulnerable to change.
- Belief change during adulthood is a relatively rare phenomenon, the most common cause being a conversion from one authority to another or a gestalt shift. Individuals tend to hold on to beliefs based on incorrect or incomplete knowledge, even after scientifically correct explanations are presented to them.

- Beliefs are instrumental in defining tasks and selecting the cognitive tools with which to interpret, plan, and make decisions regarding such tasks. Hence they play a critical role in defining behavior and organizing knowledge and information.

This set of principles informed my study of the teachers at Elena by providing a frame for deconstructing the foundations of teachers' teaching and their perceptions of the children. Objectivity is assumed to be the rule within schools, and many assume "technical/scientific" knowledge drives the decisions. But where do beliefs come into play? As they move within a school, teachers become players in the school's world. The mores and values of the school very soon become apparent, and the school's "ways of knowing" require teachers to understand their community and their place in it. If a teacher truly believes in one way of teaching reading, they will cling to it despite outside influences. I found this to be true with literacy instruction as well as with literacy assessment. The teachers were inundated with assessment tools mandated by the state and were well-versed in analyzing their validity, yet another testament to the level of their expertise and critical examination of literacy. Literacy at Elena for my eight participants was tied to their common belief that reading instruction should develop a love of reading and the ability to think critically about text.

Literacy Assessment at Elena

[Dolores:] I felt my job was as a facilitator [at the] private school. When I came into the public school settings, especially Elena, it was shocking to have students who didn't have the experiences that other children have. It was frustrating at times, overwhelming always and so I really needed to seek out some training and some help to meet their needs. It wasn't provided. I thought, the books, have them enjoy the books. [But I realized that] no, that was not going to cut it, not at Elena. So I had to learn to assess and to evaluate and try and figure out what the answers were, seek help.

Dolores contrasted the perception she had of the private-school students who were more experienced and the Elena students whom she defined as requiring more from her as an evaluator. "Enjoying the books" was not enough to develop literacy in the children, and at Elena she needed to "seek help." She saw more intensive assessment of the students' needs as a means to find answers to her teaching questions. The teachers at Elena had a great deal of access to literacy evaluation tools, and many could be aligned with Shepard's views. Shepard (2000) advocates assessing children using a social constructivist approach. She recommends dynamic, ongoing evaluation of students during instruction, not just after lessons are completed. Shepard places an emphasis on pre- and post-testing to examine students' prior knowledge and teach them what they need to know. She presses teachers to provide students constantly with feedback as to their progress and to set explicit criteria for them to follow. Shepard's model calls for teachers and students to monitor their own progress and self-evaluate, and she also explains the need to teach for transfer. Students must learn more than isolated skills: they must learn concepts that carry over into other subjects. Elena assessment plans were aligned with the tenet of assessment that Shepard proposes. Through years of training in and outside of the district, the teachers of Elena developed a common-knowledge base of how to assess their students in reading. There was a focus on specific skills and an understanding of the importance of developing more than reading and writing skills, but there was also an emphasis on ensuring that the children love reading and learn to think critically. The teachers depended on knowing and seeing their students' work for themselves.

> [Dolores:] [I assess by using] my students' class work, and their reflecting on literature, writing about it and discussing it. Then I know if they are getting it or not. That's what I base my opinion on, how well they are doing. Sometimes [with testing] you see things you didn't see because it's one-on-one, there are no interruptions, it's quiet and so you really get to focus on the child. But, at this point in the year, I'd rather look at what they are able to put on paper, what they are able to tell me.

Another teacher echoed her thoughts about the importance of using everyday classroom experiences to measure the children's abilities.

> [Devin:] I just feel like I can tell a lot from a kid's writing. If the child writes something for me, I can tell if they can read. I can tell if they actually know how to write. I know how in-depth they can write. If there's detail, if there's a story in there. I can tell a lot more in something that's more authentic than from something like [a standardized test].

During the years 1991 to 2000, the teachers at Elena used the following types of informal assessment measures: running records, writing samples, portfolios, and anecdotal records. Running records were a method of recording what children were reading and diagnosing the reading behaviors and strategies they were using (Clay, 1991). Running records gave teachers an immediate picture of what strategies the children were using as they read. They could be analyzed by teachers to assist them in determining specific teaching strategies they could use to help the children progress. Writing samples were either writing prompts given by the teachers to the students on a specific topic, or journal entries the teachers collected in order to analyze. They provided a sample of how the child spelled and used grammar and syntax. Anecdotal records were simply observations teachers recorded of behaviors they witnessed in the children. This could range from what type of book they chose to read or a spot check on their fluency. Portfolios were used for a few years to provide the students and teachers with ways to continually develop a repertoire of student work to analyze and exhibit growth and progress over time, as well as showing how well the child was able to meet the skills required by the state.

The Primary Assessment for Language and Math (PALM) assessment was designed in 1993 by teachers and area university professors of reading to replace the ITBS for first through second grades. This tool was used by teachers to study students' reading and writing by taking running records and examining writing samples. PALM was an informal measure and matched quite a few of the teaching methods teachers at Elena used during that time. Therefore, it had much validity to the teachers as a tool they could actually use without interrupting their regular routines. The PALM was far removed from the ways teachers had formerly assessed students, and the required training that accompanied the PALM increased the teachers' knowledge base in literacy instruction and assessment. The Developmental Reading Assessment (DRA) is also used two times a year by teachers in grades 1–3 to determine reading levels and record reading behaviors by having children individually read passages aloud to teachers as they record their fluency rate and mistakes. Comprehension is assessed by asking children to answer questions about the passage read. The DRA was field tested and reviewed by Reading Recovery (Clay, 1991) teachers and classrooms teachers.

[Devin:] The literacy PALM wasn't a bad thing because they had five or six different components. Nobody had to change their day for that. Nobody has to tell the kids, "Okay you've got to write a writing prompt for me." It's what we do every day. All you do is tell the kids, "Today is going to count big, try your best," and they do. I know I would say Tuesday and Thursday, I'm going to pick up everybody's journal entries and I'll choose the best one. At least the literacy PALM became something I could use. I think the actual assessment was difficult for some because they didn't teach like that. I think DRA is excellent; I like the way it's set up. [The DRA] matches up with the way I teach. So I think it's easy for the kids even though they are being tested, it's kind of easy for them in that sense.

Devin described the alignment between the PALM and the DRA's assessment methods and her classroom practice. While the PALM required teachers to evaluate students' everyday writing, and the DRA took measures of the children's reading behaviors, both instruments allowed teachers to take a look at how students constructed the final product. The end result was assessed through ongoing monitoring and teacher observation. Each tool could elicit a fairly complete picture of how the child produced the writing, how the child made their way through the text, and what strategies they were capable of using independently and what needs the teachers could address and support.

More formal assessment measures were also required by the state and/or district. My tenure at Elena was always marked by some sort of state-mandated tests and national tests. We were required to formally assess the students at every grade level twice a year. The first test, the Iowa Test of Basic Skills (ITBS)[1], was given in the early spring. The Texas state test has taken on many names and purposes. In 1987 it was the Texas Assessment of Basic Skills (TABS) test. It gradually changed and became the Texas Examination and Assessment of Minimum Skills (TEAMS), the Texas Assessment of Academic Skills (TAAS), and in 2003 the Texas Assessment of Knowledge and Skills (TAKS) will be used. The ITBS test and the state tests covered the basic skills of reading and writing. Children read passages and answered multiple-choice questions. There were some word analysis questions, and there was a grammatical section on syntax and punctuation. The TAAS test added a required writing sample for fourth-grade students. Recently, reading has been a focus in Texas. When George W. Bush became governor, the state began to follow the call of the *Nation at Risk* (1983) mentality. Believing that the country was in a state of crisis and many children were not learning to read, Bush created policy and funding to focus on the literacy of children in Texas. This resulted in the creation of the Texas Center for Reading and Language Arts, based at the University of Texas special education department, and of additional legislation to increase accountability for schools. This increase in accountability first appeared in the form of more required assessments that were used in addition to the assessments prior to the accountability system.

In 2001, Elena was required to use three informal measures to evaluate students' literacy. The Texas Primary Reading Inventory (TPRI), developed for the Texas Education Agency by educational psychology researchers at the University of Houston, is designed to assess kindergartners, first graders, and second graders in the areas of graphophonic knowledge (letter recognition/sound symbol relationships), phonemic awareness (identification of sounds within words), word recognition, listening, and reading comprehension. This tool was tested on 3,000 Texas children and developed for teachers to administer individually to each child in their classroom at the beginning and the end of the school year. The Flynt Cooter is an Informal Reading Inventory (IRI) developed by a university researcher and a teacher to determine the reading level of upper elementary grades (3–6). The inventory provides reading passages and miscue analysis of running records for teachers to look for patterns in students' reading. The Star (2004) computer assessment was used by some teachers and required students to read words and reading passages on the computer, and it gave teachers a grade level for each child's reading ability. Our literacy curriculum specialist, Natalie, provided her analysis of the use of these assessment tools she assisted teachers in administering:

> Here are all of the things the teachers are doing in reading assessment. In kindergarten, first grade and second grade, they are doing the TPRI, which assesses their phonemic awareness, their spelling, their word recognition, their oral reading, and their comprehension, but it's different at different grades. We're doing the TPRI and the DRA reading assessment in K–3, and the Flynt Cooter in third grade and above. Some teachers use the STAR assessment, the computer STAR assessment, that's just our school, not the district. The Flynt Cooter, the TPRI, and the DRA are required by the district, as is the ITBS and the TAAS . . . [T]he DRA is very helpful because it helps teachers find out very quickly what books their children are likely to be successful with. It's a quick leveler, from what I hear, teachers do not mind doing it even though the DRA takes quite a bit of time. They do have to be able to do running records which is sometimes hard for new teachers coming in. If they were here when there was a lot of running record training available, the teachers don't complain about the DRA . . . [Y]ou hear them saying, you know, I get good information from the DRA. It shows, especially in first and second grade. They see a lot of growth with their kids. They can tell where they started, where they've gone. The reason we do the DRA is the comprehension. It's the type of question I like to see on a reading test. It's just: tell me about the story. You just read a retelling [prompt] and there's little things that the teacher can check off . . . the teacher can tell me more and ask more leading questions but then it's just up to the teacher to subjectively decide whether this kid really understood the story or not. They don't have to ask these inferential questions. There's no way to say they got three out of four, let's stop. It's just up to the teacher . . . [T]he TPRI is not well designed.

As these literacy assessment measures were mandated in the past few years, teachers were required to use them with little or no training. Prior to the mandates, the state had not necessarily provided, in Illeana's words, "a lot of support. In fact, it took us a long time to get the materials, and then we ordered our own materials to supplement. They wanted the teachers to share one set of materials . . . [W]e put money into the account and said we want each teacher to have their own set." Being well versed in assessment measures, the teachers I spoke to were very analytical in their appraisal of the measures.

[Illeana:] Elena kind of started before [the state], we were doing the writing sample school wide. That was our own initiative. Then I think more people are using the DRA and the Flynt Cooter because it is state mandated, but also because we had training here where teachers learned how to do running records. As far as I know, [the teachers] didn't have any official training now for TPRI. They did, but they were those [voluntary] after school trainings where after you work all day then you go to another meeting and learn how to do it. But here on campus, I know that Natalie has offered a lot of help with that if you don't know how to do it . . . [W]hen I first got here, I'd go into classrooms and I would show teachers how to do running records and then they would take over. The assessment has both sides, the good and the bad, but at least they are doing it. At least they are doing the assessment and figuring out what the kids know and what they don't know. That's not something we did [require everyone to assess]. Although we were working on that part, but now when the state has mandated we have to do it, two or three times a year. I do think that it's really helping them learn how to do the DRA's using that material.

One classroom teacher summed up the major instruments she used to assess literacy at Elena as she provided analysis of the various reading tests she was required to give her third-grade students. A veteran teacher, she was able to articulate and critique the weaknesses in the tools from her classroom perspective. She depended on the DRA more than the other tools.

[Dolores:] We've been doing a lot of running records. We're doing DRA and Flynt Cooter. There are some conflicts with DRAs and Flynt Cooters. When I do a DRA it may show a child reading at a level 30, when you do a Flynt Cooter and it shows them reading at a level 4 which is . . . I mean that's a year's difference . . . so I'm thinking how?. . . and all of these are narratives. How do you work in informational text? That's probably the place where most of our kids have shortcomings, grasping technical and scientific kind of language. And this doesn't range it because I have students where it says level 7 and I'm going no, I don't think so. I think the DRA may be more accurate than the Flynt Cooter and then there is the STAR assessment that we use on the computer. It gives you another level. To me, it's more of a vocabulary-based test and there's no real context clues given, it's just fill in the blank and I don't really value it. We do it at the beginning of the year and at the end of the year, but it doesn't really stand up for me.

Once she explained her thoughts on the various state-mandated assessments, she relayed what she believed to be the best way to her to measure her students' progress in reading—observing them. Most teachers I spoke to depended on informal measures. Katia, another classroom teacher, illustrated how the teachers went beyond to gather additional information. She used the required tests and added journals and knowledge she gained from conferences. She was able to collect vast amounts of instructional techniques and cull the most effective practices. She was a relatively new teacher who was in her second year of teaching but had been a parent of a struggling reader and had recently graduated with a specialization in reading instruction.

[Katia:] I use the DRA, I used Flynt Cooter at the beginning, that's because it's a district thing, the Star (2004), one-on-one reading and I do a lot of reading journals. [I do] reading responses or chapter responses and summaries. I've been to a bunch of training in Natalie's room. I went to a guided reading workshop this year, it was just a repeat of everything I already know and I felt I knew more anyway too . . . It gave me extra little ideas, not that I use them all the time, but I will use some. I've been to a literature circles workshop which to me was worthless; I found out more information from the book. [I attended a] reluctant readers workshop, [a regional reading conference]. I loved it. As a mother, [I used] what I went through with my son, and I thought, I'm not going to allow that to happen with my daughter. She was reading before she went into school.

Her beliefs and knowledge as a teacher and a mother combined to inform her teaching and assessment practices. She was not only a knowledgeable teacher; she was a parent. Her knowledge about literacy was broad and diverse. She did what was required but also drew from a large amount of additional information about reading and teaching. From an administrator's standpoint, the importance of natural settings for observations of students' performance was evident. Illeana shared her view of the pull between assessment using required measures and finding a balance between more authentic assessment tools. Each assessment required by the state was done individually and took long periods of time to complete, when some of this information could be obtained by teacher observation. She felt that teachers could assess their students in more natural ways and emphasized the importance of analyzing the children through comparing scores.

[Illeana:] The TPRI (phonics test) has parts that require a quiet environment. They do phonemic awareness. You have to say words, and the child has to be able to hear you and then listen and be able to tell you about the sounds which would be difficult in a kindergarten class with 22 students. When I walk into some of the kinder classes and I see the amount of assessment, I start questioning, "Do we need all this?" And I think, "No, we don't need that much, not at kinder." I think there's more pressure on the students and its not a natural process. It's more, you can assess for a lot of those things naturally without having to test. We do our writing samples . . . [W]e're getting better about just not giving an assessment. Natalie calls the teachers in and they sit and discuss, "Okay let's look at my samples compared to your samples and how did you get your kids to do this?" We're trying to get it implemented school wide at each grade level so children are learning, or at least exposed to, the same things.

There was a tension between assessing the children's literacy through the teachers' views and the state's views, the position of the state being to gather more standardized measures of literacy and the teachers' that the daily growth of a child could not be evaluated by one test. This put pressure on the teachers. The beliefs of the teachers were evident as was their high level of knowledge about reading. These were experts in their field, professional educators who were knowledgeable and had similar views regarding literacy assessment tools. But the increasing number of required assessments by the district and state challenged these teachers in the area of reading. For the most part, the teachers at Elena remained true to their belief systems about literacy and conducted their teaching in accordance with how they interpreted their students' needs. They trusted their ability to assess their own students.

I leave this section with two basic ideas about teaching and assessing the literacy of children at Elena. The teachers I interviewed had high hopes for the children. They saw literacy as a meaningful activity, an essential tool for students to learn about themselves and the world around them. Thinking was important. Reading meant that students were understanding, questioning, and applying new information to their experiences. Assessment was viewed by the teachers as crucial to their success, but assessment had to live up to the teachers' expectations. It was supposed to inform their teaching. They tended to depend on assessments they could trust: their observations and discussions with their students. The measuring tools mandated by the school and district were implemented, but the teachers were critical and unsure about their reliability and validity. This journey led me to recognize that not only did the teachers want a high level of literacy for their students, but that they were very literate themselves. These were highly literate teachers by the definition of literacy that Freire (1987) defined as "problem-posing." The perceived "problem" at Elena, on the part of the teachers, was the difficulty the children had with literacy. The teachers developed their own knowledge of literacy and reading instruction as they sought to become critical thinkers about how best to teach the children of Elena to read. They defined and understood the context of their figured world (Holland et al., 1998) as one in need of answers to questions related to how to teach reading. The artifacts, or assessments of the children, were used to manipulate the tools, or teaching methods, to best fit the needs of the children. The teachers used their own literacy regarding teaching as power, a means with which to change the world of Elena. Natalie concurs:

The majority of [teachers at Elena] are very literate. They can read and discuss a wide variety of topics, what they read leisurely, what they read educationally, and what they read in the newspaper. There's a lot of discussion about that. You can tell they have a high level of comprehension about text.

The context of literacy at Elena was characterized by a teacher population whose desire was to instill a love of reading through meaningful experiences. To the teachers, literacy meant—and was to be used for—enjoyment and learning. Books and journal writing were necessary for the distribution of literacy. The socio-cultural conditions of the figured world of literacy at Elena were guided by the training, knowledge, and ultimately the beliefs of the teachers.

·3·

TEACHING INTERRUPTED

[Katia, a fourth-grade teacher:] [TAAS—Texas Assessment of Academic Skills] got in the way of me being able to pick up my reading [instruction] the way I wanted to . . . [My] independent reading program came in after TAAS was over . . . unfortunately the other books were always shafted and put aside [until TAAS was over]. . . It was ridiculous how TAAS was just consuming everything.

The teachers I interviewed at Elena brought up the TAAS test frequently. Spring had always been a time of testing at Elena, but in the past four years the TAAS test was emphasized year-round, and it affected almost every decision made by the teachers. In this chapter, I will outline the path of many conversations I had with teachers about the impact of the TAAS test. Although the teachers at Elena had developed a high-quality literacy program over the years, the new state assessment requirements altered the way literacy was measured and taught. TAAS was first mentioned in interviews as a time-intensive interruption of their daily teaching practices. As our conversations continued, TAAS was described as a highly pressurized event in the spring and ultimately as an inadequate measure or goal for their students. The interviews illustrated the complexity of the teachers' definitions of literacy and their constructions of the children's abilities.

Because TAAS became a major topic of interviews with my primary informants when I asked them how they taught and measured literacy, I felt obligated to explore their definitions of TAAS reading and asked them to elaborate on how they defined and how they taught in relation to the test. In order to remain true to my original inquiries, which were related to how the teachers at Elena defined literacy and described the literacy of the children and the community, I made deliberate decisions in my data analysis. I chose to emphasize the ways in which the teachers perceived the test's focus, its validity as a literacy assessment tool, and how they described the children's ability to pass

TAAS. I elected to avoid detailed interpretations of the other areas teachers discussed related to politics and more detailed analysis of reading techniques and strategies. Those areas are addressed briefly here but only in order to create a broader background in which to situate the teachers' comments related to defining literacy.

TAAS was given a great deal of attention by the teachers at Elena. It was a large part of their teaching strategy, and it became embedded in their goals. This became evident in early interviews as every participant from teachers to administrators mentioned TAAS mastery as a goal for the students of Elena. Dolores was a third-grade teacher, and she explains how teaching her students to pass TAAS was one of her top three literacy goals:

> My views on literacy? Number one, to have my students love reading, number two, to help them read so they can love reading and do it on their own, and I hate to say this but, number three, master the TAAS objectives. It is just part of reality and I know that when TAAS is on, a TAAS monster takes over me because I'm competitive. I want my students to reflect what I've done in the classroom. It's a matter of pride and I hate that because sometimes your ego gets in the way of what's best for the students.

TAAS was a compulsory state test and therefore a required goal for the teachers. It was the official measure of the state's objectives as stated by the Texas Essential Knowledge and Skills (TEKS). The state's position was clear: "It is the goal of the state that all children read on grade level by the end of Grade 3 and continue to read on grade level or higher throughout their schooling." (TEA Website, 2002). Beginning in the third grade, every child in Texas was tested by the TAAS test to determine their mastery of reading, writing, and math. Fourth graders took the reading, writing, and math test, and fifth and sixth graders took only reading and math. The teachers at Elena were well aware of the test, and many of my conversations centered around their assessment of the TAAS test as an indicator of their students' progress and the type of teaching strategies they used to prepare the students for the TAAS test.

One of the most common themes I found when discussing the TAAS test with the upper-grade teachers was their frustration with the amount of time it took for them to prepare the students for the TAAS test. Katia shared her irritation about the time she had to spend preparing her students for the writing test given in April. The TAAS writing test was centered around a formulaic type of writing prompt which was graded by a point system designed to measure the degree to which the children were able to follow the format.

> [Katia:] I think the one thing I learned at fourth grade was that TAAS got in my way too much. TAAS writing consumed my entire morning practically all the

way [from August] to February because I had Natalie [the campus literacy spe-
cialist] coming in and she spent 3 weeks working with the students for an hour or
an hour and 15 minutes. Before I knew it, it was taking me an hour and a half to
do it. We were also having to teach science and social studies, so instead of [hav-
ing] an integrated reading and writing program, which is what I would prefer to
have, that one hour and a half was spent TAAS writing the whole time.

Katia felt that her integrated reading and writing program suffered at the
hands of the TAAS practice she was required to do by the school's administration. Being a fourth-grade teacher put her in a highly stressful position, because
her students had to take the reading, writing, and math test. To ensure that all
teachers were preparing their students for the test, the common practice at
Elena was to have any teacher teaching "a TAAS grade" to be closely monitored and coached. Teachers who had proven their teaching abilities by having
their classes score well on the test were not watched as closely as those teachers
who were new or having trouble with their test scores. The principal sent the
literacy specialist to assist most novice teachers in their TAAS preparation.

With two years of experience as a teacher and numerous years as a parent
volunteer, Katia was frustrated by the amount of time she had to devote to
TAAS practice sessions. She felt she was a competent, knowledgeable teacher
fresh from her university coursework with a specialization in reading education, yet Katia felt pressured to forego her ideas about integrating her language arts block of time to incorporate reading, writing, science, and social
studies in favor of spending one and one-half hours on a prescribed TAAS
writing program designed by the literacy specialist on campus, Natalie. Natalie was another participant in the study who found herself in the position of
helping teachers teach to the TAAS test. (Later in this chapter, Natalie shares
her views about the validity of TAAS.)

[Katia:] Natalie [the literacy specialist] came in to work with the kids after she
went to some workshop on TAAS writing. She taught my students to elaborate
for three weeks. That consumed my first three weeks of school. Then it was narrative writing. I stuck to [her way of teaching], but stopped early, against her
wishes . . . These kids aren't coming to me as writers. I have to teach them how
to write before I can even [think about TAAS writing]. I told her I wasn't going
to teach narrative writing half-assed. As a parent, I'm coming with experience.
My son has been TAAS tested in writing in fourth grade, eighth grade, and in his
sophomore year. I knew the prompts that had been given during those years. I
guided my kids and taught them narrative the way it needed to be taught, and I
did the criteria charts. I ended up with nobody passing the practice test in October to 12 out of 17 passing in the spring and 7 of them got [scores of] 3's. We
were striving for 4's, but they got 3's, which was better than where they were.

Katia's story touched on aspects every teacher brought up in our discussions related to TAAS. She mentioned the amount of time required for preparing for TAAS, the loss of teacher control over the curriculum, the teacher's reliance on the beliefs they brought to Elena, and their evaluation of the children being low. Katia first criticizes the amount of time Natalie's TAAS writing program took away from her own teaching plans. In addition to sacrificing time in her classroom to practice for TAAS, Katia felt that the TAAS practice techniques offered by Natalie for writing the narrative were not enough, and she used her knowledge and beliefs as a teacher and a parent to evaluate the TAAS practices the literacy specialist prescribed for the students. She had experience as a parent helping her own child with TAAS, and she felt that teaching the children to write before teaching them "TAAS writing" was a priority. Within her statement about the importance of teaching the children to write before teaching the TAAS writing, she described the children arriving in her classroom and being unable to write at the beginning of the year. Although each section of this chapter is divided into themes, there was an unmistakable thread of the teachers' frustrations with the watered-down expectations of TAAS contrasted with their assessment that the children experienced recurring difficulty with mastering the test.

Regular teaching routines were interrupted by TAAS practice lessons, which grew in frequency and intensity over the years. To ensure that students were successful on the TAAS test, most teachers taught specific lessons focused on the test. Yet classroom teachers did not always see eye-to-eye with those outside of the classroom environment. Those differences were clear when I spoke about TAAS to an administrator. Illeana was a former literacy specialist and now the assistant principal. She felt that if good instruction was taking place, that was enough, and the students would pass the TAAS test:

> I think if you have good instruction going on all the time they're going to do well on TAAS. You still have to look at the format and you have to look at the test and what kind of test it is. If you have good instruction, which really boils down to literacy, if they can read and write and understand and communicate, they're going to do well on TAAS.

Even though Illeana believed that sound instructional practices that simply taught the children to read and write would ensure that Elena students would pass the test, the actual practices of the administrators at Elena contradicted this philosophy. Every teacher I interviewed and spoke to informally at Elena admitted to spending a great deal of time teaching the children to take the TAAS test. If the teachers and administrators really believed that the children at Elena would pass the TAAS test without specialized instructional methods devoted to TAAS, then they would not emphasize the coaching of teachers, and teachers would not feel it was necessary to directly address the test through extensive practice. This atmosphere of "teaching to the test" interrupted the teaching of literacy as it had been done prior to such high stakes being placed on the TAAS test. Whereas the teachers at Elena used to rely on the information provided by the other instruments they used to assess literacy, they now became more focused on giving the TAAS practice test in early October and then teaching to those skills required by the test.

The notion that simply teaching children to read would guarantee that they would pass TAAS is essentially the same message the policy makers sent to teachers and the public. State and policy influences and pressures on the figured worlds of Elena are crucial to understanding how the teachers' definitions of literacy were affected by the TAAS test. Hillocks (2002) states: "When the urge to do well on the tests is high and the students are deemed unlikely to perform at satisfactory levels, the knowledge base becomes even more restricted by administrative directives indicating what should be taught, how long, and in what order" (p. 102). As mentioned previously, literacy was a primary focus at Elena for many reasons. Teachers at Elena had a history of seeking out ways for the children to become successfully literate. Yet the mid-1990s was marked by the governor placing an emphasis on all children passing the reading TAAS test in the third grade. Through the course of the study, it became clear that Elena's teachers' goals and ultimately their definitions of literacy changed in response to several state-mandated, reading-focused initiatives. The state's literacy goal was to make certain that all children would be reading on grade level by third grade by implementing a new mandated state reading and writing assessment. In 2001, this standardized test (TAAS) was given to third, fourth, fifth, and sixth graders at Elena.

The definition of literacy underlying this assessment trickled down to Elena by way of state, district, and campus initiatives such as staff development, campus improvement plans, and district and state reading objectives. The Texas Essential Knowledge and Skills (TEKS) reflected everything each student should know. They were the state-sanctioned list of skills all teachers were required to teach, and they matched up directly with the objectives for the TAAS test. The summary of skills listed for third graders in Texas is as follows:

Third grade students read grade-level material fluently and with comprehension. Students use root words, prefixes, suffixes, and derivational endings to recognize words. Students demonstrate knowledge of synonyms, antonyms, and multi-meaning words. Students are beginning to distinguish fact from opinion in texts. During class discussions, third grade students support their ideas and inferences by citing portions of the text being discussed. Students read in a variety of genres, including realistic and imaginative fiction, nonfiction, and poetry from classic and contemporary works. (TEA Website, 2002)

Teachers were expected to meet these state goals for their students. These goals have remained constant throughout my years of teaching in Texas.

As described in the previous section, the teachers were very supportive of the reading goals laid out by the state. The teachers met these goals prior to TAAS through their reading instruction by having the children read and discuss books using a variety of methodologies, as mentioned in Chapter 2. Guided reading, reading and discussing quality literature, and integrating literacy throughout the subject areas of science and social studies were common practices at Elena, and teachers were well trained in implementing a high-quality literacy program based on research. Various authentic assessments such as running records and teacher observations were used by Elena teachers to monitor their students' progress and to assist the teachers in making instructional decisions as they taught, but the high-stakes state TAAS assessment began to reprioritize the hierarchy of assessment tools at Elena.

State testing had been a reality in Texas for over a decade, and the state had a history of constructing its own basic skills tests. In my fourteen years at Elena, I administered the Texas Assessment of Basic Skills (TABS), the Texas Examination and Assessment of Minimum Skills (TEAMS), and the TAAS test. All of these tests were designed for the children of Texas and administered to students to measure their progress in the basic areas of reading and math. Teachers at Elena used the state tests as another measure to enhance their picture of each child's progress, and the state assessments were not weighted to the degree TAAS was weighted. It is important to note that the children at Elena had never excelled at any of the standardized measures, but the majority of students usually passed, and there was no great concern about the students' achievement on standardized measures due to the reliance on more authentic evaluations. Elena looked at the scores as one component of a larger picture of a child's abilities, and teachers took care to place the test in relation to their own assessment tools. In the past, teachers at Elena did very little in the way of specific test preparation, and teachers had never relied on standardized tests to be the sole indicator of how the children were performing. Standardized tests were viewed as snapshots of a moment in time and not considered a true or well-rounded reflection of a student's literacy abilities. There were no accountability measures attached to the scores.

By 2001, everything had changed. The TAAS test became the measure of how Elena teachers and children were performing. Teachers were told that every child should pass the test, and other means of assessment—though still required—were rendered obsolete. TAAS preparation could not be ignored because of the power the scores had to make or break the reputation of the teacher, the school, and the principal. The idea that simply teaching the children to read and write would be sufficient preparation for a test that carried the weight of the entire school, and was the center of the instructional focus, was not realistic. Katia describes her feelings about the day her students were to take the TAAS test:

> The kids were burned, well no, the kids were okay because I think I made it okay for them. I took on all the pressure for them. I cried. I vomited. I had headaches. I did everything and they were excited. They were looking forward to TAAS writing day because my husband made tacos for them. We made a whole TAAS breakfast. It was a big deal for that day to come for everyone and they were so excited about it but on the inside I was the one going through all the chaos.

This illustrates how teachers felt the pressure of the high stakes attached to the test. The difference was in the power of the TAAS test. The state altered the weight of the test as it became the cornerstone of the governor's reading accountability initiative. By being required to measure literacy by way of TAAS, Elena became subject to the state's assessment tool. TAAS became the measure of literacy at Elena because there was no other alternative. The state set up an accountability system to evaluate literacy instruction, and the teachers had to excel.

High-Stakes Assessment Arrives at Elena

In the first year of the high-stakes accountability system, Elena teachers learned the importance of TAAS through firsthand experience. When the TAAS accountability system was new in the mid-1990s, Elena received an unacceptable rating. Our new principal found herself and the school listed in the local newspaper with the lowest rating possible and the district area superintendent and the Texas Education Agency (TEA) calling to set up site visits and school-wide parent meetings to construct a plan to improve instruction at Elena.

The faculty was greatly affected by the unacceptable rating and the events surrounding the TEA audit. Elena's third-grade teachers had elected to administer the third-grade TAAS test in English in order to measure how well their bilingual students were progressing in English. A lack of understanding about the implications of poor performance on the TAAS test caused the teachers and administrators to use the test as a diagnostic tool instead of an evaluation of mastery. The third graders' scores lowered our rating, and though Texas State Representative Dianne White Delisi stated: "TAAS is a diagnostic test. It is not an achievement test" (*Austin American-Statesman*, April 24, 2001), Elena learned quickly that this was not the case. The audit altered the interpretation of the meaning of the test and changed the view the faculty at Elena had about TAAS.

Although standardized assessments have been used by the state and Elena for many years, the state's attachment of high stakes to the assessment of literacy profoundly affected the school's center of attention (Hoffmann, 1999). The "higher stakes" arrived in the form of school ratings: every school and district was assigned a rating based on their TAAS mastery. The Texas Education Agency states: "Districts and campuses must meet all of the TAAS and dropout rate standards to be eligible for a rating category." The ratings made by the state are as follows:

TAAS Standards in Reading, Writing, and Mathematics

- For a campus or district rating of Exemplary, at least 90.0 percent of "all students" and students in each group meeting minimum size requirements must pass each section of the TAAS.
- For a campus or district rating of Recognized, at least 80.0 percent of "all students" and students in each group meeting minimum size requirements must pass each section of the TAAS.
- For a rating of Academically Acceptable (district) or Acceptable (campus), at least 55.0 percent of "all students" and students in each group meeting minimum size requirements must pass each section of the TAAS.
- Those districts (or campuses) not meeting the standard for Academically Acceptable (or Acceptable) or higher will be rated Academically Unacceptable (or Low-performing). (TEA Website, 2002)

Elena found that the demands of the rating system could override the original purpose of the test. This rating altered the focus and approach the school took toward testing and ultimately toward literacy. Faculty meetings became more focused on the state's version of literacy and student achievement on state tests. Staff development plans were tied into the state's mandated improvement plan for the campus of increasing the students' reading and writing achievement.

Once Texas schools began to be measured by their percentage of students passing the test, attention was also paid to the number of minority students passing, in addition to other variables such as dropout rates and attendance rates. School and district performance was documented in detail and published in the newspaper for the community and the state. Each school, and subsequently each district, was rated using the various criteria, and schools not meeting the criteria were audited and often reorganized. Schools that excelled received public recognition, honorable ratings, and some administrators of these schools received financial awards. TAAS was a frequent topic in the news, and the public was highly aware of its authority. Principals, school district officials, and politicians relied on TAAS performance to gauge the success of their careers. The message that schools were held accountable for children passing the test was clear, and the standards also implied that if all children could pass the test, they could all read.

The possession of a passing score reflects Guerra's (1998) conception of "Literacy as Entity" where "the assumptions underlying [literacy] still operate tacitly in notions about how literacy is conceived and how it is institutionally possible to help people become literate" (Guerra, 1998, p. 52). Schools and policy became the institutions or instruments of literacy, and therefore the characterization of "Literacy as Institution" was only able to survive within those institutions as it was defined by Guerra as "the capitalist-oriented approaches [that] recommend literacy as a currency that makes it possible for members of the society to buy their way to success" (Guerra, 1998, p. 55). In order to continue to promote the ideas that schools could make all children literate, institutions such as the state of Texas narrowed and simplified the focus and definitions of literacy.

George W. Bush's "No Child Left Behind Act" as it was presented in Texas in 1996 played a role in the use of TAAS as a measure of reading achievement in elementary children. The act focused on the idea that all children should be reading at or above grade level by the third grade. All of the teachers and administrators at Elena agreed with the premise of teaching all children to read, but the policy as it was enforced used TAAS as the only measure of the reading levels of the children.

The high-stakes use of the TAAS test as an accountability tool was one component of the governor's reading initiative. In addition to holding schools responsible, the state created a support system for teachers and schools. The state sought to educate teachers in reading instruction and created the Texas Center for Reading and Language Arts at the University of Texas at Austin. The center was designed to research and provide training for the teachers of Texas in literacy instruction and was run by the special education department, not the literacy studies department. The center soon began to implement teacher reading academies beginning with kindergarten in 1999, and then following with first grade in 2000, second grade in 2001, and third grade in 2002. A grant from the Texas Education Agency funded the kindergarten-through-second-grade academies, where teachers could attend training for four days and receive materials and a stipend of $600. The third-grade academies were implemented in the summer of 2002 and were the result of a separate funding initiative to extend the program which was granted by TEA.[1]

The third grade Reading Academy was developed by researchers at the Center for Accountability and Reading Skills, located at the University of Texas in Houston, in conjunction with the Texas Education Agency and Education Service Centers IV and XIII. Many of the resources in the Third Grade Teacher Reading Academy were designed by the Texas Center for Reading and Language Arts at the University of Texas at Austin. (Third Grade Teacher Reading Academy, 2002)

The plan was designed to train teachers in reading instruction and assist them in teaching the children of Texas to read. The reading academies were designed to demonstrate how the state skills, Texas Essential Knowledge and Skills (TEKS), were aligned with the TAAS testing objectives. The academies and materials were focused on the adoption of a "research-based" reading instruction model that matched the state's high-stakes test. From the outside, this alignment between the state skills and the state test appears to be purposeful and makes common sense. But to understand the simplistic solution to the perceived reading crisis is to overlook the negative effects of narrowing the knowledge base for teachers.

In Texas, the research chosen to drive all elementary reading instruction in the state was an educational psychology model originating from a differing stance than research conducted by many literacy scholars.[2] The special education department held a specific philosophical stance somewhat different from the literacy department, and the recommendations and research conducted by both departments conflicted in their orientation and areas of focus. This created a singular view of research that espoused a singular theory of reading. The reading academy's distance from reading scholars is evident in this statement, which was presented in the third-grade teacher reading academy:

> We are very fortunate today . . . because we can make truly informed decisions about how best to teach reading. In the past, reading experts tended to pick their favorite theories and told teachers to teach in a manner that conformed to those theories. This has led to teachers receiving confusing and mixed messages. (Third Grade Teacher Reading Academy, 2002)

The teacher-training academies aligned their material with a research focus they claimed to be different from "reading experts." Just as the accountability levels increased and legislators began to provide support, the state funded specific research programs. These research programs controlled the teacher information data base through the reading academies and the state-required assessments. Issues such as politics, curriculum, and teaching methods have come into the literacy assessment realm of Elena more than ever before. The literacy crisis mirrored other educational crises in that once a situation is deemed as requiring action by the voices in power, the action which follows brings support from policies and can be influenced by politics. Claiming that a crisis existed in literacy education benefited policy makers who wanted to "fix" the problem through the system. Berliner & Biddle (1995) state:

> Since the early 1980s, Americans have been subjected to a massive campaign of criticism directed at their public schools and colleges. We have been told that student achievement in those institutions has slipped badly, that our achievement now lags behind that of students in other industrialized countries, and that these judgments are defined by numerous studies. As a result, the critics charge, American students are now being shortchanged and the nation is "at risk." Unfortunately, these charges have often been made by the White House and other prestigious sources, and they have been picked up and endlessly elaborated on in the media. (p. 64)

The reading initiative and the TAAS test were "picked up and endlessly elaborated on in the media" in Texas as the awareness and the pressure on the teachers and administrators at Elena grew.

Bob, a veteran teacher of twenty-four years, was an avid follower of the news and shared his thoughts about the pervasiveness of the literacy rhetoric that surrounded Elena. His reference to "Mr. Bush's definition" indicates the perception by many teachers at Elena that the whole accountability system was a political endeavor. He understood how the news relayed in the newspapers was enacted at the classroom level. In Texas, the TAAS test was the primary indicator of students' reading ability. Therefore, the new definition of reading was a combination of the skills tested on the TAAS test and the surrounding factors such as the practice materials and new teacher workshops created to help teachers assist children in passing the test.

> [Bob:] It is sad that literacy has become Mr. Bush's definition. It's just one of these bumps in the road. It'll have to be removed, but it's going to take a lot of removal because they're going to put a ton of money into it. There's going to be a lot of vested interest. These testing companies and all these people will be making so much money they won't want to give it up.

Bob criticized the political and financial nature of the reading initiative. Many companies developed test practice materials for schools to purchase, and the state spent large amounts of money on research and teacher training. The political nature of the reading initiative was in the forefront as Governor Bush soon ran for U.S. President.

The atmosphere at Elena fell under the control of TAAS because of the pressure from the state, the media, and the school district. Thus the perceived crisis of reading in the state, in turn, allowed money for programs which then accompanied efforts by the state to design plans for educational reforms in the area of reading. In Texas, this "reading crisis" replicated the national movement of the National Research Council (1998) and the National Reading Panel (1999).[3] Elena had previously operated from a standpoint that valued teacher knowledge from many sources, but the emphasis on passing TAAS placed a different focus on reading instruction.

TAAS's Impact on Instruction: The Narrowing Definition of Literacy

Elena students' performance on TAAS moved measuring reading into areas of the teacher's curriculum, where the test objectives became the curriculum guide and therefore narrowed the possibilities of instruction. Once TEA visited Elena, teachers and administrators understood the gravity of making decisions based on anything other than passing as many students as possible. Since Elena was rated as an "academically unacceptable" school that one year, teachers learned the true weight of the test and began to seek out ways to teach the students to pass. "When the teacher's professional worth is estimated in terms of test success, teachers will corrupt the measured skills by reducing them to the level of strategies in which the examinee is drilled" (Madaus, 1988, p. 40). Caroline, a fifth-grade teacher, shared her thoughts about the pressures of seeking success and how she differentiated between teaching reading and teaching children to pass the TAAS test:

> There's that pressure to want your kids to do well on the test and you want them to pass the test. There's that focus on this is what they need to know on the test and then at the same time, the test is basic skills that they should have anyway. I think that a lot of the way we go about teaching the TAAS and the pressure of the TAAS doesn't really make that environment a natural learning environment for the students. I think that it's too high pressured. If you get these right, then you get rewarded, if you don't, then you're punished and you're set apart from the rest of the world . . . It's a hard thing to have to have in your classroom, that pressure . . . But I do feel that there was a lot of push [to pass the TAAS test] and a lot of it wasn't natural reading. I didn't think that the kids were learning and I didn't think that they were learning to be better educated or to be better students or to be better members of society. I thought that they were learning so they could pass the test.

Teachers and administrators learned quickly that the primary goal was to teach the children to read enough to pass the test. This impacted instruction in several ways as teachers and administrators realized the importance of teaching students how to pass the test. The Elena campus began to utilize the TAAS pretest materials in early fall as a guide to reading ability, and the teachers regrouped children based on their pretest performance. Teachers then focused instruction on testing strategies, due to the widespread belief at Elena that just teaching the children to read was not adequate preparation for TAAS. This idea, held by many teachers, became more complicated as the interviews progressed. There was constant conflict between the two contradictory notions of good instruction as sufficient preparation for TAAS and the idea that TAAS required special instructional techniques. Any other notions about what literacy might mean or the goals the teachers mentioned earlier about wanting the students to enjoy and think about reading began to fade as attention fell on passing the test. Teachers related stories regarding the ways in which they felt it necessary to address the TAAS test once I inquired about their daily literacy instruction. A marked departure from their more theoretical ideals of literacy, the descriptions of their actual students and practices altered the language they used to define literacy.

TAAS's influence could also be seen in teaching practices and curriculum changes. TAAS preparation at Elena could be classified as what Haladyna, Noel and Haas (1991) describe as test pollution. Test pollution describes several ways Elena teachers taught or motivated students to pass TAAS. These practices include:

> (a) teaching test-taking skills, (b) promoting student motivation for the test, (c) developing a curriculum to match the test, (d) preparing teaching objectives to match the test, (e) presenting items similar to those presented on the test, (f) using commercial materials specifically designed to improve test performance, and (g) presenting before the test the actual items to be tested. (p. 4)

Teachers at Elena participated and sought to become well versed in all of those activities, and the students' performance on the test improved. After the first year of being rated as an unacceptable campus, TAAS literacy scores moved to a comfortable zone for Elena and have remained there since 1994. Elena maintained an acceptable rating. Bob explained how consistent Elena's scores had been over the years: "[The scores] have been sitting right at 70 for eight years. They haven't jumped up a bit. They jump every now and then. One grade level will jump then it will settle back down. Then another grade level will jump, then it will settle back down." Elena was safe. Teachers were careful and attentive to the test, and the scores remained stable. Our scores for reading in 2001 are listed in Table 3.

Teachers and administrators at Elena had altered the instructional focus, and the students were becoming successful at passing the TAAS test. After the

TABLE 3: TAAS Reading Scores for 2001

Grade Level	Percentage of students passing
Third Grade	81%
Fourth Grade	72%
Fifth Grade	83%
Sixth Grade	80%

audit in 1993, Elena regularly began to purchase numerous TAAS practice materials published by private companies, to teach test-taking strategies such as answering the questions without reading the passage, and altering the curriculum to increase the amount of TAAS practice. In these ways the TAAS test affected the literacy practices of the teachers so as to minimize the depth and scope of the curriculum. With the stakes set high, there had to be attention paid to passing, and Elena needed to receive good ratings. Training, mentoring new or struggling teachers, and test preparation were key in the new ordering of priorities. Some teachers at Elena developed reputations for continually performing well on TAAS. They were valued by the administration and sent to classrooms to teach other teachers to be successful on TAAS. Teaching children to pass was considered an art that many times involved instructing students to actually not read the complete text. Katia explained how Maria came to her room to teach her children how to pass TAAS:

> Maria does it [teaches teachers on campus how to pass TAAS]. She is one of those teachers that if you made time for them, they'll come and you observe them and they'll come and teach your kids how to pass the TAAS. Even the principal, the first year that I was doing it, she asked me, "Are you making the kids read the passage before they answer the questions?" and I said, "No" and she said, "Don't do that. *Make sure that you're not making them read.* You need to teach them how to find those answers. You need to teach them to find the answers so they can pass."

It was Katia's first year of teaching, and the principal wanted to make sure that her children passed. Katia was a recent graduate from the University of Texas and had a specialization in reading instruction, but she was pressured into teaching the children to "find the answers" and "not read the passage." It was too important to risk allowing her to teach reading; she was supposed to teach the children how to take the TAAS test. This can be compared in some ways to what Apple (1986) describes as intensification, which may cause teachers to "'cut corners' by eliminating what seems to be inconsequential to the task at hand" (p. 42). Intensification was evident when teachers at Elena began to teach to the test and disregard other activities. Apple (1986) goes on to predict that this atmosphere may lead to what he terms intellectual deskilling, "in which mental workers are cut off from their own fields and again must rely even more heavily on ideas and processes provided by experts" (p. 42). Many Elena teachers were at that point in their pedagogy, while others I interviewed were fighting as hard as they could to remain informed and committed to the latest professional knowledge. Testing's influence was also felt in the lower grades not administering the TAAS test. Devin, a former pre-kindergarten teacher, now second-grade teacher, shared her thoughts on the impact of testing on curriculum and teaching methods:

> When it comes down to testing, that kind of changes the perspective a bit because what ends up happening is—it's not a suggestion any more. It's more of a require-ment and so I think that teachers start feeling like, "Oh okay, they want the kids to know their letters, then I'll teach them the letters." Then what happens is that program starts becoming more watered down. It again changes what you are doing. This year I had to do ITBS [Iowa Test of Basic Skills]. Well we didn't get any warning with the ITBS, so really I knew nothing about it. My kids went in and I never did any prepping or anything so maybe that's good. When I think about it, the thing is that now that I know we have it, I keep thinking, well am I going to start getting little practice booklets? Am I going to get little practice ma-terials to prep them for this? That starts changing the perspective of your cur-riculum. If you know you've got something else that you're accountable for here.

The influence of TAAS on the curriculum was profound. Even though TAAS tested the same skills the teachers had always valued, teachers felt that just teaching literacy did not guarantee that the students would pass. Devin ex-plained how once teachers understood what was on the test, they would focus on those items and, in her words, "water down" the curriculum. She embodied the notion that all teachers I interviewed agreed upon: all of the children at Elena should pass the test. There were no debates about the reading objectives of TAAS being sufficient for the children; it was felt that the "watered-down" goals should be met by the children. But the difficult finding was the conflict-ing ideas of a TAAS, watered-down curriculum, and a student population per-ceived by most teachers at Elena as incapable of passing. This deficit view (Va-lencia & Solorzano, 1997) will be discussed further in Chapter 4. Teachers expressed complex and contradictory thoughts concerning their high expecta-tions and their students' lack of achievement on TAAS. In some cases, the teachers resorted to the idea that TAAS was somewhat culturally biased and presented in a format not capable of revealing higher-level literacy skills.

Therefore, the curriculum became dependent on the practice-booklet scores. Assessment had always driven instruction at Elena, but the assessment format had changed, and to align the daily teaching methods with the assessment tool format only made sense, whether the teachers believed it was good practice or not. "Teaching to the high-stakes test is easy. It can quickly become a comfortable form of pedagogy, and students will become proficient at passing the test by mastering the tradition of past tests. Teaching becomes a defensive act" (Madaus, 1988, p. 40). Katia relates her defensive dilemma as a TAAS teacher. In defense of her beliefs about teaching, she does not want to just teach the TAAS testing skills, yet she knows her own experiences with test taking did not require reading the passages. Her view was common and continues to illustrate the underlying themes that the children at Elena were "unable to understand" and that teaching the "tricks" worked.

> [Katia:] I don't believe in teaching them the tricks to get the information but they can't get it otherwise because they won't understand. So the reason why I [practiced the tricks], relates back to my own experience. When I had to take the test that allows you to go to UR, I didn't read the passages. I read the questions and I went and found the answers and I passed the test with flying colors without reading a passage. So I took that experience and thought, "Well, I know my kids and I only have after intersession until test time to prepare them and this is the best way I know how to." That's why I went that route but I felt very pressured because I felt that TAAS writing took everything out of me as a fourth-grade teacher and then there wasn't enough left over for reading and math.

Katia's frustration reflects her understanding that TAAS reading skills have priority over her reading program, and the risk of forgoing the TAAS practice would be frowned upon by the administration at Elena and would jeopardize low students' chances of passing. All of the teachers at Elena concurred, and TAAS was perceived as a unique genre of reading.

TAAS Reading: A New Reading Genre at Elena

> [Bob:] You're not teaching for understanding. You're teaching one specific way of testing. One specific way and that's not doing these kids any good.

The teachers all agreed that TAAS was a different type of reading requiring specific techniques such as using practice materials, teaching the children to underline passages and key words, and to not think critically about the text. In Chapter 2, the teachers described their view of a literate child as one who possesses the ability to read, enjoy, and think critically about text, while the TAAS test required children to read incomplete, brief passages and answer simple questions. Teaching TAAS skills was not just teaching the TEKS skills required by the state. TAAS was its own genre. If the children were going to be successful, they had to understand how to take the test. Practicing for the TAAS test improved our scores and kept them in an acceptable range. The teachers discovered a safe method for teaching TAAS reading, but they still realized the differences between how they used literature and reading methods to develop literate students and how they used TAAS strategies to develop good test takers. Caroline explained how her image of teaching the fifth grade using literature conflicted with her need to teach the students to take the TAAS test. Reading and answering questions for the TAAS test was not the same as reading and discussing literature:

> You have these short little passages on the [TAAS] test and they're—I felt a lot of times—they're boring. They're not interesting. They don't really relate well to what the kids want to learn or what they do learn. Before, I tried to find literature that I had read that I thought was really good. I like the whole idea of how my college courses were taught with literature, those were the best courses. I think that's the best way to learn about literature, take different interpretations and talk about them and get the other kids talking and then build on those ideas and gain new knowledge that way. I tried to do that and that's one of the reasons I wanted [to teach] the upper grades because I wanted to be able to do that.

Caroline had planned to teach literature with a high level of student engagement and critique, but found herself tied to the TAAS practice formats of simply reading the passages and answering the questions. Dolores echoed her sentiments. She felt that TAAS reading was far removed from reading real literature. Her high-achieving students had trouble adjusting to the differences. She explained that they resented the practice lessons and found them boring:

> I have become aware that that may become an issue with some of my kids when you have to do TAAS passages because they are so different. I mean they really are different than actual literature, it's just not the same. So there's different strategies that kids have to use [for TAAS] that are great strategies for reading, but it's TAAS reading.

Dolores acknowledges that a few of the reading strategies she used for TAAS preparation were "great," but they were not the strategies she might use for literature lessons. The teachers at Elena felt that the TAAS test was a lower-level activity and a very separate form of reading than thinking about and discussing literature. But the bottom line was that teachers developed a tendency to overprepare and drill the TAAS skills and testing formats regardless of the skill level of the student. It was the skill level of the TAAS test that took priority. Therefore, that's what most teachers set as their goal.

Bob, and others, critiqued the skills and criteria of the TAAS objectives in light of the larger view of the kind of literacy it purports to achieve for the students. He explained that being successful on the TAAS test was not indicative of his definition of literacy as a broad concept that utilizes critical thinking and a high level of competency:

> [Bob:] I think [teachers] do think that it's a little body of skills. As far as TAAS is concerned, it's eight little skills or six or whatever it is, and if you can do six you're a literate person. But none of those things, if you look at them: main idea and word recognition. That's all it is, [testing] details. You can be a TAAS whiz. That's the kind of people we're developing.

Unsatisfied with what he considered to be a watered-down version of literacy, Bob continued by describing how a student new to his class had a difficult time adjusting to his style of teaching. His story about her reluctance to participate in his classroom discussions illustrates the behavior of a student new to reading critically. In her previous classroom she had not been required to participate actively and critically. He taught reading using guided reading discussion groups that required the students not only to understand the readings but to participate in book discussions, a way of teaching he sees as being separate from TAAS.

> [Bob:] It's the way she's been trained . . . [Her old classroom] was a large group . . . She could just sit there and not have to speak—ever. Well in here, when we do our friendly little guided reading groups, they all have to talk. I don't let anybody sit. They all have to respond. So when she first got in here, she would just giggle and put her head down and not respond. That was it. But now, after a while she's figured out that usually would work with the other teachers. They would leave her alone because they would think they were doing her a favor, being nice not making her talk. I wouldn't let her do that. I made her participate. When it was her turn, she would be asked a question. Well after about a week and a half she started answering the questions and I thought, "Well okay you're answering the questions. That's the way it should be."

If Bob is teaching literacy as a classroom discussion of issues and trying to "untrain" the students to be passive receptacles of information and regurgitate answers, then he is moving outside of the idea of teaching to the test. Madaus (1988) writes, "How do teachers teach to the test? The answer is relatively simple. Teachers see the kind of intellectual activity required by previous test questions and prepare the students to meet these demands" (p. 232). So once teachers were familiar with the test requirements, they began to teach to these requirements. Penny, a special education teacher, described how some children had been conditioned to read "for TAAS":

> You see them, the kids who are in the TAAS classrooms. Sometimes you can spot those kids that are in the classroom for TAAS work because you give them that TAAS and they are underlining, circling, numbering, and doing all of this. They've got those strategies down, but they don't know quite what to do with all of them but you can see the ones you've taught do this, and the teacher's like, "I'm going to be walking around with a clipboard. If you're not doing these things I'm just going to mark it on my little thing and those of you who did it get a pizza party."

The idea that children were taught to underline specific sections or words as they skimmed test practice passages and then were rewarded for it with pizzas was common. The TAAS reading program unofficially sanctioned the use of TAAS practice materials and teaching for mastery of those behaviors. Here is where one aspect of the high-stakes nature of TAAS comes into play: rewards and punishments were given according to performance. Rewards at Elena were pizza parties and trips to the local water park for the children. While teachers' names and scores were circulated and used for their teaching evaluations, administrators and schools received awards through publicity. TAAS rewards and practice materials had become so pervasive that one Texas lawmaker felt it necessary to propose a bill. "House Bill 1646 would bar the use of TAAS study guides as an instructional tool except in intensive programs designed for students who have failed the exam. It would also prohibit school employees from giving students material rewards based on their test scores" (*Austin American-Statesman*, February 23, 2001). TAAS is the primary goal for administrators, schools, and teachers. Incentives for success, unheard of prior to TAAS, consisted of trips to water parks, pizza parties, swimming parties, candy, or tacos. Students at Elena learned to find specific answers for rewards rather than read multiple texts for enjoyment and learning.

Elena teachers' view that TAAS reading was different from their regular reading program can be compared to the concept of literacy as adaptation. This theory focuses on literacy as a pragmatic tool for survival. TAAS was touted as a measure of how the state's children were reading. A school was doing well if their reading scores were acceptable, but Elena teachers held the view that the TAAS test was not able to provide them with information detailed enough to guide instruction because of their extensive knowledge base. TAAS, to the teachers at Elena, was little more than an additional measure of *if* the children could read or not. Natalie described how the information on the TAAS test was not adequate for teachers, as the test did not provide valuable information to inform their teaching:

> The test itself, I don't have a problem. I do not have a problem with the way the reading test is done. It's a reading passage. The questions are fine. A child who is

literate at their grade level should be able to do that. It doesn't give very good information to the teacher. First of all, most of the teachers know going in whether the child is going to pass or fail the test. They don't need the test to tell them, especially at third grade. I have a lot of experience at third grade, it didn't give information about what the child was doing, whether it was oral reading they were having problems with, or decoding, or whether it was a comprehension problem, or they don't have the vocabulary. All it measures is whether they can answer questions about the passage.

When asked if TAAS measured reading, Katia concurred with Natalie. Both believed that any child reading at grade level should pass the required TAAS objectives, and they both discount the value of TAAS as an informative way to illustrate a child's reading proficiency.

> [Katia:] No I don't think [TAAS measures reading] because at this point, I haven't gotten the scores. But it wouldn't be a true reflection of what they would know in reading. I think it would be lower because I think what TAAS does is teach them how to take a test. Here at this school anyway. We don't teach them how to read for information. We teach them how to take the test. I can say at this school I am teaching so that the kids can pass that test, teaching them how to pass it. I'm not teaching them to read the passages and understand them. I'm teaching them how to find the information and take shortcuts so that they don't end up brain dead half way through the test because they've read and reread.

Katia refers to the ideas other teachers mentioned as they described the TAAS test. Their opinions centered around the ideas that TAAS was not a true reflection of the children's literacy but was a separate form of reading and had to be specifically addressed through explicit instructional methods. As an assessment tool, the teachers at Elena felt that TAAS did not give teachers valuable information beyond how the children could perform on the test itself. Darling-Hammond (1991) supports this view: "Because of the way the tests are constructed, they ignore a great many kinds of knowledge and types of performance that we expect from students, and they place test-takers in a passive, reactive role, rather than engage their capacities to structure tasks, generate ideas, and solve problems" (p. 220). Elena teachers were knowledgeable and adept at using various reading assessments in order to monitor their students' growth. The TAAS test contributed little to the portfolio of a child's work. These two quotes show the complexity of the views the teachers held and are similar to Hillocks's (2002) research with teachers under high-stakes assessment pressure. TAAS was a unique genre and measured basic skills, but teachers felt it was not a true measure of literacy, and students had to be coached to achieve adequate scores for these lower-level skills. Natalie discussed how

TAAS could not be used as an assessment tool for teachers. Once TAAS was defined as a yes-or-no type of monitor for a student's reading ability, it was critiqued for all it did not measure.

> [Natalie:] I don't think it gives teachers enough information. You look at the results and you can say, "Oh this many of these third graders can't read." Okay so what? Are you going to fix them? You can jump to assumptions that are wrong. You can say, this child can't decode words, but that's not their problem. They could have read orally and fluently with no problem, but they can't answer the questions because they have a problem with comprehension. So then, if you're putting a program in place that teaches them how to decode words you may be wrong. So it doesn't tell you exactly what the child's problem is. Yes, if they fail the test, yes they are having some problems with reading. What problems are they having? It's not there. There's not enough analysis.

The teachers at Elena believed that they knew their students, and scores were rarely a revelation for them. The teachers' arguments about TAAS as a unique reading genre focused on lower-level or functional literacy skills mirrors what Illeana states:

> I think we're getting better at getting them to write for a purpose and read for a purpose, more than just to pass the TAAS. I would say looking at our TAAS scores most of our sixth graders are at the point where they can pass the test *but I think they still need to continue working on being fluent readers and writers.*

Illeana states that passing TAAS is not a criterion for all of the skills that the students need, and even though most of our students pass, she reveals her judgment that they need more, another indication that meeting the standards for TAAS is not enough. She also implies that they are able to pass TAAS yet need to work on being fluent readers and writers. This mirrors what the teachers hinted at regarding the notion that passing TAAS did not require the students to be fluent readers. In light of the amount of knowledge the teachers at Elena had about literacy instruction and assessment, the TAAS test was not a useable source of data. Students read passages of text and answered questions about the main idea, events, and a few inference-type questions, but as far as being a source for teachers to turn to inform their teaching, TAAS came up short compared to assessment tools the Elena teachers used on their own. Teachers must still rely on taking running records to analyze actual reading behaviors so they have a diagnostic evaluation of where the children are and how to assist them. Some teachers saw the extensive assessment requirements as a waste of time when the only measure was TAAS. Illeana reiterated what most teachers said about TAAS's ability to support teachers in appraising their students:

Well, I think if it didn't have so many passages it would be okay. You don't have to have 20 different passages to know that this child knows how to read and comprehend, but of course it's not the ideal way to test either. I think the ideal would be getting a running record, [but] who is going to come in and insure that that's done? If they would let us turn in our running record scores, that's the better indicator of whether the child can read or comprehend.

Illeana agreed with teachers I interviewed that the priority at Elena was on TAAS, not running records, teacher observations, or the DRA. Therefore, the power of other assessments in the teachers' eyes began to fall. The accountability system preferred TAAS, so the teachers began to follow suit. TAAS did not inform the teachers' literacy instruction; it informed teachers about the children's ability to pass the test. There was consensus that TAAS, in most cases, would mirror teachers' overall assessment of whether a child could read or not, but none of the teachers were surprised by the TAAS results. Many times, the teachers explained that the test was requiring a minimum and very low level of literacy for the children. At Elena, the teachers had high expectations for the children, and the TAAS test lowered them. Bob explained the difficulty when the children were faced with a question aimed somewhat at higher-level thought processes. Some passages required that the students be able to read and infer the feelings or thoughts the characters had and then reinterpret those thoughts in order to answer the questions.

[Bob:] If you look at the TAAS questions, the only TAAS question that even gets anywhere near [critical thinking] is inference. That's the only one, but inference is not really a thinking skill. It's using thinking to get answers but it's not really this independent thinking we're talking about. It's not even mentioned anymore. It's regurgitation.

Even though Bob had spent time discussing literature with his students, when it came down to the test, he had to redirect them to "just keep it simple." They had to switch gears and remain true to the test-taking tricks of underlining and marking the areas of text that answer the question. Dolores shared her views on the limitations of the TAAS test for students' learning in the long run. She believed that TAAS was simplistic and limiting, and she fought to disrupt the expectations she felt the test placed on her students.

[Dolores:] These are our worker ants. We want our worker ants to be able to problem solve and these are the problems that we want them to solve and this is the way that the problem will be worded. You know, is this real life? And then we want them to be able to pull things from text and this is the information we want them to pull. And these workers, in order to be good workers for us, must be able to do the following skills. That scares me because—so is that what public schools are going to become? We're going to be the feeders to this industry and this industry and this industry? Or are we going to really create quality citizens who can make decisions on their own and who will have a chance to make those choices? I don't want worker ants. My babies are not worker ants. They are thinkers. But the TAAS says, "Don't think. Don't question. Just do it." And to that I say, "No no. You better question. You better question, even me.". . . I tell them, "You have every right to question."

Whereas Dolores had taught her students to read, think, and discuss, a major goal of most teachers, the TAAS test wanted less. The test required one answer. I heard teachers say, "Don't think about it too much" when they spoke to the children about the test. "Just underline the skills." defined this simplistic view of minimum literacy skills as a metaphor of literacy as adaptation or functional literacy. "This metaphor is designed to capture concepts of literacy that emphasize its survival or pragmatic value . . ." As the teachers' interpretations were narrowed, they began to resemble one explanation of literacy as adaptation in that the literacy demands of the students were adapted to the functional or minimum reading skills required by the test. In order to survive in the world of school, the students and teachers had to reach "the level of proficiency necessary for effective performance" (Scribner & Cole, 1984, p. 73).

The Classification and Organization of the Children at Elena

When I spoke to the teachers about TAAS, they emphasized the uniqueness of the children of Elena. There was an overwhelming view that the children of Elena were different from the children at other schools, and this factor affected the ways teachers taught and organized their classrooms. Not only did TAAS affect the literacy methods the teachers used, it affected the groupings of students. Bob describes his feelings about the way the test looks to many of the children he taught:

The last three weeks before the test, I told them, "Excuse me, your answer makes a lot of sense and I know where you're coming from and I see you've been doing a lot of thinking on this answer, but the reason it's wrong is it doesn't come from this little story." A lot of kids have trouble with that because some of the answers they give will make sense from an "other world" standpoint. A lot of our kids have sort of another world aura about them. They're not really focused on what you're doing so they'll read the story about the sheep and all of a sudden, in their mind, will come this big [idea]. That's one of the reading skills, according to Andrea, the idea of visualization. But not if you're going to visualize yourself right out of the test . . . I read somewhere in one of these [test booklets] that you have them read the question, just quickly read the question, not look at the answers. You look at the question and you ask them, "Is the answer to that question right there? Or do you have to think about it?" and it really did work. I could see a lot of them really link into that for some reason. I don't know why, and they wrote RT (right there) on the question and that meant go back to the story and find it.

Bob's story is complicated and was repeated in many ways through conversations with other teachers. The "other world aura" appeared as students drew conclusions about test passages that were not correct. Bob described how he could follow the children's train of thought, but he still had to back them up and require students to use the test-taking strategy of reading the question and then determining where to find the answer. This implied that the children could not simply read a passage and make inferences, one of the only high-level skills required on the TAAS test, without specific strategy coaching, a belief that could be compared to Delpit's (1995) idea that children of color may require more explicit skill instruction than children from homes more aligned with mainstream culture. Other teachers mentioned the children's lack of familiarity with the vocabulary or the use of vocabulary in passages. Many teachers also claimed that the test was culturally biased in the subject matter and language patterns used. Bob made the statement that "substituting Jose for Joe" did not make the test culturally appropriate. Language, especially discourse patterns, is culturally specific as explained by Heath (1983):

> In each community, by the time they go to school, the children know the sounds, words, and grammatical systems of the language spoken around them. They have learned their community's ways of using language to get along with the people and to accomplish their social goals. They have used language to acquire the knowledge their community has judged they should know at their age, and they have learned appropriate ways of expressing that knowledge. (p. 145)

The culture of the neighborhood was specific in that it was primarily a low-income, inner-city area with a Latina population. There were cultural and language-specific discourses unique to the children that did not necessarily match the language of the test. The idea that the Elena children had what Bob called an "other world aura" was repeated in various ways when the teachers talked about TAAS at other schools. At other schools the children seemed to be able to do both—read and answer questions and read and think without getting off track. As Katia explains her students and their abilities, she vacillates between seeing their strengths and their weaknesses:

I think you need to teach them (Elena children) how to take the test as opposed to my daughter at Cypress Hills Elementary. I can't teach my daughter what I've taught them to do here because it would make her go crazy. It's too much. It would be too much work. She reads . . . To me, it's more confusing for the [Elena kids] . . . [TAAS] is them reading for information and reading and being able to find that information in there and/or inferencing.

If Katia had taken her daughter through all of the steps she took her Elena children through, she states that it would frustrate her. She felt that the children at Elena needed to be developed into strong readers first and then given TAAS preparation techniques. But, as with most teachers at Elena, she felt that was too risky. Teachers focused on teaching the test-taking strategies of not reading the passage, underlining the key phrases in the questions, and finding those phrases in the passage to answer questions before or in place of straightforward reading instruction. TAAS practice tests were given in early October to see where the children were. Any child who struggled on the October test was targeted for more practice, and in some classes, that was the majority of children. Therefore, classroom routines were interrupted to a large degree. Dolores, who has a son at another school, explains the difference in the quality of literacy education the children receive at different schools:

[TAAS is] perform reading. It's just two totally different feels and when you go to other schools, like when I talked about TAAS with some of my son's teachers, who taught in [other schools]. I asked them what they did to prepare for TAAS and they say, "We teach. We don't have to worry about the TAAS. Our students pass the test." And so I was just like, "Oh nice". . . but in my classroom it doesn't work that way.

Even though TAAS did not measure reading in Dolores's eyes, she acquiesced to its demands by preparing students for the test, because of the enormous weight attached to TAAS. It was crucial that students were literate in TAAS reading, but it was not crucial that they were literate in a broader sense of the concept. The focus of this study was to explore the teachers' definitions of literacy at Elena, and the complexity of their responses was dichotomous and extremely circuitous. One line of argument that organizes the teachers' overall logic as far as how they rationalized the children's lack of ability and the teachers' need to teach to the test can be found in Hillocks's (2002) breakdown: "(1) When a teacher covers everything to be learned, any students with appropriate background should be able to learn what is required. (2) I have covered everything to be learned. Yet these students fail. (3) Therefore, the students must have inadequate backgrounds" (p. 13). Teachers knew that just teaching them to read did not guarantee they would pass the TAAS test, and they tended to look beyond the classroom to the students' backgrounds to explain the struggle with TAAS. Since other schools did not have to prepare their students to take the test as the Elena teachers did, the teachers placed the responsibility outside of the classroom. Knowing that some teachers did only teach TAAS all year, Dolores attempted to balance her teaching with both literature and TAAS instruction, but she still built her teaching around the practice test results and sent TAAS homework.

> [Dolores:] No, [TAAS] doesn't measure reading . . . We do practice [for TAAS]. I do expect them to do well but there's no recipe. Sometimes it's panic. It's like, "Oh my God. Look what you did on your practice test." I do use the practice test to monitor the objectives that my kids are having trouble with . . . and then I look for every student's strength. And yes, we do TAAS homework so they become familiar with the format of the test. It familiarizes them with the way they are being asked questions because it's not quite like the literature circles I use where we sit down and discuss what is going on in the book and whether you agree or disagree. No, there is a right answer. So it's very different and you just have to train them, I hate to say that, you have to teach them how to take a test.

Teaching a "TAAS grade" at Elena was stressful, and three of the teachers I interviewed longed to escape the pressures of their grade levels. Dolores had requested a pre-kindergarten assignment for two years and been denied because her students' TAAS scores had been above average every year. Caroline spent one year at fifth grade and then moved back to second grade, and Katia applied for a transfer to Cypress Hills Elementary. Here she compares Elena children to the children she tutored at Cypress Hills Elementary:

> [Katia:] Fourth grade over there is easy. It's a piece of cake because you don't have to drill the kids in TAAS. They all pass the first time. In October, they all pass with the exception of a couple and over there you can implement a writing workshop as opposed to TAAS writing. There is a difference in their writing program. It's not TAAS driven. The people that teach at fourth grade should be given a break. You need to move, either move up with your class or move them somewhere else but give them a year break. Then let them come back to it. To me, that would be the only effective way to do it. I was burned out by February. I was so burned out. I wanted nothing to do with that grade level.

Katia also reiterated the tremendous pressure on teachers at grade levels focused on TAAS. She was a successful teacher according to her TAAS scores. Katia's frustration with the amount of time she had to spend on TAAS at Elena versus the amount of time spent on TAAS at her son's school had brought her to the point of putting in for a transfer. Her feelings were an example of how teachers at Elena felt TAAS preparation interrupted what they considered to be good teaching of reading and writing. TAAS reading was perceived and defined by teachers as a separate form of reading requiring extensive practice. Dolores shared her concern over the TAAS pressure. She explains how Elena began with little attention to the TAAS test seven years prior to the high stakes of TAAS and compared it to the recent situation. Dolores worried about her third graders and the growing pressure of the test:

> The first year I came to Elena I asked someone about the test. I did look at our TAAS scores and I asked one of the teachers and he commented and he said he didn't worry about it. I was like, "Wow, you don't worry about it?" And then that kind of concerned me, not that I want to be at a school that's TAAS driven, but I do think you need to be aware of what you're being asked to do for students. [TAAS] loses sight that these are children and at the third grade level it is much more because it's the first year that they have to tackle this kind of task. You're just made so much aware of it when you're at the third grade. I mean it's your score, too. What your kids make is what you make and it's hard on parents, it's hard on teachers, and it's hard on kids.

Dolores had enough experience with the high stakes attached to TAAS to realize that the school needed to be aware of its objectives. She ended her discussion by expressing concern that those very TAAS objectives would be used to determine if the third graders of Texas could be promoted to the fourth grade. Teachers perceived that Elena children were harder to teach than other children, and they had to be trained. TAAS had a profound impact on the teachers I interviewed and the teachers I knew in the district. Every school I visited as a university supervisor of student teachers at the middle-school level plans around TAAS. During the month of April it was mentioned almost weekly in the newspaper. Administrators were hired and fired based on how well children performed on the test, and it was the center of most conversations, faculty meetings, trainings, and evaluations of children.

One way teachers dealt with the pressure was to construct ways to organize the children into groups according to their abilities on the TAAS practice tests. Teachers tended to teach to the ones on the edge. Students who were exceptional or performing on grade level were placed in groups, and the students who did not pass the practice tests and did not read on grade level were either placed in special programs or grouped within classrooms to received extra TAAS practice. This form of tracking is described by Bob as he explains how children who are easily passing the TAAS practice tests are left alone, and teachers concentrate on the middle group—the group who is within passing range. The lower children are either referred to special education or left out altogether:

[Bob:] The trouble with TAAS is that TAAS is what you call a mastery test. So if you're teaching to TAAS at your grade level, you're only doing half of your class. The other half is sitting there with not a clue and unable to do it because we only have a 70 percent pass rate. If you are into TAAS and you are taking the TAAS Bible and using it and trying to do it all year long then you are only teaching half of your class. So the other half, who are not going to pass, and who are not up to that level . . . are out. There's only half of the middle that really knows what they are doing.

Bob describes how the students who received the most instructional attention were the ones who had a chance to pass. This tendency on the part of teachers to categorize children according to their ability to pass the TAAS test made instruction easier. Top students who were believed to have the ability to pass the test were not worried about. Low-performing students were sent for TAAS tutoring, and the middle group of students, who were thought of as capable of passing TAAS, became the focus for most teachers. This tracking occurred in various ways. Teachers grouped students within their classrooms and across grade levels to focus instruction on the needed skills for TAAS. The stakes were high, and the freedom to alter instruction to help students pass—in any way—was embraced. Natalie sums up what effects the high stakes attached to TAAS have beyond literacy education. She thought that the actual reading objectives were appropriate goals for the children, but she expressed concern over the peripheral changes in Texas schools connected to the pressures of TAAS. She mentions what she calls the "unintended effects" of TAAS:

[Natalie:] I do not have a problem with the TAAS objectives, especially the reading objectives. They're fine. I think kids should be able to do those things. I don't have a problem with high standards for everyone. I think they need to be in place. I have a big problem with the high-stakes nature of the TAAS. Now especially with 2003 high stakes being the threat of failure, not just graduation, but failing in third grade. I've seen its effect on teacher evaluations. Fortunately, not so much at Elena, but I've heard of stories about other principals and other schools doing horrible things to kids and parents to get their kids to pass the TAAS. At one school the principal called in all the parents of all the minority students and asked the parents to sign a permission [form] to get them tested for special education. The principal was not aware that this parent was a teacher in the district and the principal was trying to get her child tested for special education just because of her race. That made me sick. So the unintended effects of TAAS are very disturbing. I think they're going to get worse. I think the teacher shortage is being affected now by TAAS and more so because evaluations are being so closely tied to TAAS and because of the pressure. The stress of high needs schools and high needs kids is so dramatic that teachers are getting out as fast as they can. It's going to get worse. I see very dedicated, experienced teachers who are counting their years to retirement trying to go to a school that's easier because we have a hard job. We have a really hard job.

Teachers at Elena did "have a really hard job," and in some ways the TAAS test made it easier. Due to the fear that the students at Elena would be unable to pass TAAS with the "regular" reading instruction models, teachers at Elena began to spend greater amounts of time defining "TAAS reading" and prioritizing the teaching of "TAAS reading" over other genres of reading. Rather than worry about teaching high-level skills using multiple materials and methods, teachers became increasingly dedicated to finding out more about the TAAS test and how to help children excel. The teachers slowly succumbed over the years to the stress created by TAAS and aligned instructional goals and methods to the test. All of the education, knowledge, and beliefs the teachers possessed about the definition of literacy and how to teach students to be literate became reprioritized by the high-stakes assessment model established by the state. The TAAS test cannot be the sole bearer of fault for the changes at Elena over the past fourteen years, but the multiple references the teachers made to TAAS could not be ignored. TAAS found its way into almost every conversation I initiated about literacy, and the coding and analysis of themes brought out the intricate nature of how the teachers defined the test and the children in relation to its measures. The next chapter takes a closer look at how the teachers' analysis of the children, their families, and their performance on TAAS affected programs and practices at Elena beyond individual classrooms.

THE EROSION OF
A FIGURED WORLD

As Natalie, the campus literacy specialist, shared her thoughts about the unintended effects of the Texas Assessment of Academic Skills (TAAS) test, she referred to the changes that had occurred at Elena and other schools in the district over the last decade. As high-stakes accountability became a reality in 1997, the figured world of Elena became more influenced by outside forces. TAAS cannot be named as the sole cause of any of these changes, as altering of the focus of literacy instruction may have occurred without the impact of accountability. However, it can be said that in 2001, passing the TAAS test was the most important goal at Elena. Prior to the TAAS test, Elena operated under a philosophy shaped by the principal, the teachers, and the community that had been open to various methods of instruction and assessment and was targeted to embrace a love of reading and a high level of engagement by the children. High-stakes accountability changed the "field" of the figured world at Elena as described by Bourdieu, cited in Holland et al. (1998). Bourdieu defines a field as "a separate social universe having its own laws of functioning independent of those of politics and the economy" (p. 58). Elena moved from establishing and maintaining "its own laws" to viewing the students' TAAS scores as a "cultural artifact" and recognizing "the force of [TAAS's] use in practices—practices responsive to [the] changing historical circumstances" (Holland et al., 1998, p. 63).

Literacy assessment was changing in the state, and, subsequently at Elena, many of the teachers and administrators understood that the TAAS test measured everything—the effectiveness of a teacher, a principal, a school, and the entire school district. The teachers had learned from their past experiences of being audited that nothing else about Elena was weighted with such importance; nothing else meant as much to the district and the state as the TAAS scores. The district did not measure our special education program, our bilingual program, or our community involvement in ways similar to the assessment of literacy through TAAS. These endeavors were maintained and recorded for documentation purposes, but they were not given priority in the accountability system and subsequently were not a top priority for many of the teachers.

As Elena learned to pass the TAAS test with greater and greater success, teachers' attention turned to maintaining our "acceptable" rating status, and in 2002 we reached the status of being "recognized" by the state in all areas. We were one step away from being an "exemplary" school, the highest achievement the state of Texas bestows upon its schools, its teachers, and its principals. Yet the figured world of Elena was becoming a reflection of the changing culture and goals of state policy. The erosion of the figured world of literacy once complexly defined by Elena as focused on the culture of the community, the development of children literate in both languages of the community, and a teacher population open to diverse learning theories and new ideas, was eroded by the streamlining and simplifying of goals required by the TAAS test. As I interviewed my primary participants on the topic of literacy, several other areas of schooling came to light. Although the following topics are not directly related to literacy, they are relevant to illustrating the teachers' attitudes about Elena, the community, teaching in general, and the teachers' and school's changing beliefs about the role of the children and their families in literacy acquisition.

Special Education Expands

One way TAAS altered the focus of literacy instruction at Elena was evident through conversations I had with teachers regarding the special education program and how it related to those children struggling with reading. Special education was a complicated system, and in order to concentrate the attention on the literacy questions of the study, I did not pursue the area beyond how it related to literacy and the construction of the children's and families' literacy abilities. The pressure of the TAAS test was one reason the teachers began to refer more students to special education. This was a reversal of the school's philosophy in the early 1990s, which was characterized by higher expectations of classroom teachers and children. The expansion of special education at Elena illustrates the view that struggling readers could not be served in the regular classroom.

When I first arrived at Elena in 1989, I was explicitly instructed by our principal that our special education program was used only as a last resort and only after extensive discussion with various teachers, parents, and administrators. Holding fast to Elena's philosophy that "all children can learn" and all teachers could teach meant that I was to meet the needs of children in my classroom by being informed about educational practices and having high expectations for myself and my students. The campus had one special education teacher at that time, and her role was to teach those few students identified as special education students officially by the assessments and to assist teachers in meeting the children's needs in their own classrooms. This section is designed to illustrate the changes over time in the meaning and use of the special education program at Elena and how the teachers viewed the abilities of the students. The most prevalent philosophy exposed through these discussions became the overriding theme of what Valencia & Solorzano (1997) characterizes as deficit thinking.

Over the last five years, the supporting structure for struggling readers at Elena had expanded exponentially. In 1989, Elena had one resource teacher who served a handful of students. In 2001, we had three-and-one-half resource teachers, one full-time aide, one literacy support specialist for classroom teachers, two full-time Reading Recovery teachers, and one half-time Reading Recovery teacher (myself). In all, the students at Elena served outside of their own classrooms for literacy had dramatically increased, supporting the claim that literacy continued to be a focus at Elena. Although this increased focus on literacy brought welcome resources such as books, training, and support staff, the other side of the story can be viewed as detrimental to the students and the teachers. The intense pressure to have all children pass the third-grade TAAS test affected every grade level. More children were referred to special education courses, and they were referred earlier in some instances to avoid the test, while more teachers were frustrated with the perceived slow progress of children struggling on standardized tests. An unintended effect of TAAS at Elena was a dramatic increase in our special education program since 1998, soon after accountability began. Penny, one of our special education teachers, shared her thoughts about the growth of special education at Elena:

> I've only been here four years and it's gone from just Mary, she was the only one here before me. By Christmas, there were so many students that they had to get Lila. By the beginning of that next year there were so many students referred, they had to get me. By the end of that second year, we had to get another half-time person and we're probably going to have to get another full-time person. Right now, we're allotted three and a half resource teachers and that's when your numbers get up to 20 or so apiece. We're hitting the speech therapy limit too. We just had to get another speech therapist. We now have two because there are so many students. I think part of it is TAAS, the danger of [the students] possibly failing, teachers know it.

Penny explains how quickly the program grew and how teachers were hired mid-year to meet the needs of all of the students qualifying for remedial services. Penny felt that teachers were increasing their referrals to special education because of the increased pressure of the TAAS test. This was because special education students did not take the TAAS test. There was a separate test for those students, and their scores were not aggregated into the scores that determine the school rankings. Not only was each campus rated, but each teacher's TAAS results were profiled and scrutinized more closely each year, which dramatically increased the pressure on teachers to make sure the students performed well on TAAS by third grade. Teachers were measured by their individual classroom scores; each teacher received a printout of their students' performance on TAAS, and scores were given close attention in each teacher's official evaluations.

Natalie also compared Elena's use of special education prior to the onset of TAAS pressure to the increase in the number of students perceived by teachers to require intervention outside of the regular classroom. She explained the shift in philosophy as a move toward the norm in the district. Whereas Elena was below average in its rate of referral of students to special education in earlier years, the special education program had expanded since the early 1990s and was now in line with the numbers referred by other schools in the district.

> [Natalie:] Special education has grown since I've been here. We used to have a staff that was very anti-special education and anti-labeling children. I think in some ways that worked against kids for some individual children who needed some extra services. I've talked to people district wide; I have a friend who is a tester. Our numbers were always way below average for the entire district. Now they are average. Almost 100 percent of our referrals are good ones. They qualify. Most schools have a much higher number of not qualifying.

Natalie states that the number of referrals at Elena was not excessive as compared to other schools, although considering the history of Elena, the increase in the special education program was swift and dramatic. She also indicates that most of the children referred were "good ones." A "good referral" meant that most children the teachers recommended for testing ended up being eligible for special services; there were few, if any, misdiagnoses by the classroom teachers.

Fourteen years ago, Elena teachers had smaller classes and worked with children who were behind. There was a philosophy that all children could learn and all teachers could teach. Classroom teachers formed small committees to problem solve when children were behind, and teachers visited and observed in each other's classrooms to assist each other in meeting the children's needs. Several indicators were taken into account when a child struggled. Teachers at Elena explored the child's language dominance and worked to make sure that all possible avenues were taken to keep the child in the classroom with his or her peers. It was only after all interventions were attempted that the child was referred for testing.

In 2001, committees still met and discussed possible actions for children struggling with reading, but there was a leaning toward special programs intervention rather than improving classroom instruction. Therefore, where once Elena teachers had made a conscious decision to avoid the testing whenever possible, they now sought out testing and viewed the special education program as a primary resource. Some teachers referred to the ways the earlier avoidance of testing children for special education placed some children at a disadvantage.

Literacy Knowledge of the Special Education Teachers

Another reason for the increased use of the special education program, unrelated to TAAS, was the perceived improvement in the ability of the special education teachers. A poorly trained special education teacher can also have a detrimental effect on the educational development of a child. Penny recalled how teachers had not trusted the previous special education teachers and attributed the increase in special education referrals to the teachers' new faith in the fortified program and the increase in the student population:

> I think that special education, before Mary was here, five years ago, was a horrible thing. I heard it was a nightmare and there was not a lot of trust among the faculty. We worked so well as a special education team together and we really built a lot of community within us before we went out to the classrooms. People started trusting us. They see those huge jumps [in the students' progress] and they're also getting a lot more kids in their class. We went from 400 to 600 students so of course you're going to have more referrals.

The special education staff was a tightly organized unit for a few years between 1997 and 2000. There were three teachers who worked together, and regular classroom teachers began to trust the program as they saw the children's progress in reading. This point in time ran parallel to the increased pressure of TAAS and an increase in literacy training alignment on the campus. Here is where the complexity of the growth of the special education program can be seen through the eyes of Penny. Earlier she stated that the special education program grew because of TAAS pressure; then she stated that teachers began to see progress in the children, and that was cause for the higher number of referrals. Therefore, the increase in special education referrals is not exclusively in response to TAAS, but it can be given some credit for enhancing the perceived need for the program and its use as a way to exempt struggling students from TAAS and eliminate their scores. This argument echoes Natalie's earlier statement that a lack of referrals in the past prevented children from receiving assistance.

The strengthening of the special education program at Elena was due to the focus on literacy instruction by the special education teachers and was one reason, in addition to TAAS, that the referrals increased.

> [Natalie:] I feel like we have some good special education teachers, so those kids can get some extra help. I like seeing someone like Penny who is in special education and got her master's degree in reading. I think there should be more reading [education] required of the special education certification. I see special education teachers using the Directed Reading Assessment [DRA]. But I still think they need more reading training.

During the expansion of our special education department, Elena was unique in that one of our special education teachers, Penny, had her Master Reading Teacher Certification[1] and received her master's degree in literacy studies. This type of knowledge and literacy education was valued by the teachers at Elena and mirrored the knowledge many of the classroom teachers held regarding literacy. Other special education instructors Elena employed were trained in special education, which is not traditionally viewed as dependent on literacy instruction. Elena administrators valued the literacy training provided for classroom teachers and expressed satisfaction that our special education teachers were attending the trainings as well.

> [Illeana, our Language Proficiency Assessment Committee chair:] They have attended the guided reading training [the literacy consultant for the school district] did. Some are going to Project READ[2] training, but I don't know how helpful that is. They are using more of the guided reading approach, too, so I think that's a move in the right direction, but again the problem I see there is connecting with the classroom teacher.

Illeana recognized the strength the literacy knowledge provided the special education team at Elena but was concerned about the tendency for special programs to disconnect children from the classroom teacher, and she felt that having the classroom teachers and the special education teachers receive the same literacy training was unique and important.

At the time of the study, there were two special education programs divided by grade level. Penny managed the branch of the special education program for the primary grades (1–3) and another teacher taught the fourth-, fifth-, and sixth-grade students in special education. Classroom teachers in the lower grades trusted Penny and her knowledge of literacy instruction, and many teachers consulted her.

On the other hand, the teacher in charge of the upper grades' special education program was not seen as a viable alternative for supporting students by Bob and Katia, upper-grade teachers. They both indicated their preference for keeping their students in their own classrooms. Bob allowed the special education teacher to come into his room, while Katia fought to not recommend services for her students because she felt competent in meeting their needs.

These two teachers demonstrated the views and philosophies of Elena prior to 1998. Bob was not a proponent of special education as it was commonly used at Elena. He required the special education teacher of the upper grades to come to his classroom. "If you were to walk into my classroom, you would not be able to tell [which kids were in special education]. She services everybody. I wanted to do it that way because I can't stand them going down there." These two teachers felt that they could help their students more by keeping them in the classroom. Bob allowed the special education teacher to come in and assist all of his children under his guidance while Katia, who planned to move up with her class, wanted her students to remain in her classroom as much as possible:

> [Katia:] I've got a special education teacher telling me, 'We want to pull these students out," and I said, "No. They're not going to have you their whole life." They will have me for two years and they'll have that much of a better chance because I differentiate for them to the point where they are successful. I feel one more year with me will make them that much stronger. I told her [the special education teacher] it would shock the principal to find out that I want to keep this student . . . because I know I can make a difference with one more year.

Bob and Katia were upper-grade teachers, and the special education teachers at the upper levels were not trained in the literacy methods. These teachers, who felt confident about their abilities, did not want to send their students to the special education teacher. They wanted the students to remain in the classroom, and they wanted to teach them themselves. Every teacher was left to their own interpretation of the meaning and use of special education; the use of the program depended on how the teachers viewed the children's abilities and their own teaching.

As the figured world of Elena changed over the years, teachers became more receptive to using special education programs to assist struggling readers. Bob and Katia were unique in their views of special education and reminiscent of the views the school held prior to the increase in students, the improvement in the education and program, and the onset of high-stakes accountability.

There were cases where the special education teacher and the classroom teacher were not operating from similar perspectives. Special education teachers did not always view the children the same way the classroom teacher did. Penny described the progress of one student in her room and contrasted this description with the lack of progress the classroom teacher saw. She felt that the classroom teachers were not meeting the needs of the struggling special education students and not viewing them in a positive light.

> [Penny:] I've seen some just tremendous jumps [in the students' abilities]. I just don't know how it carries over into their classroom and their everyday lives. I see it here. I had one [student] that I've been working with—he was one of the first kids that walked in my door in second grade. He's now in fifth grade and just this year he jumped from a [reading] level 6 to a level 26 just like in a week. He just got it. I don't know what they're doing in their class. When I hear their classroom teachers they are talking differently about these kids.

Penny implied that classroom teachers had contrasting views of the children in relation to her views. The idea that special education was designed to assist children struggling only as long as necessary was important to Penny. In the past, once students were placed in special education, they stayed there with little thought as to exiting them back into the regular classroom. Penny saw special education as an intervention designed to catch students' difficulties early and then exit them as soon as possible, stating: "In four years, I've dismissed one. We're about to dismiss probably two or three others . . . We're really trying to work with getting these kids out. These kids are showing great improvement." Penny also knew the children did well in her classroom, but she expressed concerns about the experiences her students had in their regular classrooms:

> The kids know all of those things and when they get to their rooms they are so scared sometimes or they're so bad out there that people don't even want them and like them. And I'm like well, wouldn't you be bad if your teacher asked you to read and you couldn't? Wouldn't you be goofing off so you didn't have to do that? But, when you see them in here, they produce nothing in class, [but in here they are] producing books upon books.

Penny knew where the children needed improvement, and she was committed to having them read as much as possible. She understood the stigma of special education and made her room a safe, nurturing place for them.

Penny's comments also reveal the complexity of many teachers' views. Even as she cared deeply about her students' experiences and was protective of their feelings, she continued to exhibit shades of low expectations. These types of feelings were common as I spoke to teachers about issues surrounding student abilities. Penny thought that most Elena students would qualify for special education services as she stated: "All of [the Elena students] are high needs. If you tested this whole school, half of them would be special education." She also questioned the cultural validity of the testing instruments and said: "I think that there's something biased in the test." As a result, Penny illustrated the intricate search for reasons behind the special education program enactment at Elena. She felt that one of the reasons for the increase in referrals was the increase in student enrollment and a shift in attitude from an "all children can learn" philosophy to more of an "all children need help" notion.

Since Elena had always been classified as a Title I school by virtue of our high number of Spanish-speaking children and the socio-economic status of many of the families, most of our students were technically considered "at-risk" by the federal definition, and most of the teachers agreed. Special programs were viewed as a way for teachers to send students not performing on grade level out of the classroom for assistance. Conversations regarding referrals centered around TAAS many times. If children were struggling in first grade or second grade, it was common knowledge that they needed to be referred before third grade, the first year the TAAS test was taken.

There were times, however, when teachers did not know how to help children who were struggling, and they avoided them. As a Reading Recovery teacher, I was in constant contact with first-grade teachers worried about the progress of their children. The negative side of the drive for early referral was the idea that many teachers had when "specialists" were available. The classroom teachers ceased teaching the children who were pulled out for remedial assistance, and in many cases they left instruction to the specialist. This never afforded the classroom teachers the opportunity to learn how to address the reading difficulties of their own students. Toward the end of the year I attended a meeting to make a decision about referring a student to special education. The classroom teacher claimed that Noel could not read and needed to be tested for special education. When another teacher asked her what Noel's reading level was, the teacher replied: "I don't know. I haven't listened to her read since October."

Teachers at Elena varied in their interpretation and use of special education, but not in their tacit references to the deficit construction of the children. Two of the tenets of Valencia & Solorzano's (1997) theory can be used to describe the teachers' attitudes toward children and families at Elena.

Deficit thinking is a persons centered explanation of school failure among individuals as linked to group membership (typically, the combination of racial/ethnic minority status and economic disadvantagement). The deficit thinking framework holds that poor schooling performance is rooted in students' alleged cognitive and motivational deficits, while institutional structures and inequitable schooling arrangements that exclude students from learning are held exculpatory. Finally, the model is largely based on imputation and little documentation. (p. 9)

Penny's belief in a deficit model is evident in her feeling that just about any child referred to testing would end up qualifying for special education. Penny was the only primary informant who was a special education teacher, and she spoke extensively about the special education program and its relationship to literacy education and Elena. Her thoughts were in line with the shift in the Elena belief system that encouraged the placement of students in special education rather than using special education as a last resort. Penny's thoughts are also reflective of the complexity of the teacher's views. In this story, she described the views she held that the testing procedure was biased and that all of the students in the neighborhood met the criterion the program holds as "lacking educational opportunity." The myriad topics she touched on in this one monologue serve as a foreshadowing of the remaining two sections on how the teachers' ideas about the children's and their families' abilities and possibilities guided teacher decisions, beliefs and actions.

[Penny:] I think that there are inherent biases in the [special education] testing. There's one thing in here that I have to check off that says the eligibility decision was not based primarily on lack of instruction in reading and/or math or LEP status. Well, when you're talking about a kid who didn't pick up a book until they were five or six years old, well isn't that lack of educational opportunity? I have to check it. I get my paperwork sent back if I don't or I have to say I don't agree with the eligibility placement. I don't know what would happen then [if I didn't check it]. I would have to just disagree with the eligibility decision. [The special education] paperwork says, "This criterion was not based on home factors or lack of educational opportunity." It flat out says that they did not qualify because of lack of educational opportunity. What are they talking about? We are overflowing with lack of educational opportunity in these neighborhoods. Their parents can't read. They can't speak English. They're working two or three jobs and if they're not doing that they're drinking two or three cases of beer every night. I mean, it doesn't mean that they can't do it, but does it mean they're disabled? No, but what do you do? Say I don't agree with it and let them be in regular education with thirty kids? I don't know. I had a class last semester with Dr. Gonzales that really punched my buttons about it because she was saying but that's not a reason to put them in special education. I said, "Then you come to my school and you do something else with them because I can't."

Although Penny expressed her frustrations and was critical of the special education criteria and her role, she also revealed her deficit views about the families of Elena children that were also reminiscent of the deficit theory tenet that "the major myth that low-income parents of color typically do not value the importance of education, fail to inculcate such a value in their children, and seldom participate . . . in the education of their offspring" (Valencia & Solorzano, 1997, p. 190). Penny voiced the complicated view she held of the children throughout this section. At times she defended them and their families even as she stereotyped them into a rigidly defined deficit construction. It would be easy to fault her for these views, but in order to understand the positioning of many teachers at Elena, Penny can be used as an example of how the teachers loved and cared for the children yet truly believed them to be lacking the background to excel. "In light of the 'victim-blamers/victims' nature of deficit thinking and the lop-sided power arrangements between deficit thinkers and economically disadvantaged minority students, the model can be oppressive. As such, the deficit thinking paradigm holds little hope for addressing the possibilities of school success for such students" (Valencia & Solorzano, 1997, p. 10).

The notions of deficit theory will be revisited throughout the remaining chapters. They will be intertwined with cultural and racial factors to paint the multifaceted and layered relationships between the teachers' views and their ongoing struggles with teaching the children of Elena under the pressure of a high-stakes accountability system focused on literacy. In many ways the feelings of the teachers at Elena can be seen in Trueba's (1988b) statement:

> Racial prejudice in schools, whether unconscious or not, is deeply rooted in the misperception by mainstream persons that minorities are academically incompetent . . . [T]he concept itself of disability as applied to culturally different persons must be defined in specific domains, otherwise further stereotyping will follow its inaccurate use . . . [N]ot all chronic reading problems of minority students are enough grounds to classify a child as learning disabled. (p. 149)

In the past, Elena had elected to refer only students in the greatest of need, those students whom the classroom teacher could not possibly reach. Over time there was a dramatic shift toward the view that it was necessary to refer children not on grade level according to a standardized test and an absence of impetus to improve classroom instruction.

The Erosion of Bilingual Education

Just as the increase in the special education program became an additional theme in the conversations I had with teachers, bilingual education was also brought to the fore in several discussions regarding literacy. Language learning decisions were touched by the fact that 38 percent of our students were limited English proficient and 93 percent of our students were Latino. In order to maintain a focus on the relationship of bilingual education to literacy definitions and the changes over time, I did not pursue the greater questions lurking in quite a few of the teachers' statements in relation to the benefits of the various models of bilingual education or detailed arguments of methodology in bilingual and English as a Second Language instruction. Instead, this section will reflect the administrators' and teachers' changing attention, education, and knowledge about bilingual issues related to literacy over time and how the bilingual program became a reflection of the priorities, or lack thereof, of the state's reading initiative and accountability system as it related to bilingual education.

Mitch, our computer lab teacher, gave an overview of the role English-language education played in instructional practices at Elena in an email directed to the entire staff:

> I devote 15 to 20 hours each week observing and assisting with instruction of the entire 600-plus student body in the school's computer lab, which gives me both a perspective somewhat unique among the staff and at least some standing on which to base comments. This is my eighth year at Elena, and I'm becoming more alarmed every day that substantial numbers of Elena students who are patently non-functional in English are being prodded—required, in many cases—to conduct research, take quizzes, compose written work, and perform similar tasks in English when they haven't a clue as to what they're reading or writing. As I noted last November in a moment of frustration over a lack of Spanish-language material for the school's website, there are "LEP-A" (students speaking only Spanish) student folders on the campus file server with hardly any work in Spanish and at the same time loaded with unintelligible, half-finished work in English. This isn't especially surprising when, as recently as last week, I watched a very bright, articulate, third-grade Spanish speaker—a U.S. resident of less than a year—staring blankly at the computer screen, trying to make sense of the English heading he had just transcribed from the board to his paper. When I asked him if he understood what he was supposed to write, he said he didn't; when I asked the teacher if he should get started in Spanish, she said she'd help him do it in English . . . Elena has traditionally had a strong [maintenance] bilingual education program—is there not some way to improve our school's TAAS scores without totally denaturing the bilingual program?

Models of Bilingual Education

Mitch was a strong supporter of the bilingual program. He expressed how bilingual instruction on campus was altered to a great extent by 2001 and connected this transformation to the attention placed on TAAS. Spanish and English literacy was the foundation of bilingual instruction and assessment at Elena, but from the time I was hired until 2001 it was swept to the side by other priorities to become focused on English mastery. In 1989, the bilingual program at Elena could best be portrayed as a maintenance model that attempted "to foster the minority language in the child, strengthening the child's sense of cultural identity and affirming the rights of an ethnic minority group in a nation" (Baker, 1996, p. 173). The teachers and administrators at Elena had made a conscious decision to focus not only on valuing the Spanish the children and families brought, but the school also specifically addressed the culture of the community through a developmental maintenance model which "develop[ed] a student's home language skills to full proficiency and full biliteracy or literacy" (Baker, 1996, p. 173).

This philosophy went beyond the basic requirements delineated by the Bilingual Education Act. The Bilingual Education Act amendment of 1967 was designed to assist native Spanish speakers who "were seen as failing in the school system . . . [T]he underlying aim was a transition from a minority language (e.g., Spanish) to English, rather than support for the mother tongue" (Baker, 1996, p. 169). The transitional model proposed that the school "shift the child from the home, minority language to the dominant, majority language [where] social and cultural assimilation into the language majority is the underlying aim" (Baker, 1996, p. 173).

Elena teachers, with support from the school's administration, were more aligned with the 1974 Supreme Court decision in

> Lau versus Nichols [that] outlawed English submersion programs for language minority children and resulted in nationwide "Lau remedies" [that] included English as a Second Language classes, English tutoring and some bilingual education . . . [These remedies] rarely resulted in heritage language enrichment or maintenance programs as the accent was still on a transitional use of the home language for English language learners. (Baker, 1996, p. 169)

In 1996, Elena received a grant to implement a Dual Language program that increased teacher education in second-language acquisition and created a complete biliteracy program focused on fully developing and maintaining both English and Spanish for all students. Baker (1996) characterizes two-way bilingual schools as allowing the two languages of the school to have equal status. The school's philosophy was clearly in support of this bilingual aim, as confirmed by the use of both languages for announcements, letters, assignments, curriculum, and training. The campus took care to ensure that Spanish was given equal attention in all school activities.

Prior to the Dual Language program implementation, Elena had a bilingual and English as a Second Language (ESL) program that served all of the children. Though required to teach bilingual classes, teachers could decide the amount of time they spent on each language. In the past, the design favored supporting both languages equally. Each bilingual teacher had a class of about half Spanish-dominant students and half English-dominant students. Monolingual English-speaking teachers, such as myself, were given all of the children classified "D" or "E," those children who were categorized as proficient English speakers. We were paired with bilingual classes and switched classes daily to ensure that "D" and "E" students placed with monolingual English teachers would receive Spanish instruction for a small part of the day. All students began to transition to English by third grade so that they received only English instruction for the remainder of their schooling, but at Elena, it was important that all children receive instruction in both languages until the sixth grade, and the school had the personnel and the desire to meet the needs of such a model.

Procedures for Student Placement

Elena followed the same procedures for executing the bilingual program that all schools in the district implemented. The first step required by the district was the language survey questionnaire administered to parents as each child registered for school. A simple form, the home language survey, was used to document the language used at home most of the time by the family. If any language other than English was designated as the dominant language of the household, then the child was given the IDEA Proficiency (IPT) Test (2002). The IDEA test was an oral listening and comprehension test used to determine the child's level of language competence. This test was and is still used to determine the listening and oral proficiency of each child. The scoring gave each child a language score between A and E. Spanish-dominant children were labeled "A's," and English-dominant children were "E's." Once labeled along the continuum according to language proficiency dominance, children were placed in heterogeneously grouped classrooms. Bilingual teachers received the "A," "B," and "C" students, while ESL students, labeled, "D" and "E," were placed with ESL-certified teachers. If the child qualified for bilingual services, the parents had to give permission for their child to be instructed in Spanish. All children listed as A, B, C, or D were monitored monthly by the Language Proficiency Assessment Committee (LPAC), since they were receiving either Spanish instruction or ESL instruction.

To maintain this model, the hiring practices at Elena were set up to require teachers to be certified to serve the children. In 1989, every teacher hired was required to be either bilingually certified or ESL-certified by the state. This was a condition of employment, paid for by the district and clearly articulated during interviews. Twelve hours of coursework and the completion of the state certification test gave teachers their ESL certification within their first two years of teaching. Gradually the school began to disregard the ESL certification. Now the certification is not required, but teachers can simply take the state certification test. If they pass, the state certifies them as ESL teachers. Illeana acknowledged the need for ESL-certified teachers: "I think it has to be on the contract. I think it's needed. All of the new students we're getting are all speakers of other languages." Yet by 2001, some teachers were hired in spite of their refusal to teach in a bilingual classroom. Katia was adamant about not teaching Spanish, even though she was bilingual, and she made her feelings clear before she was hired:

> I will not get [my bilingual cert.]. I won't get it because to me, it is a lot of work and I have my own beliefs and arguments even within my family . . . I will not get my bilingual certification. That is not the reason I went to school. I went to school because of my son. My focus is literacy and giving these kids a chance.

If Katia had interviewed in 1989, she would not have been offered a contract, and her comments show how the policy at Elena had changed over time. The bilingual program now functioned with less emphasis on teacher education and certification in areas previously required. Other areas of the school also began to show an absence of dialogue attending to bilingual issues, and the program was no longer at the forefront of school conversations during faculty meetings, there was no longer a bilingual cadre to develop and guide bilingual instruction, and the LPAC committee rarely met. Bilingual education was not a primary focus any longer, as attention turned to developing English mastery so the children would pass the TAAS test.

Transitioning Children to English Instruction

Once the Dual Language grant was approved in 1995, this model remained, and materials and education for all teachers were enhanced. After five years, the grant had run its course, and a large number of new teachers had been hired. There was a lack of interest in maintaining the classroom instructional design and the training elements of the program. Illeana, our LPAC chair, described how Elena determined when children transitioned to English and how they were placed. The LPAC committee was in charge of reviewing all bilingual students' programs and placements. She adhered to the transitional model of bilingual education where the goal was to transition students to English.

> [Illeana:] The ones who are literate in both languages are the ones that are in the bilingual program, the actual bilingual program. Usually, they've been here since pre-kindergarten and by the time they get to second grade, just like the research shows, they're ready to transition into English. It's a real natural transition. We have a lot of children who were bilingual who have exited, which means they've passed TAAS in English [at their grade level].

The bilingual model Elena followed was the same basic formula that was followed years ago, except the TAAS test became the unofficial exit test rather than the district-provided language assessment tool. Once the students passed the TAAS test, they were moved to English instruction because their remaining years would be measured by their performance on the English TAAS test. The program had been left with a minimum compliance design. However, Elena used to go above and beyond what the state and federal laws required, and now the school was perfunctorily meeting the minimum requirements set by law.

Transitioning to English became crucial, even though there was a TAAS test for Spanish-speaking students. The new push was for students to take the test in English, since the Spanish test could only be taken once, was not used in the accountability ratings, and was therefore not a focus of instruction. In many instances, if a student was successful on TAAS, they were quickly moved to an English-only model. Devin, a fifteen-year veteran of bilingual education, recalls how one parent felt that her child was not prepared to move into English-only instruction, while the principal and the teacher wanted to transition the child to English because he had passed the TAAS test.

> [Devin:] I think the teacher had decided to transition her child. The parent still wanted him in a bilingual classroom in fourth grade, but he was placed in a monolingual [English] class. She called [the principal] up and said, "You need to move my child out of that class because he's bilingual." [The principal] said, "No. Your child passed TAAS." And the parent said, "Look, I can't help him with his homework if it's in English for one thing and two, he's only been transitioned for part of last year. Maybe he did well on TAAS, fine, but it hasn't even been a year." And [the parent] said, "I just don't think that we're ready for that."

Devin's story is an example of the influence of TAAS on bilingual instructional decisions. Decisions to exit children used to rely on multiple indicators such as teacher recommendation, work samples, and the IDEA test. These assessments provided a wide range of information on each child's language abilities. Over time, the TAAS test became the default measure of language proficiency because of its importance in other areas of school accountability. The principal moved students out of bilingual classes according to their TAAS performance, even though TAAS was not designed to measure language proficiency. Everything the school was judged on was based on TAAS, not on IDEA scores. This shift in policy at Elena was not documented anywhere, and the bilingual policy remained intact on paper. Illeana continued by explaining the strength of allowing children to maintain their first language of Spanish and how Elena used the IDEA test for student placement, even as the school began to use TAAS as a foundation for placement decisions.

> [Illeana:] It's all based on the [IDEA] assessment. We have to go by how they score on the [IDEA]. It can't be our own choice, unless of course the parent denies the program. So we test them and if it says they need bilingual instruction, then they are placed in a bilingual class.

To move a child into English before they are literate in their home language of Spanish can affect their literacy deeply (Crawford, 1989). Teacher knowledge is crucial in the preliminary and the continual assessment of language within the bilingual and ESL programs. Students are always progressing in their language proficiency, and teachers must be adept at recognizing their growth and struggles. As a Reading Recovery teacher, I had two first-grade students referred to me because of their teachers' concerns about their lack of progress in reading. Once I began instruction and became acquainted with their families, I discovered both students were fluent Spanish speakers, and I should not be instructing them in English. Their teacher was new and did not understand the bilingual program. To further complicate matters, the office staff had misplaced the students in all-English classrooms. Teacher education in the areas of bilingual and ESL instruction and theory was losing its value and place as an important part of the culture of Elena. As a result, decisions about individual students' literacy instruction suffered.

During the years 1987–2000, most teachers understood and accepted the theory of second-language acquisition espoused by Cummins, who

> hypothesizes that children must attain cognitive-academic language proficiency (CALP) if they are to succeed in the "context-reduced, cognitively demanding" activities of reading, writing, mathematics, science, and other schools subjects. CALP typically takes five to seven years to develop . . . and is best nurtured by

building on the linguistic foundation that language-minority children bring to school, rather than trying to replace it." (cited in Crawford, 1989, p. 107)

This idea that students may master conversational oral and/or written aspects of the second language, but that they are not proficient until they have mastery over academic language, was embraced and guided many decisions at Elena. To transition students prior to the onset of mastery of fluency in the academic language of their first language was to rob them of a strong base with which to access the second language. This can result in interrupting the language development of both the first and second languages. According to Rodriguez (1998):

> Children coming to school speaking Spanish already have a communication skill that should be capitalized on rather than minimized or eliminated. The Spanish-speaking student who is not literate in Spanish should be given the chance to develop and maintain the native language. The student should also be allowed to progress academically in the native language while simultaneously receiving systematic, sequential, and regular instruction in English. (p. 35)

Elena teachers aware of the complexity and importance of proper implementation of a true bilingual program held fast to the belief that teacher knowledge was necessary and should be nurtured. Devin explains the complexity involved in learning how to administer the IDEA test to determine language dominance:

> One of the things that worried me so much was initial identification. We've had all of this turnover in pre-kindergarten and kindergarten teachers. You really are getting teachers in there that are identifying our kids that really don't have enough experience with administering the instrument or working with children. I know during my first year, I was very lucky that the former pre-kindergarten teacher brought me up and she said, "I'll go help you," and I said, "Oh really?" I sat there with her as she evaluated a few kids and she observed me evaluating a few kids and then we talked about it. It was a wonderful situation. It was an ideal situation for a new teacher like me, somebody kind of walked me through it. She spent the whole day doing that, and I don't know if our teachers do that enough.

Knowing the community and the needs of children, Devin continued to reiterate the high level of understanding and knowledge required to adequately interpret the needs of children and balance the multiple interpretations of program requirements. Devin also pointed out the coordination necessary to serve children well. In this case, the LPAC committee did not meet to assess and monitor the instructional needs of this child until the end of the year, which resulted in individual interpretations of the language services this child should receive.

> [Devin:] It is difficult in our school where we're 90 something percent Hispanic, I would say most of our kids here speak Spanish, some of them will say, "I don't know Spanish," but they do. A lot of people don't understand that. A lot of people, I mean everybody in bilingual [education], they don't understand that in a community like this that's a necessary thing. If you're not a bilingual teacher, then you better be an ESL certified teacher because there are some real particulars that happen and you have to have background or ideas on how to handle this. I had a child in my class where I did instruction in Spanish and I just realized he's a "C" and when I talked to Illeana, she kept insisting ["C's" had an option of choosing English or Spanish]. I guess she knows more than I do, but I told her "C's" are supposed to be instructed in English. I said, "I've been doing instruction in Spanish" and she said, "No, 'C's' are supposed to have an option." And I'm thinking, "I don't ever remember there being anything about an option." She's the LPAC chair and I'll go by whatever she says so as long as I'm not doing anything wrong. I told her I didn't administer the ITBS [Iowa Test of Basic Skills] and I didn't give her instruction in Spanish and at this point she's transitioning. At the beginning of the year, I felt she was much more dominant in Spanish and yet she had a lot of skills in English, but it's not until now [that we had discussed it].

Devin and Ileana did not converse about this child until the end of the year, suggesting a lack of attention to and the eroding importance of the bilingual program through decreased monitoring of not only the initial placement of students but also of their progress and instruction.

Elena's LPAC committee used to meet throughout the year to reevaluate and discuss the children's placements. There was a continual dialogue about language in the forefront of all teaching decisions. Now the LPAC committee rarely convened. Caroline, a fifth-grade teacher, lamented the increasing focus of weekly meetings centered around TAAS issues instead of the bilingual issues she thought needed attention:

> Now what's happening every week is we have a TAAS meeting [in lieu of bilingual committee meetings]. The push is to get the kids speaking English so they can do well on the TAAS test. You saw the support we got when we asked for a bilingual assistant principal. We didn't get one. We have a monolingual assistant principal, our new principal is not certified bilingual, our counselors are not bilingual, so we have a whole administration that is not bilingually certified. And we have the entire district office not supporting bilingual education, too. I think any push to get a bilingual principal or assistant principal is from the staff, but the interesting thing is it took a monolingual teacher to get the whole thing situated and get the letter turned in.

Bilingual education at Elena was an issue for some teachers, and they were fighting to keep it in the forefront. Caroline refers to a letter many teachers signed criticizing the district for not hiring the necessary personnel to support a bilingual program. The administration had changed since 1992, and priorities had slowly shifted from developing and maintaining a strong bilingual program focused on developing both languages to a program aimed at English mastery.

A recent event suggested how policies within the school had shifted. Ms. Hernandez was our principal from 1992 to 2001. In the spring of 2001, the district hired a new principal and assistant principal because of Ms. Hernandez's retirement. In light of the new administrators, some teachers saw a gap in the representation of bilingual interests. At one faculty meeting, some of the bilingual teachers became concerned that the new governing Campus Action Committee (CAC) would not have a bilingual teacher on board. Devin described how she brought up the issue at the meeting and then pressed the principal for an answer. She did not understand why the special area teachers were seen as needing representation and bilingual education was not.

> [Devin:] When I brought up the whole bilingual issue at the faculty meeting, I wasn't looking for an answer at that moment. I was looking for somebody to say, "Well you know what? You're right. It is a problem. Let's sit down and brainstorm about this." I can accept it. I may not like everything that they are going to say, that I have to do, or all the decisions, but I can at least feel like we got heard. I had an argument with Ms. Hernandez down the hallway . . . [I told her] "I'm just going to put this out there so everybody can talk about it. There is no bilingual representation." She said that special area and special education had to be on there. When you look at the guidelines for CAC, it says there that all professions need to be elected. So basically even though they were on the ballot, they weren't opposed, which comes down to being politically appointed. Why were they even on the ballot? There was no point to having them there if she was going to do that for them. She needed to think of doing that for bilingual.

Because of the absence of a determined campus-wide focus on bilingual education and all of the complicated decisions involved in correctly assessing and implementing instruction, the bilingual program at Elena became defined by three views: (a) teachers who felt it was important to maintain both languages; (b) teachers who pressed for and accepted the earlier transition to English; and (c) those new teachers unaware and uneducated in the language development of bilingual children and limited English-speaking children, who thought that language issues were irrelevant to teaching reading.

At Elena, deep within a Latino community where the billboards were in Spanish and the halls of the school were covered with Spanish and English bulletin boards, the influence of the community seemed to be disappearing within the school's walls. The Dual Language program faded out with sighs of relief from many teachers who felt that it required too much work and interfered with TAAS. As procedures and attitudes changed in the past few years, Elena children were moved into English reading hurriedly to pass the state tests. The teachers' views were reflections of the overall emphasis the district and the state placed on TAAS and its lack of specific attention to bilingual issues. The teachers of Elena were merely enacting their world as they felt they should in response to the broader goals of the policy community.

The figured world of Elena had eroded into a very different view of teaching. Rather than emphasizing the complexity and culture of the students and seeking to maintain their culture and language as much as possible, the school became highly focused on streamlining the curriculum to match the states' objective of passing the TAAS test. The figured world of Elena was eclipsed by the figured world of the state's accountability system, and the beliefs of the teachers were transmitted invisibly by and through them to the children. The lack of importance attached to the bilingual program can be attributed to a lack of teacher knowledge, a lack of support from the administration, and the absence of a state accountability component addressing bilingual issues.

CULTURE AND RACE
AT ELENA

The altering of the bilingual program and the growing special education program at Elena could be viewed through a theoretical frame
based on Critical Race Theory. Critical Race Theory (CRT) views
the role of White culture in schools and casts its eye toward the constructions
of race and power in society. CRT moves race into its covert, institutionalized
enactment in everyday school life (Delgado & Stefancic, 1997; Scheurich &
Young, 1997). Fourteen years at Elena had shown me a variety of teacher attitudes toward the children and parents. My first few years at Elena were
marked by many explicit conversations I had with Latina teachers there. They
explained not only the culture of the community; they also interpreted things
other teachers, the district, and I did from their point of view. For example, my
first year teaching a fellow teacher was in my classroom, and she explained that
my parents and children may not feel comfortable with the chart that listed my
"hired hands" or classroom helpers. She went on to let me know that many of
our students and their families were migrant workers and that my description
might be hurtful. During my first meeting with the principal, he explained the
importance of learning to pronounce the children's names correctly, making
two home visits per year, and attending PTA meetings. He also assured me
that the school would support me as much as needed in those activities. As a
White woman, these topics were things I had not thought about. There were
no optional methods of conducting business at Elena. The directives were
clear and explicit, and teachers were held accountable and were required to
document their home visits. The principal always asked teachers if they had
completed all of their home visits, and he was present and visible in the halls,
teacher's lounge, and classrooms daily. The assistant principal met with me

within my first month to explain in great detail the bilingual paperwork involved in placing the English as a Second Language students in my classroom. I soon realized that teaching Latina children required a greater understanding of teaching than simply working my way through the curriculum. I was learning how race and culture impact teaching.

Several scholars have illustrated that schools do not consistently recognize the impact of race on instructional decisions (Delgado-Gaitan, 1986; Delpit, 1995; Ladson-Billings, 1994; Oakes, 1985), and they have seen and documented the cultural and racial dramas within schools (Guerra, 1998; Schaafsma, 1993; Spindler, 1998; Trueba, 1988, 1999; Valdes, 1996; Winfield, 1986). From Kozol's (1991) depictions of inner-city schools to Trueba's (1999) examination of how Freire's "pedagogy of hope" affected two different classrooms of children to Valenzuela's (1999) "Subtractive Schooling" and Nieto's (1999) "The Light in Their Eyes," these studies cry out for teachers and schools to reform their views of children of color. These studies and many more relate the importance of understanding the racial attitudes, identities and subsequent actions of teachers with countless examples of teachers such as myself not understanding the children they teach, which brings me back to Elena.

Whiteness

Since many teachers and I were White, I was interested in how race affected both White and Latino teachers' beliefs and knowledge at Elena. In 1987, the staff was primarily Latina, and the Latina teachers had strong opinions, voicing them frequently. In 2001, the staff was 50 percent Latina and 48 percent White. The Latino culture of the community was often brought up in school meetings about holidays, families, and literacy practices, but Whiteness was never directly discussed. The idea of Whiteness as a culture with specific ideas and practices was not talked about. During data collection, I decided to bring it up. With four of eight primary informants being White and the other four Latina, I was curious to know how they would react to my direct inquires about race. Only three of the eight were willing to discuss race as a factor in their teaching. The others simply thought it was irrelevant. These variations in response to discussions about race are common and documented in various ways. For the purposes of this area of the study, I will use Helms's model. Helms (1984, 1990 as cited in Derman-Sparks, 1998) constructed a hierarchical model depicting how the racial identity of Whites is developed:

- Contact: "awareness of the existence [of people of color] characterized by naiveté, fear, and lack of knowledge about people of color; unawareness of oneself as a racial being; tendency to ignore differences or regard them as unimportant (colorblindness); and lack of awareness of cultural and institutional racism" (p. 30).

- Disintegration: "becomes aware that racism exists and if forced to acknowledge his or her Whiteness and the part he or she plays in perpetuating racism, feelings of guilt and depression arise . . . Helms postulates three ways of resolving these uncomfortable feelings: (1) attempt to overidentify with people of color, (2) become paternalistic, (3) retreat into the predictability of White culture" (p. 31).
- Reintegration: "Two reactions may occur at this time. One is a withdrawal into Whiteness, and the other is further examination that leads to anti-racism" (p. 31).
- Pseudo-Independence: "individuals make a conscious effort to disconnect themselves from racist behavior and covert acquiescence to White power, seeking instead to replace conformity to racism with a world view that affirms the value of all people and cultures and, further, seeks to share power and resources" (p. 31).
- Autonomy: "[individuals] have learned how to be autonomous Whites, functioning as self-actualized individuals and joining with people of color and other exploited groups to change racist systems" (p. 31).

This model illustrates the views many teachers at Elena shared—or avoided sharing. Most of the teachers could be viewed as maintaining a level of racial awareness described by the contact stage. Being in a community and a school of color, the White teachers were aware of the children's race, not their own, and they were fearful of the community, demonstrating a consistent lack of awareness of cultural or institutional racism. Penny, one of our special education teachers, became the most vocal of all of the teachers when the topic of race was broached. Although her honesty and forthright answers reveal her tendency toward "othering" and stereotyping the community and children, she was quickly moving toward the reintegration stage. Where the other teachers were more silent or covert regarding the racial aspects of teaching at Elena, Penny was willing to express herself uncensored and was therefore moving herself into the most difficult part of recognizing the role race plays in teaching. I will use her here as an example of one teacher willing to tackle the minefield of racism in schools. Penny, a White teacher, was the most willing to discuss how seeing herself as a White teacher affected her daily existence at Elena:

> My biggest chasm is language. I could be a White teacher and speak fluent Spanish and be able to operate more within the parental area. But I don't speak

Spanish. I try. I do what I can. I think I'm pretty down to earth with them . . . I tone down my . . . I guess some would say professionalism, my teacherism. Working here and in these places, I know in my outward appearance, I know that definitely I do not fit in. When I was a first year teacher and I went and bought whole new wardrobes, I had those big long leather boots, that lasted about a month. I started feeling horrible because my kids were wearing clothes they wore all week. Brothers and sisters clothes too and parents coming up here in sweat stained, working construction and stuff. I felt bad. I can't do that. They would look at me different and I would feel bad as a parent too, if I worked in the field all day or worked in a kitchen and came up dirty and looked at Miss Perfect with her jewels. My voice, my speech, I've definitely dumbed down my professional language. I don't say phonemic awareness, Vygotsky, proximal development, I don't say those. I say she's working at this grade level. She's reading these words. I'm very specific because if it's not their language and they don't understand what I'm saying, they don't understand the vocabulary. I guess you would say, and not in any mean way, I've had to and I feel comfortable doing that. I still think that I maintain my position as a teacher with that.

Penny was aware of the differences between herself, her students, and their parents. It altered her feelings about how she saw and conducted herself. Although she focused on the socio-economic differences, there are inherent aspects of race that she avoided. Race is difficult to discuss, and Penny came the closest to articulating how she felt she was viewed and how she tried to adjust herself to her surroundings when at school. Frankenburg (1993, 1997) explains Whites' continued failure to see Whiteness as a force in society. She explains that Whiteness is defined primarily by referring to those of *other* races; Whites do not see White culture as a culture but are able to see who is *not* of the White culture. Penny was beginning to see herself as White and privileged, and she was aware that the parents might view her in certain ways. She wanted to make them as comfortable as possible, although in her desire to even the playing field she exposed her feelings that the parents were not capable of understanding her professional language, which is not necessarily race-specific and could be a nod to the deficit theory ideas espoused by Valencia & Solorzano (1997).

Why engage in talk about culture and race? The main reason is because it was so often avoided, and the unspoken, avoided issue can be the most critical and powerful of all. "Race, like gender, is 'real' in the sense that it has real, though changing, effects in the world and real, tangible, and complex impact on individuals' sense of self, experiences, and life chances" (Frankenburg, 1993, p. 11). Kincheloe & Steinberg (1998) relate the importance of a focus on White culture as it affects education:

Whatever the complexity of the concept of whiteness, at least one feature is dis-
cernable—it cannot escape the materiality of its history, its effects on the everyday lives of those who fall outside its conceptual net as well as on white people
themselves . . . [S]cholarship on whiteness in general should focus attention on
the documentation of such effects. In a critical multicultural educational context, the study of whiteness should delineate the various ways such material effects shape cultural and institutional pedagogies and position individuals in relation to the power of white reason. (p. 8)

Within the walls of Elena Elementary, race was a constant factor in the attitudes and interactions among the teachers, families, and children. Although
the teachers were individuals acting on their own, they were also part of the
larger community inside and outside of the school. Elena worked inside of the
larger context of the city, state, and society in general. The relationship
between the school as an institution and the teachers as part of that establish-
ment can be viewed through the idea of institutional racism. Institutional racism, as described by Scheurich & Young (1997), "exists when institutions, including educational ones, have standard operating procedures (intended or
unintended) that hurt members of one or more races in relation to members of
the dominant race . . . if a school's standard pedagogical method is culturally
congruent with the culture of white students but not with the cultures of students of color" (p. 135). The powerful nature of working in an organization
that preferenced the dominant culture's ideology about literacy, schooling,
and parenting was evident in Elena's shift away from the community.

Fourteen years ago, Elena was staffed primarily by Latina teachers. They
emphasized preserving Latino culture through their attention to issues they
felt were unique to the community, such as maintaining Spanish and actively
fighting the deficit views so often expressed in the school district's policy.
Upon my arrival, I learned much about the community from explicit and im-
plicit directions from the principal and the teachers. By 2001, many new
teachers at Elena had arrived, and most were White. The bilingual program
was almost gone, and there had been a transformation in the type of communication expected between parents and teachers. Most teachers communicated
through notes home instead of making home visits. Natalie, the campus literacy specialist, arrived at Elena the year before I did. She spoke of the influence
of the cultural differences she felt:

I grew up in a White middle class culture at home but my dad was military, so we
moved around a lot . . . when I was hired I was asked if I would be willing to get
my ESL certification. I said yes and so after my first year, I spent the whole summer in school. That was the first time that I really started to see my perceptions

as a different race teacher. The teachers really affected the way I felt about language and about learning . . . I had one professor who especially talked about how standard English is what we decide as a society and culture. That it's not the right way to talk it's the standard way . . . now I have to say I've noticed a big change in our staff over the years. [A group of teachers] we used to have here . . . had chips on their shoulders because of race and because of their upbringing. That influenced the way they got along with other teachers, how they felt about education and I was made aware of race. I always kind of felt included in that group, but not completely . . . It's not like now. A couple of Hispanic teachers who I feel like they have a chip on their shoulder and they're always looking out to see if they're getting the short end of the stick. Not all of them, just a few. I've noticed that more with the Hispanic teachers than with the other teachers.

The Latina teachers' tendency to speak explicitly and directly about race made some teachers, including Natalie, feel uncomfortable. They were outspoken about their world view and disrupted the discussions at meetings by sharing their views of how race was related to decisions and issues at Elena.

Over the years, many of the outspoken Latina teachers have departed, and the campus is back to a relatively quiet existence. One of the teachers became a principal and hired three of the teachers and the parent training specialist to go to her school to work for her. Two of the teachers who went to the new school were Latina, and one was White, but they shared a common ideology. They were disgruntled by the changes in focus of the school and sought to re-create the philosophy of what they felt was a more child-centered, dual-language program. Not many bilingual issues were raised in 2001, and they were not supported by more than a handful of teachers. Whereas a decade ago there would have been extensive discussion, debate, and research to design and fortify the program, now most teachers were not involved in debate or discussion on the topic.

In the past, the Latina teachers made race an open topic as they spoke about the children and families. They made the connections between decisions and labels applied to children obvious, and the idea that race affected teaching was emphasized. Some teachers welcomed and understood this point of view; some teachers saw their viewpoints as "chips on their shoulders." When viewed through Helms's model, racial issues between White teachers at Elena in the past were more explicit, and the White teachers found ways to ignore the direct focus on how Latina issues were raised by Latina teachers (Contact) or White teachers came to overidentify with the Latina teachers' ideas (Disintegration). In 2001, the overall pattern of behavior of White teachers at Elena was to maintain the elements characteristic of the contact stage of racial identity as they carried an awareness of the existence [of people of color] characterized by naiveté, fear, and lack of knowledge about people of color; unawareness of oneself as a racial being; tendency to ignore differences or regard them as unimportant (color-blindness); and lack of awareness of cultural and institutional racism. (Derman-Sparks, 1998, p. 30)

Since most participants did not think race was an issue, I did not push the topic; instead I turned the conversations to the community. By discussing the community, the teachers revealed their thoughts about the culture of the families. The conformity expected of the families was apparent, first by the expectations set up by the school and the teachers, second by the distance between the teachers and parents, and third by the conclusions the teachers drew from their knowledge and beliefs in relation to the community.

It was clear that many of the White and some of the Latina teachers viewed the families in the Elena community in a general, essentialized way. These views were not always clearly marked simply by race, as Katia, a Latina teacher, placed the same expectations on the community as the White teachers did. I did not press her for her views or inquire as to her deeper feelings, but her attitude may be due to the dominant view held by the school regarding parental expectations. The teachers spoke of the families as a separate category of people in language that may be defined as "raceless." Teachers elected to use socio-economic status, neutral terms or references to language differences, professional differences, or lifestyle differences. Such practices are what Feagin (1998) describes as talking about race with "code-words." Code-words serve to relay basic ideas about the social construction of race without naming race. Feagin's (1998) examples include vocabulary such as "welfare mothers," "inner city," and "at-risk." He agrees with Frankenburg (1993) that Whites will not often directly discuss race because they feel bound by the idea of "hyperpoliteness" Moon (1999). The teachers I interviewed at Elena illustrated these theories of "hyperpoliteness" and "code-words" throughout the study. They were not willing to discuss the children as racial subjects directly or to talk about themselves as racial subjects. The most common words or phrases used by the teachers as codes for race were the simple "they," "their," and "those." These words served to indicate a great separation in the way the teachers did things and the way the parents did things. The delicate dance around racial factors in teaching was conducted in broad language in order to avoid saying Latina, Hispanic, or White. Penny was the only teacher who used any direct references to race and who did not shy away or avoid the topic. The following sections relate to the topic of race and culture at Elena in that these are the words the teachers used to describe their feelings about the families and the children they taught.

The Road to School: A One-Way Street of Parent Expectations

[Illeana, an administrator:] One of the best things we've done is have the parent workshops. We've done a lot of workshops where we talk about literacy, especially the [television station] one. This year they went to the public library and they had the classes there and so when the parents go they get trained on not only how to use books, but how to watch TV effectively and it's all connected to books. We know that the children are watching a lot of TV so if we can make it a little more effective that'll help but it also got the parents in the library to get library cards. We also have workshops here on campus for reading and also the Reading Recovery teachers had a workshop for the parents that explained the program so they understood a little bit better. Then we had literacy week and that night we had things for the parents. We had a storyteller come that night and we had book walks for the children so that they could get more books. I think the other thing we do for the community, a lot of the teachers now are sending home information on how to read with your child, how to open the book, what are the different parts of the book. They are sharing more of that with the parents in the younger grades. School-wide we're still doing the read at home program where everybody is supposed to read. Of course now we have more resources; we have more books available in Spanish. We've really purchased a lot of materials so that they can do that. Don, the librarian, lets parents get their own library card so they can check out books from our library and he has a section for young babies and young readers where they can check out those hardback books so they can start teaching the children earlier. Whenever we have a PTA meeting, I always remind parents that they can get library cards. We don't get a big turnout [at parent workshops]. . . most of the time we get maybe 8 parents, but at least it's 8 parents. A lot of them are repeats but that's one thing we need to try to do is to get the ones that need to be here. I'll help everyone but we still need to target the ones that need to be here.

Illeana indicated that teachers and administrators communicated with parents in two ways: notes home and phone calls. With parent literacy workshops being the focus of outreach attempts, all measures of parental communication were dependent on the perception that the workshops Elena provided and the reading teaching tips were the key to communicating with the children's families. Illeana summarized how Elena supported literacy in the community by offering workshops, library cards, and meetings, but she also revealed how few parents attended these events and that the attendees were usually the same parents.

Elena had a history of being uniquely connected to the community through home visits that allowed the teachers to become familiar and meet with the families in a more intimate personal way. By 2001, Elena's procedures of sending notes, calling, and providing the occasional workshop was the standard issue method of conducting business, a way of conducting business that may be seen as an institutionally learned way for teachers to contact parents similar to what Feagin & Vera (1995) define as institutional racism. Institutional racism can be seen in the "ritual nature of racist events . . . [S]ocial practices that dissipate human resources and energies are often ritualized, that is, they are routine and recurring actions distinguished by symbolic meanings that pervade and guide their performance" (Feagin & Vera, 1995, p. 9).

Most teachers did not think twice about the parent communication measures at the school. They often compared the way the parents at Elena responded to the notes and calls to the way their own parents responded. It was important that the parents should take more initiative. Caroline, a fairly new teacher, felt that sending notes home and using the school's parent training specialist, Ellen, whenever there was a problem, was the way to communicate with parents. Although she admits to being uncomfortable with the process of interacting with parents, she did think sending a note home should be enough:

> [Caroline:] That is definitely one of my weakest areas, parent communication. I'm young and I know that a lot of parents are young, as young as I am. I've gotten a lot better, just being more comfortable in what I'm doing . . . I feel more comfortable explaining it now. I feel like I can explain better to the parents, but when I do communicate, it's either through a note home or a telephone call. Mostly a note home, some [respond]. I think a note home about a child misbehaving in class and having problems with their behavior should result in more than just a small note back. I think my parents would have been up at school.

Caroline, a White teacher, describes the parents' way of interacting or lack of reacting to her notes as not being what her own parents would do. She typifies what Derman-Sparks (1998) describes as ethnocentrism, a characteristic of the first stage of racial identity:

> When Whites control all the institutions of a society, White "norms" become synonymous with what is natural, normal, and universal. [Teachers] taking a colorblind stance assumed that racial and cultural background was irrelevant, they also assumed they were being nonracist if they judged everyone by the same norm even when they then found others wanting. (p. 52)

When teachers talked about the families, there was always an expectation, an expectation that led them to compare what the parents did to what they believed they should be doing, what White parents would do.

Just as teacher identities can be obscure, recognizing the effect of race and culture in teachers' identities is difficult and complicated but crucial. Critical race theorists of color set out clear pictures of how Whites cannot see the culture they live within (Bell, 1992; King, 1997; Mahoney, 1997a). There is a tendency to believe that there is not a "white culture." At Elena, White culture had become the dominant force it always has been in the U.S. Teachers controlled the social mores and values of the figured world at Elena and applied those social expectations to the parents. Parental behavior and student achievement were measured by what the school's culture felt was necessary for the continuation of the status quo.

The primary evidence of the school's vision for parents was visible in the teachers' comments regarding how involved the teachers thought the parents were in their children's lives within the school's walls. Since most communication between parents and teachers was relegated to phone calls and notes home, there were ample opportunities for misunderstandings. This limited form of communication is revealed in Caroline's comments. Caroline, a relatively new teacher, described her thoughts about how she tried to communicate with one parent. Frustrated with the parent's lack of response, Caroline sent the parent training specialist, Ellen, to "get onto her."

[Caroline:] I think that right now with Ms. Garcia and Illeana, I think they generally do a really good job of reaching out to the community. I think just being here for so long they have that connection with a lot of the families that have stayed in the neighborhood. We have a lot of transient families and I think that's really difficult, not only for Elena, but for other schools too. They have the same problems to reach those people. We have a parent training specialist and she does get involved, usually only when there is a problem though. I do use her quite a bit just because I don't feel like I have time and I don't feel as comfortable going and pressuring parents into doing things. An example is, this year, I have a student who came in after I got back from maternity leave. He came in towards the end of the year, he's supposed to have glasses and evidently they were broken. His mom didn't have money to take him to the doctor, so we sent her the papers and she wouldn't return them, so I had Ellen get onto her about that. Then when they had the papers turned back in and they had their appointment set up, they missed the appointment. I had Ellen get onto them about that and then he had his glasses and he wouldn't wear them. He said they were blurry. His mom had put them up and said she was going to take them back. So, I sent Ellen and nothing happened. Finally I just walked home with him after school and told his grandma to tell his mom to get his glasses. She wanted the nurse to check him and see what was going on and now he's wearing them.

Developing parent communication is difficult and requires guidance. Caroline never directly communicated to the mother, and her first course of action was to send Ellen, the parent training specialist, to "get onto her." Ellen was a secondary informant, and when I asked her about her job, she indicated that this was the way all of the teachers used her. Ellen was sent to homes to have notes signed and check on any "problems." If teachers rely on notes or "sending Ellen," the potential for two-way communication is limited. Children lose notes or parents cannot read; children may travel between divorced parents. Although Caroline did not state that the child's mother did not care for her son, there is an implied message that it was Caroline who had to help the child get glasses, and if she had not stepped in and sent Ellen to the home or spoken to the grandmother, he would not have worn the glasses.

A lack of response to a note may not indicate a lack of care. I continually heard conversations in meetings, in the teacher's lounge, or at faculty meetings depicting the parents as not caring about their children. Some teachers at Elena fell into operating from a distanced perspective. They relied on knowing what they expected rather than what might really have happened. Using Ellen as an intermediary allowed even more distance, and since Ellen's errands were always due to some negative event, such as the parents' lack of response to the school, parents may not have viewed Ellen's visits in a favorable light. By using Ellen and relying on notes and phone calls, teachers did not attempt more personal communication with the parents, and they assessed parents' responses based on White culture, which so dominated the teacher culture at Elena that it was virtually invisible to the White teachers there. Teachers were operating under the assumption that what worked in their lives would work in the lives of the parents at Elena. Therein lies the danger that if teachers do not see Whiteness as a cultural factor, they will never perceive or recognize what impact it has on those who are *not* White.

One example of this process occurred when Katia, a Latina teacher who embraced many of the same views of parents as White teachers, described the difference between the predominately White, middle-class parents at Cypress Hills versus the predominately Latina, low socio-economic-class parents at Elena. Katia described how she felt Elena parents were easier overall because of their tendency not to get involved. This sentiment was a common theme with many teachers I knew at Elena. They appreciated the fact that the parents did not challenge the teacher's ways or ideas.

[Katia:] As far as parents at Elena versus those at Cypress Hills, this is a very relaxed atmosphere. Here you don't have parents in your face, over there you will. You get to do more enrichment over there, there's a lot more to do over there with those kids. I still want the challenge [of Elena]. I still have the energy, but I don't feel like having parents in my face right now . . . I have yet to have a parent come challenge me. I've challenged, many times, my child's teachers on many things that I feel, "Hey, wait a minute you're doing what?" I think it's the level of education and the priorities. I think a lot of them don't have the level of education that we have and that's why they're intimidated and that tends to hold them back.

Katia's feelings mirrored those of many other teachers I interviewed and teachers I knew at Elena. Teachers did not want the parents involved in making decisions, yet they wanted parents to show up for conferences and respond to notes home. In other words, they wanted parents' involvement only to serve their ends, not to form a partnership with respect to the children's schooling.

With an abundance of White teachers teaching children of color, to not expose Whiteness as a school culture within the community's culture, with its own communication and perceptions of parents, avoids understanding why there were such differences between White teachers and families of color. This avoidance of critical analysis allowed teachers to essentialize the community group without asking questions of themselves or reflecting on their positioning. Frankenburg (1997) claims that to engage critically in discussion about Whiteness is to "perpetuate a kind of asymmetry previously unexamined." Teachers at Elena had no means of analyzing their communications because of the nature of the powerful set of beliefs they had about the community, beliefs that were shared throughout the campus. No one disrupted the talk heard around the lounge, in faculty meetings, or in the halls. Race was not directly named as an ingredient for teachers' formations of the children's identities, except for the teachers of color, and these teachers were dismissed by some White teachers as "having a chip on their shoulder."

The expectations placed on the families were very much aligned with the traditional role of parents in schools. Even though Katia and other teachers recognized that the parents might be intimidated, they did not mention ways in which they sought to place the parents at ease. Penny's earlier description of how she dressed informally and spoke with less professional jargon was the only instance of a teacher identifying ways in which she understood the impact her presence or race may have had on parents. Mahoney (1997b) depicts race as a social construct that Whites create: "Whites also define Whiteness, albeit in ways that we cannot fully see, and they impose that vision on the world as much as [they] can" (p. 306). White teachers at Elena did not directly talk about Latinos, nor did they talk about being White. The avoidance of naming Whiteness as a race with its own cultural expectations exempts the teachers at Elena from seeing how their world view came to dominate their evaluations of children and families. By using the word Whiteness, we "assign everyone a place in the relations of racism" (Frankenburg, 1997), just as Latinos and African Americans are "assigned" labels. The balking at this label by Whites who claim to be "just Americans" illustrates their quest for individual recognition before racial identification, a view rarely afforded people of color. It is White dominance's final frontier in the avoidance of its own place in race relations.

As Natalie, the literacy specialist, revealed her feelings about the relationship between the school and the parents, her desire to educate the families is clear. Although she feels that the school could do more for the parents, she views the challenge as teaching the parents more about school, rather than teaching the teachers more about the parents. Natalie had taught at Elena for fifteen years, and she had a historical view of the school's relationship with the families:

> That's the one area I think we are weak in. I haven't seen a dramatic change in that over the years. To me, it seems about the same. We've done workshops for parents on reading to their kids and those are ongoing. I see our librarian, our parent training specialist, and maybe me too in my role, needing to do more. I think it's very difficult to change a culture and that's really what you are talking about. I know there are people doing things around the country trying to get literacy for 0–3-year-olds. It's one of the hardest things, going into homes and saying change the way you live, [laughs] read to your kids, read yourself, turn off the television. Literacy night is something new and we have parents attending. I did a thing on fourth grade writing. Do I see a lot of kids coming from literate homes? No. If so, it's because of the change in the demographics. I think we're probably doing more than we did ten years ago, but I don't know how much impact it's had. I'd like to know what else we can do. We're not going to have dramatic changes in literacy until that starts happening.

"Difficult to change a culture" sums up contemporary notions teachers at Elena held about the families at Elena. Any interaction the school or individual teachers had with the community was in the form of a directive or expectation.

Like many schools, Elena perceived parental communication as a problem to be solved. Illeana, an administrator, acknowledged that the relationship between parents and the school could be improved, as she lists what Elena did to communicate and involve parents in the schooling of their children. She mentioned the parent training specialist going out to the neighborhood to share knowledge about literacy, but there was no mention of teachers going out to learn about the community.

> [Illeana:] I think its getting better, but I still think we have a long way to go. We need to reach out to the community. If we had Ellen, who really should be in a house everyday, sharing books or techniques or something. But not just Ellen alone, I think I like the home visits. We didn't do it this year, but I think we should do that. I just think we need to do more things to bring the parents in but sometimes it's the time factor. A lot of them work and have more than one job. We'd try to do things like morning noon and night even so that they'll

have different options but still it's hard because then they'll have the children. Now we're providing baby sitting but we still need to do more. We need to find a way to bring the parents in more to learn, to learn about reading, to learn about literacy.

Illeana's comments implicitly indicate that communication between school and home was overwhelmingly a one-way street, both literally and figuratively. Reaching out to the community meant educating the community, reflecting a desire to give information rather than as an interest to exchange information and knowledge. But the history of Elena can be characterized as more of a two-way street. Teachers used to go to the homes of children and meet their families through home visits twice a year. Devin, a second-grade teacher, recalls the relationships between the community and school during the years 1989–1991:

> We had to get together to get what we needed here. The district was not going to hear us if we didn't unite. We were fighting with the parents [for a new school in 1989]. We were helping them out, organizing things, documenting things that were going on with the building. There were a lot of things that were happening in the building during that time period. I don't think it's fully together [now].

Then she recalled that teachers used to be required to go to PTA meetings and that the previous principal motivated and supported relationships between teachers and the community. He built a bridge between the school and the community by expecting teachers to show up at PTA meetings. He made his expectations very clear; there were no questions as far as what teachers should do in community relations. Devin, a Latina teacher, discussed the way the principal enforced the Elena philosophy during the early 1990s:

> I don't think we're as active as we used to be. One of the good points about that particular principal, he was much more charismatic and much more motivational in getting parents here and motivational in getting teachers here. Sometimes it wasn't in a very nice way, but for the most part, I think he made you feel like you had a stake in this. We had home visits, we had these other things we have now, but it was a different kind of feel. It wasn't quite the same . . . It's a formally structured type of interaction all the time. If we did home visits in lieu of doing conferences the first time around, I could see us doing that.

Over the years, as principals and teachers came and went, the teacher culture of the school changed. Where once teachers were told what, and how, to interact and contact parents, now it was relegated to the traditional methods of notes home. Caroline compared her relationships with parents as a White teacher to Devin's relationships. In her eyes, race was a factor since Devin was Latina and able to speak Spanish to the parents, and Caroline perceived Devin's interactions with them to be easier. Caroline also recognized that she did not make the effort to know the parents of her students better:

> I see Devin and I see how easy she has it with the parents, not only because of communication barriers between myself and the parents and she does have that but, she's what they are used to. They don't realize that I grew up around them. This is the kind of school I went to. But they don't know that about me. I don't give them the opportunity to know that because I don't make the effort. It's definitely something that I want to work on. It's something that I've wanted to work on since my first year here.

In the absence of not being directed as to how to interact with parents, even teachers such as Caroline, who would like to develop relationships with the parents, did not know how to establish them.

By 2001, the only directive from the administrators was to conference with the parents twice a year on the designated conference days. Home visits were brought up by the veteran Elena teachers who remembered the required visits, but when I asked teachers about their feelings about visiting the children's homes, many issues arose. The teachers began to speak about their feelings about the community and their place in it beyond literacy practices. Penny described the community with references to the physical spaces, the language, and the feelings she experienced about one of her students once she saw his home:

> This is the first year in fact a month ago where I had to drop a letter off to a parent. I was trying to talk to a parent of one our newer students and I got in Ellen's car with her and she drove me around. The parent wasn't there so we didn't have the meeting and while we drove she said, "Hey, do you want to see some of your other kids' houses?" I'd been here four years and it was the first time I'd ever seen some of my students' houses. That was when I found out one of my students was no longer here. There were six children, five or six children, and then both the parents and then like a grandmother and aunt and an uncle living in this one bedroom house. Nicely kept, pretty, but I was like . . . they all lived there? All of them? It made me have respect, made me have more respect for them. I guess because they work so hard here. They may, I don't know how hard they work in there out there in their regular [classroom]. One of them got two awards. You're like, "Student of the year! Here you jumped two grade levels in reading, you're a math whiz, you're this, you're that!" and I just saw where he lived.

Knowing the children's homes, rather than the neighborhood as a collective whole, made a difference for Penny. When I spoke to teachers about the community, I noticed a clear distinction in the way they described the neighborhood and the way they described individual children in their classrooms. The veteran teachers remembered the home visits, but the new ones had never done them. I asked them to share their thoughts about visiting their students' homes.

Keeping a Distance: Home Visits

Home visits were a complicated concept. They could be extremely invasive and were to be approached with sensitivity and care. In the past, since every teacher at Elena visited homes, it was not a stigma for the children who received a visit. Seeing a teacher at your door was not cause for alarm, because the teachers went to everyone's home every year. It was a part of the school year that was designed to be positive. Teachers were instructed to go as early in the school year as possible simply to meet the families and establish a relationship with them. I later realized how crucial this visit was to all of the subsequent interactions teachers had with the parents. The first visit was early enough so that there were no academic or behavioral concerns. Teachers introduced themselves and asked the parents to share any information they thought might help the teacher know their child better. There were times on home visits when I was asked to stay for dinner, and there were times when the parents and I met out on the front porch. Some parents were not comfortable with teachers seeing their homes, and teachers knew to let the parents be their guide as to how and where the visit occurred. Knowing the role home visits used to play in teacher and parent relationships, Bob, a White, 24-year veteran teacher, described the interactions between teachers and parents as being limited and more removed. The degree of parental involvement had eroded to a more traditional model of sending notes home and calling parents.

> [Bob:] Pitiful. It's totally pitiful. There's nothing going on now. Everything is done just for the form, to say that we've done it. You know people send notes home. But if you really want something to happen, you don't send notes home. The home visits were a wonderful thing and they really did put the neighborhood with the school . . . There's absolutely nothing happening. You send the notes home, that doesn't do anything, and you can drag the parents up here for the conferences and you can chit chat with them about all that, but they're not really involved in what's going on. That's the whole point. They're supposed to be involved in what's going on.

Even though all of the primary participants agreed that home visits would increase communication between parents and teachers, no one relished the idea of going. There were many reasons given: time, safety, and simply the concept of having too much information were the main themes. Knowing the neighborhood could result in views that distanced the teachers, as evidenced in the views of the teachers I interviewed at Elena. White teachers can experience what Frankenburg (1993) describes as the "social geography of race." They may feel thrust into a new culture. For as Frankenburg (1993) states, ". . . for many [White] women, to be caught in the act of seeing race was to be caught being 'prejudiced'" (p. 145). Yet teachers continually used their own culture and environment as a reference point, and it all began with the assessment of the neighborhood. Penny described what she would imagine other teachers would say about the community if they were asked to go on home visits:

> No one's going to go for a home visit. They are going to scream, "That's on my own time. I'm not getting paid for it." They're going to scream, "That's dangerous. I'm not going into that house alone by myself with the drunken father." And they're going to scream, "Gross, I'm not getting lice and sitting on their couch." It will never happen.

Teachers were allowed the opportunity or privilege (Delgado & Stefancic, 1997) of not having to go to their students' homes. The traditional role of teachers and schools is to do exactly what Elena teachers were doing. Teachers are supposed to send home notes or call homes to inform parents about their children's progress. In turn, parents are supposed to answer the notes and the phone calls and come to school activities, but Elena used to do more. Teachers made more of an effort. Bob recalled the way he conducted home visits in the past. He described how he also visited homes of students during the school year if he needed help with a child. He did not rely on the parent training specialist, Ellen, to go for him. He knew the parents and dealt directly with them.

> [Bob:] If you want good parent cooperation, you can get it really easily, but you have to work at it, you, yourself. You have to work at it. You'll have to go make some visits like what I do if I have somebody who's really having problems. We just walk home in the afternoon and that's what people have traditionally done. Not many people do that anymore and in the past that's the way it was. The kids knew it. So if they had a problem, they knew that they were going to get a walk home, even during the day. I'd walk them during planning period in the past if they lived real close. We'd just go at 10 o'clock. I think these telephones are good but part of the problem *is* the telephones. People just get on the phone but it's not the same as you standing on the front porch with one arm on the kid and the mother with her mouth wide open. She gets a real good message that something's not right because here is Mr. Hollis standing on my porch with my

kid and something's not right. I know I'll have to do something because he's going to come back. It really makes them talk to you. On the phone, they know they don't have to answer, but as long as they know you'll show up on their front porch, they will turn around a little bit and they will do enough to get you off their back, which is what you want and that's basically all you're looking for. But, most people don't go in homes anymore. They don't make the visit and I really don't do it now unless I need to, unless I have to because I'm just as lazy as everybody else. I just have the home visits for the new ones. Basically, I know most of my parents already before they even get in here. Since I've been here so long they know I will come over so it makes a difference. I think the new teachers should make the effort to go home because it's so easy to do.

Bob described how he interacted with parents and how relatively easy it was for him to establish relationships with parents. He was male and had been a teacher during the years that home visits were mandatory. Once the teachers had met and visited with the parents at the beginning of the year, it was easier to address any concerns or questions because of the prior relationship teachers had with parents. Knowing the parents and making an effort to meet them was the way Elena was when I first arrived in 1987. It was an expectation that communication between parent and teacher was a two-way endeavor.

Natalie, also a teacher at Elena during the years home visits were required, shared her views on the importance of home visits, suggesting that they gave her insight into her students:

The home visits changed my world view and beliefs. When I went to a couple of homes, especially with some kids I was having real problems with. I don't know if you remember, Luis? Oh my God, he gave me so much trouble. So I went on a home visit to his home. And I sat down with mom. We started talking about something and she brought him in the room and she laid into him verbally. She might have even hit him in front of me. I can't remember. It's been 13 years, but I think she hit him. I saw him just shrink as she called him names and I was almost in tears crying and thinking he deals with this all the time. I remember she had brought him to me before school started when they were registering and everybody was saying he was bad. I remember thinking, oh my God. But it made me treat him differently. It really did. I had a totally different understanding of where he was coming from. I didn't feel as angry towards him. There was another home I went to where this little girl she wasn't really doing her homework. She never did her homework. I went to her home and I found out that she, I guess I could have found this out without a visit, but I found out that she was basically the mom. She had four or five other siblings. She was the oldest. She was cooking. She was cleaning. She was doing everything a mom would do in that household. I was like, I am not going to give this child grief about homework anymore. So there's this, I know the teachers we had before, there was this kind of . . . this, make the kids feel good bring up their egos. Don't have high expectations. Now it's the opposite. Some of our teachers say, they don't care where they are coming from. My expectations are up here and I'm not going to lower them for anybody. You have to have an understanding of where they are coming from, you still have to set a standard and have the expectations, but you have to do it with a lot of support and understanding of where they're coming from.

Bridging the gap between home and school by going out to the home rather than continually asking parents to come to the school allowed the teachers to know more about the children they taught. Natalie explained how knowledge of the homes of the children could evoke sympathy from teachers to the detriment of maintaining high expectations, but she also stated that knowing where the children came from could also create a fair amount of empathy and balance out the teachers' feelings of understanding with high academic expectations.

Time and safety were brought up several times by all of the teachers as deterrents to home visits. Driving through the neighborhood brought up strong reactions. Feelings fluctuated between feeling sorry for the children and being afraid of their surroundings. Bob, the only male participant, was also the only teacher not concerned with safety. Every other teacher expressed both sadness at some of the conditions and fear that they were not safe. Caroline felt that developing close relationships with her students was important, and she invited them to her home.

[Caroline:] If you didn't have any concerns about safety issues, I think it would be a great idea. We never did this when I was in school. I never saw where my teachers lived. Teachers were just completely, even though my mom was a teacher, it was just completely different. You don't go to their house, but I'm taking my kids to my house on Thursday for a swim party and barbecue. So I do think it is important that they see your house, that they see outside of school and they can see you as more than just a teacher. Especially these kids, they need somebody that they can feel like is more than somebody who gives them work to do. I think I would enjoy feeling closer to my parents and feeling more comfortable around them and I think you would get that by visiting with them and spending time with them, but I also think that having to go way out of your way in order to do that is something that shouldn't be asked of us just because we have so much to do.

Caroline was willing to make an effort to bring her students to her home because she felt making a connection with them was important, but she was concerned about the amount of time it would take for her to go to their homes. Caroline was also willing to discuss her feelings about being sensitive to the parents' feelings about having her in their home. This also shows her tendency to dramatize the home life of the children from a distance. Ellen fed her fears by discussing how "she felt like she was in danger."

[Caroline:] I've gone to one student's home because the mom didn't come for a conference. Ellen was going to go and it was my conference period. I decided to go with Ellen. I think it's the worst house, from what Ellen said. It's a horrible situation and I felt extremely uncomfortable. I don't know, I think that, but I can't tell you what the mom would have thought if she had been home, maybe she would have felt ashamed. I think the student would have been too. It's not really [a good idea to go] but I can't tell you how they would have felt about that. That might be superficial of me to think that they would be embarrassed. I never got to meet with her. That's the only time I've been to a parent's house and I've also talked to Ellen a little bit about it because I've been curious. She talked about situations where she felt like she was in danger. If you have that kind of situation, then I don't think that is a good idea.

Caroline felt that this was a home where the parent might have been ashamed of having her visit. Based on her one "near visit," she constructed a view of the idea of visiting homes as unsafe. Ellen, our parent training specialist, often fed this view of the community in the teacher's lounge. There were many occasions when teachers and administrators shared "horror stories" about the neighborhood, even though in my fourteen years at Elena nothing had ever happened on our campus or in the neighborhood that was remotely frightening. Caroline expressed interest in one new teacher's lack of fear about entering the neighborhood. Barbara began teaching at Elena a few years before Caroline. She had student-taught at Elena and had a comfortable way with her students and their families.

[Caroline:] I noticed one thing about Barbara, because she and I were the same age. So I always would kind of watch what she did and I always noticed that she had a very good rapport with the parents. That she could talk to them easily and I remember her saying on conference day that she was going out to a parent's house because the parent wasn't able to walk. It was a matter of fact and she wasn't stressing about it, she wasn't upset about having to go out, it was just a duty and she was going to go do it. I thought that was really admirable.

Caroline's feelings that Barbara was going above and beyond professional expectations to visit a child's home indicated how the standard modes of community interaction were clearly defined so that Barbara's actions appeared out of place to Caroline. What was once a common way of interacting with parents was now rare and almost non-existent.

One drawback of not conducting home visits made understanding the families on a deeper level virtually impossible. By avoiding visiting their homes, teachers missed attaining knowledge of the children and families beyond where they lived and what their homes looked like. Knowledge of the children's homes was a powerful experience for every teacher who did go out past the school's walls. Penny simply drove by a child's home—she had never been in one—and she felt moved enough to contemplate the lack of knowledge she had about her children's private lives and the effect that knowledge had on her teaching.

> [Penny:] I haven't gotten to do [home visits] and I'd like to. It's a piece that I think that is . . . I don't know, I'm torn on that one. Hurting and helping me. Hurting me because I don't know and helping me because I don't know. I don't want to say, "Oh you live there, so I guess you can't do that can you?" I feel that I would. Instead of being the hard-ass that I am and basically saying, "No, I don't care where you live. I don't care what happens. I will stay after school and help you or we will find a way but you will do the same thing as everyone else."

Penny described the constructive and harmful aspects of teachers going farther than the school's walls to get to know the children and families they interacted with daily. She revealed the complexity of emotions that knowledge of the children can evoke in teachers and how that knowledge can shape their expectations of the students in the classroom. Teachers' constructions of the families and children will be discussed further in the remaining chapters.

A balance between maintaining relationships between the school and the community was missing. Teachers were distanced from the children's lives outside of school, or they dwelled on the negative glimpses they had and generalized them to the entire neighborhood. Home visits, which enlighten, can be intrusive for families and unnerving for teachers. Teachers need to be guided, since home visits do impact teachers' beliefs about the children by adding to their knowledge about how the children live. On the other hand, keeping a distance between home and school can leave the teachers to draw their own conclusions about the literacy of the children and their parents. Among the eight participants, only two had actually been to any students' homes, yet the teachers had drawn many conclusions about how the families lived, what they thought, and what the children were capable of learning as a result of their home lives.

Every teacher I interviewed thought that the families were not involved in their children's education and had virtually no educational goals for them. The basis of these decisions appeared to be the conference interactions, overgeneralizations based on hearsay from the teachers' lounge, past experiences, or the lack thereof. The positioning of the teachers as professionals with no required involvement with the community bred a teacher culture of decisions based on distance and myth. There were a handful of parents who were very vocal about their opinions on school policy, yet most of the teachers could depend on conducting business with little involvement from the parents. The privileged positioning of teachers as they made decisions and evaluations, based on the norms of White culture, was pervasive at Elena. Wildman & Davis (in Delgado & Stefancic, 1997) connect Whiteness and privilege by unraveling the way White culture defines the norms of society and how we can decide to engage or not to engage in talk about our race. Many would like to explain success as the result of hard work and place the responsibility on individual attributes, all the while disregarding the power societal forces have in continuing the racial hierarchy begun so long ago. White educators hoping to aid or save the children of color they teach bring a White cultural practice encased within privilege that may prevent them from seeing their own positioning outside of White culture:

> Absent their awareness, White children who become adults of goodwill most often oppose racism by helping people of color to help themselves. Albeit well intentioned, this form of White anti-racism never challenges the racial privilege on which it relies—because it emulates from the intersection of conscience and a non-reflexive racial consciousness. (Marty, cited in Nakayama, 1998, p. 52)

Elena teachers were privileged by comparison to the parents at Elena and by the nature of their job descriptions, their economic status, and their knowledge about schooling. Teachers were the professional educators, and many thought they were "adults of goodwill." Teaching at Elena was a challenge. All of the teachers I interviewed loved the children, but they felt that the children and the community were not adequately involved in the children's lives. Parents were not seen as educators of their children, and the additional effects of race on power relationships between parents and teachers added weight to the teachers' position.

White teachers' interactions with families of color created tension that no one at Elena discussed. McIntosh (1988) wrote of her privileges as a White person, listing in detail the ways she moved among the White world effortlessly as compared to people of color. The White teachers did not always realize the ways they moved with ease in the world they controlled. Penny noticed the fact that she could berate the "Mexicans" in one instance and then defend them the next:

> It's hard for me to admit as well that I do this. I still can drive down the street, turn on the street and a stupid guy just cuts slow in front of me and I'll be like, "Mexicans, they do that all the time." [laughs] Fifty percent of the kids here have

lice. It's giving me the idea where most little Mexican kids all have lice. I made some judgments too that I shouldn't have. It's shameful for me to admit that but I've got to admit my biases. I don't think that I can conquer my biases unless I just admit that I have them. I've seen where working here has changed my vision a lot because I got into several knock down drag out fights with my family and my friends. They don't have those experiences and I'm like you can't talk about it that way, you don't live it every day. You don't see this every day and they just don't work, they are just lazy people. I have to contend with my family and it makes me feel Whiter. It makes me ashamed in some ways. I can't believe you're my family and this is what I work with every day and you're speaking about this *this* way.

The ability Penny has to move in and around the stereotypes of the unsatisfactory driving or grooming habits of the Latina culture she then defends against her family is indicative of the unique power of White culture. Whites are rarely subject to carrying such negative identities. Penny validates the stereotypes through joking and then berates her family for similar stereotyping in their characterization of Latinas as lazy. Either situation makes Penny come out in a positive light to her White audience. She would not be thought to have lice or to be lazy, and her proximity to the Latina culture gives weight to her opinions, for other Whites, because of her first-hand exposure to the Latina neighborhood.

As our interview continued, she went on to explain how the parents were very respectful and that they would not hurt her. When her friends asked her if she were "getting shot at," she combined her explanation that "no, she does not get shot at" with her feelings that her friends should not be so judgmental about the Elena parents.

[Penny:] Teachers are a different status in their culture. You don't share your family. The teacher is the teacher and she is almighty teacher and you don't talk back. That's why I'm very shocked when my friends are like, "Oh God, you work in East Austin. That must be horrible. Are you getting shot at? Are you?" Well, we don't have any behavior problems. The behavior problems we have are the White kids, not ever the Mexican Americans, the Hispanics, wherever they come from, never. They are just very respectful and I found that in Mexico as well. They are very respectful.

Penny described the common passive role parents took at Elena. The school virtually depended on parents not questioning the system. Penny was struggling with her positioning but was still subject to her own views of the families and children of color. She appreciated their respect but also knew that the respect she garnered was because of her race and its power. She was a teacher and was viewed as a person who could teach the children things their parents could not. The idea that White teachers were saviors and crucial to the families can be framed within the definition of identity as described by Holland et al. (1998):

> People tell others who they are, but even more important, they tell themselves and then try to act as though they are who they say they are. These self-understandings, especially those with strong emotional resonance for the teller, are what we refer to as identities. (p. 3)

Combining the idea of the privilege of White teachers to avoid talk about race or to talk about it in ways they find flattering to themselves is crucial to understanding how the teachers' construction of the children at Elena could become a way for the teachers to see themselves as the children's only hope. All of the teachers avoided race directly and did not explicitly acknowledge their privileged positioning. The Latina teachers, except Devin, did not speak of race when discussing the children or themselves. In all, three teachers— Devin, Natalie, and Penny—named race as they related their stories and feelings. Framing the teachers' views within a CRT theory frame of Whiteness as a dominant force in shaping expectations could be inclusive of even the Latina teachers' adherence to the ways and mores of White culture's expectations as they related to school behaviors.

Whiteness is a package tangled up within privilege. Frankenburg (1997) defines Whiteness as "a location of structural advantages, a standpoint for looking at us, others, society and a set of unmarked markers and unnamed cultural practices" (p. 1). Wildman & Davis (in Delgado & Stefanic, 1997) define privilege as ". . . characteristics of the group defining the norm, [where] privileged group members can rely on their privilege and avoid objecting to oppression . . . [F]or both reasons, privilege is rarely seen by the holder . . . [T]he privileged group members gain by their affiliation, often thought to be individual merit" (p. 316). This combination of Whiteness and privilege allowed teachers at Elena to view the culture of the children from a distance while ignoring the pervasive White culture of the school's ways and mores. Katia described how her husband and a university course assisted her in dealing with what she perceived as the challenges at Elena. Some teachers actually used the distance as a refuge, and Katia's husband advised her to keep a distance from her students, although one of her university courses had taught her to be aware of the students' home lives.

> [Katia:] He helped me to ingrain that in my head. He said, "If you're going to make a difference in somebody's life for the future, that's where you're going to do it, not outside [of your classroom]." So once I was able to internalize that and

come to realize that yes that's all I can do and not more. I think I was able to accept every challenge that I got and I was able to accept that if this child didn't bring their homework in today I wasn't going make a big deal out of it. Especially if I knew where that child went home, what kinds of problems were at home. The other eye-opener was that [university] community class with Sarita, always thinking about their homes before you mark an x on this kid and think the worst of them, go back and see why is this not happening for you and so I take that into consideration.

The combination of feelings that the parents weren't interested and that the teachers should avoid pushing children could be heard over and over again. Katia had decided that she could not do anything about the home lives of the children and would not press any student she perceived to have a difficult time at home. This view was common at Elena. Teachers' high expectations sometimes came at the expense of any sensitivity toward the children, or teachers became so concerned about the home lives the students led that they backed off and lowered their expectations. The idealistic teachers had a realistic view, yet they strove to keep the expectations high and had very high goals for the children. Bob respected and cared for his students, but he still believed they had low aspirations:

> There's no desire to move up and move on. We've got the little comfort zone here. Momma's going to take care of me forever. She doesn't care if I come [to school] or not and she really doesn't care if do my homework or if I do anything else. I've heard that a lot over the years. Kids will come in and say, "My dad doesn't know how to read. He's doing all right." I've heard that a lot. It's really the neighborhood. It's really not an intellectual atmosphere. They're not a moving up neighborhood. There's a little small pocket of them, but most of them are just comfortable as hell. Their little house. Their little cousins. Their little niche in life. They don't want to bust out of that. They're comfortable, but it sure puts the hurt on the kids.

Once again, Bob's comments show how the Elena parents were measured by expectations based on the teachers' conceptions of appropriate life goals. The school sought to teach all of the children to read with a goal of graduating. Bob felt that the parents did not share those goals and that it was detrimental to the children.

Many teachers at Elena felt that the students and families were not interested in or aware of how to teach their children. Devin and Katia discussed how they felt about parents in the community not working with their children at home. The basis for this discussion was their own family experiences. Devin and Katia, both Latina teachers, wanted the parents in the community to do more at home in the way of learning. This attitude demonstrates how the racial aspects of teaching at Elena were overwhelmed by the structure of schooling and achievement. Whiteness was not always the direct guiding force of these expectations, because even the Latina teachers shared the dominant view that families should be doing certain activities with their children. Devin, a Latina second-grade teacher, talked about her niece and how she knew how to count at an early age, whereas the pre-kindergartners at Elena did not:

> For example, with our kids, it's like a catch-22 situation. Some of our kids if we don't expose them to something they never get exposed to it at home . . . The thing is with our kids, no one is ever going to count with them. It's unfortunate but we sit there and count with them up to 100. No one's going to sit and count with them by 5's, no one's going to talk to them about the days of the week.

Similarly, Katia thought that the parents did not read with their children at home. The underlying message in the statement that follows is the notion that all of the parents had "other priorities," and she was the sole source of her students' literacy development.

> [Katia:] There is not enough reading [at home], too many other priorities at hand. So to me, there is not enough literacy in the home, but I feel that I've made a difference this year in maybe changing that in my classroom because I ordered the *Time for Kids* magazine. It works well in my class but I do have those students who have absolutely no support at home. So with those students it was okay. I was flexible and they could work on it with someone here.

Katia advocated that reading was important and implied that if a child came to her classroom not reading it was because the parents did not prioritize literacy. Yet she explained how reading at home with her own son failed to help him learn to read. In her eyes her son's struggle in literacy was not seen as a measure of her priorities as it was of the parents at Elena. Once again, her comments illustrate the teachers' beliefs in deficit theory (Valencia & Solorzano, 1997). Katia, a Latina teacher, did not blame herself for her son's reading struggle, yet she did fault the parents in the community if their children struggled with reading. Her feelings demonstrate the overall lack of critical reflection in the teachers at Elena:

> [Reading at home] is important, but I know that from experience with my child. Even though I was an avid reader growing up and I learned how to read quickly, my son didn't. Somehow I missed that one as a parent and I was like, well I read to him and there were books around. I don't know, so to me it's important that parents read to their kids.

Katia explained that she had missed "that one as a parent" but that she *did* read to her child. Yet her evaluation of the Elena parents was that they were not reading with their children and subsequently undermining the literacy efforts of the school. In the past, most Latina teachers would give the parents more leeway in interpreting their actions or perceived lack of actions, but the changes in Elena teachers altered the discourse to a degree that almost all teachers—regardless of race—held the same attitudes. For instance, each teacher I interviewed talked about the importance of reading at home, and the underlying assumption was that most of the families of Elena students did not read with their children at home. When I inquired about the literacy practices of the families, the teachers relied on their beliefs rather than on information from the families themselves. There was no real knowledge base for the idea that these children were not involved in literacy practices at home.

The tensions created by such beliefs were magnified when the Texas Assessment of Academic Skills (TAAS) test was mentioned. Although the neighborhood around Elena had not changed much in the past fourteen years, the nature of accountability had. The increased pressure of high-stakes testing placed a new emphasis on school achievement that trickled down through teachers who then attempted to pass the pressure on to students and parents. TAAS made literacy at home a factor for the teachers, because the teachers perceived the parents as not being concerned about literacy. Perhaps this came about because the parents did not share the same sense of alarm about the TAAS test as the teachers did. Bob explains how he felt TAAS was not a high priority for some of the parents because no one had set up the expectations for them:

> If we didn't say TAAS at the conferences, I feel like they wouldn't even ask about it. I don't think they give a sh—. I don't think they care a bit about TAAS. I really don't because we make a big deal about telling them because you have to pass. You have to graduate, but the parents, I don't think they give a hoot. It's not something like on the West Side of town. I've [told] lots of parents . . . "I really think he's going to do great and you should really expect him to graduate from high school." And they'll say well, that would really be interesting, nobody else has said that. You forget that the expectations are not there.

Bob brought up the idea that the parents had low expectations, and he connects the parents' perceived low expectations with failing their children by not encouraging them to pass TAAS. As a sixth-grade teacher, he spoke to parents about the future of their children and stated that the parents did not expect their children to graduate from high school. I heard teachers say that families did not read every night with their children and complained that parents did not show up at conferences. By contrast, the complaints directed at the children were softer. The teachers looked at the community and asked why they did not respond to the school's communication efforts.

By contrast, I never heard any questioning of our practices as teachers. I did not hear any comments searching for new definitions of teacher involvement, only vast numbers of directives to the parents. I believe this is due to the overwhelming support Elena gave to the dominant culture's view of what school should be, how roles should be defined, and how children's school identities should be constructed. Racism is a word many fear to use. Most people are comfortable labeling overt acts perceived as racist. The act of naming what we are not, rather than what we might be, is common. In the case of Elena, racism operated on a much less visible plane.

King (1997) uses the term "dysconscious racism" to describe how Whites may be unaware of the breadth and scope of what is considered racist. It was common to walk the halls of Elena and to hear conversations about children littered with a language of blame. Teachers would explain the failure of the students to meet academic or behavioral expectations by casting an eye to the community or the parents rather than their own teaching abilities. The combination of pressure from TAAS and the distance between families and teachers left spaces for the building of a view determined to find fault outside of the school's walls. Katia, a Latina teacher, and Natalie, a White teacher, talked about how other teachers used such blaming language, and although they did not characterize it as such, their descriptions suggested thoughts aligned with the notion of dysconcious racism. They were aware that such extreme negative attitudes by other teachers were harmful, yet they were unable to see the role race played in the underlying constructions of such events or the role their racial views might play in their own notions of the children and parents.

[Katia:] I think we [the teachers] have different goals and visions. There's a lot of degrading of students and parents. Anything that's negative in that respect, I'm going to stay away from it . . . I don't like the views that people have when they come to you and say, "Oh you know, he's so stupid." You don't get anything done. You spend your whole 45 minutes complaining.

[Natalie:] [The teachers] do blame parents. They are quick to blame the parents, more so than before. I've noticed that change. Yesterday a parent was here at 3 and her meeting was scheduled at 3:30. The teacher came in complaining. I was thinking about the parent. She's got five kids. She has to come here for a meeting. If she doesn't come back it's not because she doesn't care about her kid. It may not be just because it's inconvenient. Inconvenience is a reality but I think we see less tolerance towards the families. I think there does need to be training for teachers to remind them where some of the families are coming from and some of their situations just to soften them up a bit.

In her statement, Katia related how she avoided the teachers' lounge because of the way the teachers spoke about the children. At one point during the spring of 2001, the principal addressed the negative teacher attitudes in the lounge through the weekly faculty meeting. Then, in 2002, the new principal asked teachers to "keep confidentiality respect in mind when they spoke about the children." Elena was becoming a campus fraught with negative attitudes toward its children and families.

On the other hand, Devin, a long-time member of the Elena staff and one of the Latina teachers, was still willing to speak up about issues. Caroline spent a great deal of time with Devin and thought she had learned a lot from hearing her perspective.

[Caroline:] You have to look at the teachers I'm in with. I'm in with Devin more than my new team so I've just heard a lot about bilingual education. So I've heard a lot about the bilingual status here, but I think a lot of the newer teachers that are bilingual. I don't see that in them. You have some newer teachers who aren't Hispanics, but they are bilingual and it's not that they didn't appreciate the culture because they did, but they didn't grow up in it so it was different.

Race affected how teachers viewed the world in and around Elena. Devin's influence on Caroline was dramatic in some ways. Caroline was one of the few White teachers to step up in support of maintaining a bilingual administration for Elena. However, such relationships had steadily dwindled over the years. The Elena of the early 1990s could be characterized as a school striving to match the culture of the community. The teachers had high expectations, and they were very race cognizant rather than colorblind. Colorblindness (Frankenburg, 1993) refers to the idea that race is not a factor and allows for the idealistic view that we are all the same. It is a common view of teachers and schools that if everybody works hard, everybody is rewarded. If you fail to work hard, you deserve what you become. Meritocracy rules the ideology, and meritocracy is based on effort. Race cognizance was an idea espoused in the 1970s that found groups such as the Black Power and La Raza movements (Frankenburg, 1993) raising awareness and becoming involved in the civil rights movement. Ethnicity was recognized by people of color as an asset, and differences were enhanced and embraced, similar to the way teachers and administrators at Elena operated the school in the past.

Overt racism is easily recognized and causes most people to shake their heads in disbelief. Whites quickly recognize the racial slur, the derogatory remark, and recoil at its bluntness. But it is covert racism (Bell, 1992; Frankenburg, 1997; Rodrigo, 1997; Scheurich & Young, 1997) that was embedded within the everyday practices at Elena and the social reproduction of such racism that

I explored in the figured world of Elena. Covert racism is cloaked in many disguises. At Elena it was the avoidance of naming race, it was the politeness of not defending those subject to being racially ostracized, and it was the way teachers simply let race go by unnoticed, as though they had no power to alter the order of lives they touched every day. Wildman & Davis (in Delgado & Stefancic, 1997) concur from a White perspective: "I simply believe that no matter how hard I work at not being racist, I still am because part of racism is systemic, I benefit from the privilege that I am struggling to see" (p. 317).

Elena is one example of how schools in general suffer from systemic racism. The teachers' attitudes were not a result of their lack of caring about the children; they originated from larger forces in society in general such as the dominant views of the school district and the state, which I will cover in more detail in Chapter 6. Race was a topic directly avoided at Elena, and as difficult as it was to get teachers to engage in conversations about race, it was even more difficult to choose to struggle with racism. Our views of racism are colored by our racial identities and by our personal beliefs, as Devin relates how she views many of the White teachers at Elena and our Latina principal:

> I don't think they have enough information. Even when they say something, I don't think they take it in. They don't really do anything with it for example, it's just because it looks good on paper. Our principal, she's Hispanic and everything, but she's rich Hispanic. I'm not going to say rich but maybe middle-class or maybe more privileged than most. In her background, she came from a small town. Her father was the owner of a store. I know she wasn't out picking cotton. I know she wasn't having to. Her mother didn't have to clean houses or she didn't have to clean houses. I never got to pick cotton, but my brothers did and my parents had to be migrant workers. So I didn't grow up rich. My dad worked. He's a city worker and he worked out in the streets and stuff and so it's different. You grow up differently. You grow up appreciating things a little bit differently, empathizing with people.

Although teachers at Elena empathized with the children's perceived lives and lowered abilities, some transformed their empathy into lowered expectations and distance. The erosion of the literacy program at Elena can be linked to the events and attitudes surrounding the increase in the special education program, the decreased emphasis on the bilingual program, and the withdrawal from the community. A school once rich with culture and the belief that all children could learn and all teachers could teach became a reflection of the times in Texas. Pressures from high-stakes testing, changes in staffing and a lack of focus on the strengths of the children and their families resulted in teachers adopting a colonized (Street, 1995) view of the literacy goals for the children. The children of Elena were not educated to be become literate in the sense of a broad and powerful critical view of literature once espoused by the teachers. Rather they were educated to ensure that they would pass the TAAS test. Passing the TAAS test was the most important literacy goal of the teachers. Focusing on mainstreaming students in their regular classrooms, maintaining a strong bilingual program, or developing and sustaining ties to the community was not worth the risk. All energy and focus—instructional and administrative—was geared to passing the TAAS test. Elena was rewarded year after year by rising to the comfortable status of being rated an acceptable school by TAAS scores and then, in 2002, to a recognized school because of the concentrated efforts of all staff to attain the goal of raising TAAS scores.

·6·

THE COLONIZATION OF
LITERACY AT ELENA

The greatest revelation during my study is reflected in Greene's (1988) statement regarding freedom: "When people cannot name alternatives, imagine a better state of things, share with others a project of change, they are likely to remain anchored or submerged, even as they proudly assert their autonomy" (p. 9). The state was proud of the rising Texas Assessment of Academic Skills (TAAS) test scores and claimed that Texas children were receiving a better education than before the accountability system, while the teachers and administrators of Elena rejoiced the day our scores arrived and we were finally recognized by the state. This celebration was a significant event in the figured world of Elena that would serve to measure how completely the views of teaching reading at Elena had changed. The fact that the school spent time organizing a pep rally, throwing parties, and celebrating the percentage of students passing a standardized test was amazing when contrasted with the La Raza parade for Caesar Chavez in 1987, the parties for Diez y Sies, and the celebration each week for children who had exhibited good classwork and behavior.

In order to organize these changes, I chose to view the transformation of literacy definitions at Elena through the definitions and enactment of literacy education the teachers and administrators held. Holland et al.'s (1998) defining factors of figured worlds touch on many of the events and ways of using and interpreting activities and resources, as did the comparisons between beliefs and knowledge. Because of the historical reflections I used to contrast the figured world's evolution from one definition of literacy to another, I thought it necessary to place the literacy metaphors within the theoretical frame of figured worlds.

By "figured world" then, we mean a socially and culturally constructed realm of interpretation in which particular characters and actors are recognized, significance is assigned to certain acts, and particular outcomes are valued over others . . . The production and reproduction of figured worlds involves both abstraction of significant regularities from everyday life into expectations about how particular types of events unfold and interpretations of the everyday according to these distillations of past experiences. (Holland et al., 1998, p. 53)

The figured world of Elena was socially and culturally constructed within and across the four walls of each teacher's classroom and influenced by the production and reproduction of the figured world of the national, state, and district policies. The events that unfolded and shaped the gradual alterations in the conceptions of literacy at Elena are important to understand because of their strength and influence on the teachers and ultimately the school.

Each chapter of this book has drawn a picture of how the conversations with the teachers evolved. The chapters have been somewhat chronological and thematically ordered to illustrate the complexity and contradictory nature of the ever-evolving transformative nature of the teachers' responses to the simple query about the literacy of the children and their families. Chapter 1 described the teachers, the school, and the community of Elena from 1987 to 2001. The teachers' current "ideal" literacy definitions and goals for the children were illustrated in Chapter 2. This was followed by Chapter 3's demonstration of how TAAS interrupted the daily instructional routines and altered the literacy goals of the teachers because of the accountability measure attached to the school's results. In Chapter 4, the erosion of the figured world of Elena was evident as teachers began to focus on TAAS and categorize children according to their performance or potential performance on the TAAS test, and subsequently reorganized the functions and priorities of the special education program and the bilingual program at Elena. Chapter 5 revealed the teachers' and the school's relationship with the community and the underlying avoidance of race and/or culture as a factor in literacy acquisition and development. The conclusions drawn from each chapter's relationship to the larger findings of the study are best tied together through the most common threads found within each teacher's story. In this chapter, I will begin by defining what I believe to be the most significant discoveries of the study and then attempt to place these larger ideas into perspective by way of a review of data and a theoretical frame based on a socio-cultural definition of literacy. Further contextualization of the conclusions will be drawn with regard to events in the figured worlds of the school district and the nation and will complete the chapter, mapping out areas for additional study and clarify the limitations of the study.

Elena offered a unique perspective on the complexity and the ongoing transformation of this particular group of teachers' definitions of literacy and how these definitions were subject to internal and external forces. Views of literacy held by the teachers at Elena were shaped by the culture of the community, the culture and beliefs of the teachers themselves, and the outside influences of policy makers at the district, state, and national level. The view of literacy held by the teachers of Elena in 2001 can best be described by Street's (1995) definition of colonial literacy. Street proposes that literacy has been a monolithic idea pushed into developing countries ignoring the local, social literacies already in place. He describes literacy as an ideological practice caught up in power relations and anchored in the cultural meanings and practices of the dominant culture. Street also writes of the educational aspects of "providing" literacy to specific societies as a colonial literacy model. This is, by nature, proposed by outsiders in the community to teach those within the targeted community deemed illiterate; and while they receive the technical information needed to become literate, those groups "receiving" literacy were also learning about the culture indoctrinating them.

Literacy as a Monolithic Concept

According to Street's (1995) definition, Elena operated under many of the ideas of colonial literacy. Literacy became a monolithic idea in many ways. The teachers held fast to the reading and writing skills espoused by the state mandates and the TAAS test. These skills were described clearly, concisely, and aligned to TAAS very tightly with no specific attention to broader ideas or culture. The idea of literacy as a monolithic, one-size-fits-all notion was espoused by the teachers and the state. At this point, I want to be clear in my belief that I do not in any way place blame or judgment on the teachers for these views. I believe they were subjected to the view of the district, state, and broader national trends, a process that I will continue to illustrate throughout this chapter. This lack of awareness of the importance of culture in dialogues about literacy at Elena can be illustrated at a macro level by George and Louise Spindler (1998). They echo the idea of how reaffirmative trends reinforce monolithic curriculum designs in their description of the effect the dominant White culture has on educational theory and practice:

> Education has been hit directly by reaffirmative trends. The antagonism to bilingual programs, second-language programs and any other program that departs from the Eurocentric center of cultural transmission, has been active for

some time. All moves, such as English as the official language of America, can be considered reaffirmative, and are supported by the White ethniclass. The antagonism extends well beyond the language arena. Lately there have been attacks on multicultural education, efforts in the schools to raise the self esteem of minority children, any hint of an Afrocentric or Latinocentric curriculum, and in fact any addition of materials about the cultures of immigrants or minority children into the curriculum, or any "multicultural" emphasis. (p. 38)

This could easily portray events and unspoken attitudes at Elena. Although there were no "attacks" on multicultural education at Elena, it was decidedly a non-issue, so much so that it was never directly brought up by the teachers I interviewed. Elena enacted a narrowed view of what constituted literacy achievement by its evolving sophistication in tracking students into special programs and its slowly turning attention away from the bilingual and English as a Second Language education programs. The rhetoric is more forceful at the national and state level of debate, whereas at Elena, some of the teachers' attitudes demonstrated a lack of specific attention and understanding about the ways the cultural aspects of literacy were being played out through the school's ways of conducting everyday routines and making decisions.

The powerful nature of the TAAS accountability system promoted an ideology the teachers at Elena labeled "TAAS reading." This ideology simplified and narrowed the definition of literacy to a simplistic pass/fail measurement similar to Guerra's (1998) metaphor of "Literacy as Institution" where "learners have to be provided with the necessary scaffolding and are judged on their ability to meet certain institutional expectations" (p. 56). Many attempts to measure children's literacy skills *en masse* are not without discrepancies or voids between the truth of test scores and the knowledge of teacher observation. The power TAAS held over teachers increased the tendency for teachers to adopt the test's literacy goal at the expense of their own professional judgments. The state, through the teachers, imposed a specific set of literacy practices in the children without attention to local contexts or practices. Scribner (1984) wrote of the difficulties in defining and measuring literacy and how it can become a simplified "yes or no" standard:

Each formulation to the question "What is literacy?" leads to a different evaluation of the scope of the problem (i.e., the extent of illiteracy) and to different objectives for programs aimed at the formation of a literate citizenry. Definitions of literacy shape our perceptions of individuals who fall on either side of the standard (what a "literate" or "nonliterate" is like) and thus in a deep way affect both the substance and style of educational programs. A chorus of clashing answers also creates problems for literacy planners and educators. (p. 71)

Within this "chorus of clashing answers," teachers simplified their instruction and definitions and held on tightly to TAAS. The question "What is literacy?" came to be known and defined by TAAS, and the definitions of who was literate or nonliterate were simplified as who passed or did not pass the TAAS test. Since teachers felt that Elena's students and families were as a whole "non-literate," and since this underlying theme was present in almost every interview, discussion in the lounge, and debate about instruction, then the goal as set by the state was clear. The students needed to be literate in passing TAAS; "TAAS reading" was the goal, and, therefore, the teachers taught so as to meet that need. Defining by an either/or assessment of literacy narrowed the connection of literacy into a monolithic idea that needed to be provided for the children lacking literacy. The teachers at Elena began to realize the need for addressing the reading format and objectives of TAAS in order to ensure that students could score high enough on the test to be labeled as literate. The alteration of the teaching routines to meet the TAAS aims aligned the teaching practices at Elena with Street's (1995) intimation that one aspect of colonial literacy is the role power plays in shaping practices. The figured world of Elena was considerably altered by the power of TAAS.

Literacy as an Ideology Encased within Power Structures and Cultural Meanings

Street's (1995) tenet that colonial literacy is an ideological idea pushed into developing countries where the local literacies were not addressed or valued can be seen in how the teachers at Elena thought they should teach to the test. National, state, and local discourses were aligned with the notion that the Latina children of Elena were at risk of dropping out of school and were in need of assistance through accountability measures. This influential alignment replaced the sophisticated discourse in local settings such as Elena with the simplified dialogue of policy.

One of the greatest impacts on the literacy definitions of teachers was how Elena as a school was measured. In spite of having multiple instruments to measure the reading abilities of the children, the TAAS test was what teachers talked about most. Even as they assessed the children's literacy with tools required by the state, most teachers began to focus solely on the TAAS test, because this measure was what principals, district administrators, and the state focused on. An understanding of literacy's complexity was not necessary in order for teachers to prepare children to answer simple questions for TAAS assessment purposes. Where once teacher training and education was dedicated to literacy theory and practices tied to a wide range of views, literacy training was now closely tied to TAAS practice, and TAAS was becoming a political force through the expansion of the accountability system. Governor Bush's reading initiative in 1996 was followed by a national movement to reinforce schools through accountability:

> In October 1998, the Senate passed the Reading Excellence Act (H.R. 2514). Although many of its aims are commendable—it provided grants to states for inservice training of teachers, after-school tutoring in schools with high numbers of poor children, and family literacy programs—its major potential impact on literacy education was in its explicit definitions of reading, reading instruction, and "reliable" research, all of which emphasize teaching skills and might find their way into other reading legislation and teacher education. (Coles, 2000, p. xv)

One answer to the perceived reading crisis addressed by then-Governor George W. Bush's reading initiative in Texas was the Teacher Reading Academies. The reading academies were designed to supplement the accountability plan that harbored the high-stakes TAAS test and the state's literacy goal of having every child read by third grade. The underlying assumption behind this movement was that teachers were not teaching children to read, and the state's plan could remedy the problem with training and testing. The training offered to teachers was conducted through the reading academies described in Chapter 3. The reading academies were the official product of the state's reading initiative and set up explicit ideas about what was valued for reading education in Texas. This marked a change at Elena, because the campus had previously been able to seek out various teacher trainings and venues for further teacher education. The state did not require teachers to attend the reading academies, but teachers at Elena were increasingly being asked to go to the trainings, in which the new principal placed great faith.

To further illustrate Street's (1995) colonial literacy tenet, which connects power and a specific ideology to literacy, I will analyze the views behind the sort of information that drives the decisions about the use of research to train teachers. This connection is crucial to understanding and interpreting the philosophical stance behind the state's and district's adoption of specific programs and teaching models related to literacy education, the most important point of which is that a distinct view was espoused by the state and subsequently controlled all choices.

Coles (2000) explains the differences in approaches to teaching, differences that have been given political power due to their sometimes falsely created dichotomies. One example of the ideology of the state's approach to reading instruction can be seen in the position taken by the No Child Left Behind Act of

2002 (PL 107–110). The act clearly distinguishes between two types of reading research. The first section defines the preferred and state-sanctioned orientation to reading research by emphasizing the scientific approach to research, while the second section criticizes the "unproven fads" of reading research and claims that literacy research conducted outside of the "scientific parameters" identified by the state has not served the reading needs of children or teachers.

Proven Methods—The Science of Reading

The No Child Left Behind Act provides grants for state and local school districts in which students are systematically and explicitly taught five key components of early reading.

- Phonemic Awareness: The ability to hear and identify individual sounds in spoken words.
- Phonics: The relationship between the letters of written language and the sounds of spoken language.
- Fluency: The capacity to read text accurately and quickly.
- Vocabulary: The words students must know to communicate effectively.
- Comprehension: The ability to understand and gain meaning from what has been read.

Unproven Fads, Untested Ideas Have Hurt Our Kids

- For many years, educators have been subject to many unproven fads and fashions in reading instruction.
- As a result, many teachers have not been prepared to teach reading to America's children with methods developed from scientific research.
- America has arrived at a literacy crisis with only one-third of fourth-graders able to read at a proficient level. This means that nearly two-thirds of fourth-graders have a greater likelihood of dropping out and a lifetime of diminished success.
- Too often the system has failed to offer teachers the very tools that scientific research demonstrates actually work in America's classrooms. (http://www.no childleftbehind.gov/start/facts/reading.html)

This position regarding the research used for all state-supported trainings illustrates how literacy in Texas was narrowed into an ideology encased within power structures and cultural meanings (Street, 1995). President Bush developed the No Child Left Behind Act based on the policies of the Texas Reading

Initiative, and the ideologies were similar. Prior to the Texas Reading Initiative, Elena teachers had selected many of the trainings they attended. As the state became more involved not only in assessing literacy through high-stakes accountability but in training teachers and holding them accountable, there was little room for a diverse, well-balanced knowledge of literacy research.

Another assumption of the state is that the TAAS test actually measures literacy. Multiple factors about this assumption have not been thoroughly explored. Does TAAS measure reading? And if so, for whom? As literacy definitions are established, the focus inevitably leads to how to properly assess literacy. Most policy makers would disagree with Scribner & Cole's (1978) statement that

> Although attempts to arrive at some overall measures of literacy competencies may be useful for certain comparative purposes, the conceptualization of literacy as a fixed inventory of skills that can be assessed outside of the contexts of application has little utility for educational policies. (p. 459)

I agree with Scribner & Cole (1978), but I also know policy makers will not be able to wrap their statistics around views of literacy that do not provide standardized literacy information with which to measure children's progress. Educational policies begin outside of schools. They trickle down to teachers through mazes of federal decrees, state standards, district policies, and finally through principals' dictums.

At Elena, this occurs differently every year. Power structures are altered, personnel transfer, but the children keep coming. "The danger is that challenging standards, like standardized tests, will not have a positive effect on the achievement of students of diverse backgrounds but will simply serve as another means of identifying students of diverse backgrounds as losers in the educational game" (Au, 2000, p. 844). Hillocks (2002) quotes President George W. Bush's plan as presented during his presidential campaign:

> if scores are stagnant or dropping, the administrative portion of [the school's] federal funding—about 5 percent—will be diverted to a fund for charter schools. We will praise and reward success—and shine a spotlight of shame on failure . . . without testing, reform is a journey without a compass. Without testing, teachers and administrators cannot adjust their methods to meet high goals. Without testing, standards are little more than scraps of paper. Without testing, true competition is impossible. Without testing, parents are left in the dark. (p. 9)

Teachers at Elena never stated that they did not believe in standardized tests; yet when teachers criticize standards, there is an implied sense that they are avoiding accountability. At Elena the teachers' criticism of the test was its limited view of literacy. The above statement—that without a standardized test learning was not occurring—was not true at Elena. Prior to the high-stakes testing system, Elena was a school rich in dialogue, adept at parental communication and aggressive teacher education. Bush's idea that without testing there is no chance for reform, no meeting of goals, no standards, no competition, or information for parents, is misguided, threatening, and simplistic. It negates the ability of teachers, researchers, and communities to educate children in professional and highly informed ways. When coupled with the teaching methods espoused by the No Child Left Behind Act, it also negates entire realms of literacy research now defined by harsh political boundaries. The underlying assumptions that the test and standards are up to par is confounded by the supposition that testing is needed in order to assist educators to "adjust their methods to meet high goals" (Hillocks, 2002, p. 9). If the goals are set high, then it would seem that the tool to measure such goals should be as complex and render more valuable data than if a child can read or not. But the constant subjection of Elena to the state requirements gradually shaped the teachers' viewpoint to match that of the Texas Educational Agency's as depicted by Valencia & Solorzano (1997). "[TEA's] rating policy is grounded in deficit thinking" (p. 5).

The language of the state and national positions trickled down to Elena in various ways. TAAS was the main impetus, and the district's blueprint followed suit. The superintendent proposed a plan to increase TAAS scores at schools deemed unacceptable according to their TAAS scores. Although he states that "all children can learn," he also implies that there is one way to reach the goal of teaching children to pass TAAS. In an excerpt from the document, the superintendent remains true to the idea that more control and rigid adherence to specific modes of teaching will ensure that all children, teachers, and parents will perform:

> It's easy to say, "All children can learn," and I'm sure most of our teachers and principals believe that. But from this point on, if there are any teachers or principals or other AISD employees who look into their heart of hearts and find they don't believe this, then I am asking them to consider looking for employment somewhere else for next year. As a district, we have high expectations for all our students . . . We will focus on all schools in the district deemed low performing by TEA.
> 1. We will require a specific curriculum in math and language arts, with specific blocks of time.
> 2. We will require two extra weeks of staff development this summer with stipends. There will be additional training and support throughout the school year.
> 3. We will require a written compact with teachers and principals guaranteeing that they will deliver the proven curriculum prescribed for these schools.

4. We will not hire rookies to fill any open positions. All new teachers in these schools will be trained, certified in their subject area and experienced. (Austin Independent School District Website, 2002)

Every teacher I knew was aware of this blueprint, as it was highlighted quite frequently in the media. I also had colleagues in two schools who fell under the blueprint plan. While the general public and the school board felt secure with the language, the amount of security, and the implied guarantee this plan asserted, the level of intimidation and threat to teachers was apparent, and many teachers understood the deeper meaning of this plan. The first part of the plan was based on success on the TAAS test, evidence that the school district has made the TAAS its entire focus for measuring the effectiveness of a campus' ability to teach children. Teachers also understood the implications of the first point: Open Court was to be the "weapon" of choice here, as echoed by Barbara Foorman:

In Texas, a beginning reading program called Open Court, which emphasizes phonemic awareness (the awareness of sounds within words) and related skills, was reported to be extraordinarily more successful than other instructional approaches, especially whole language, in teaching poor children. "You can take [this] classroom program and get all but 4.5 percent up to the national average—that's astounding," commented Barbara Foorman, the leading researcher of an NICHD-supported study that made the comparison. (Coles, 2000, p. xiv)

Foorman's comments illustrate the discourse that provides unequivocal guarantees to root out failure and suggests that what had been done before had not prepared students adequately. This idea is an example of the information shared previously in Chapters 2 and 3.

To develop a complete picture of what this means, however, one would have to be privy to many figured worlds. To the teachers I knew at the two blueprint schools, it meant teaching from a specific textbook not currently adopted by the state and therefore requiring extra funding. To the researchers at the university Center for Reading and Language Arts, it meant that the head of their department's advice had been taken by the Austin superintendent and was used in the letter presented to teachers at a faculty meeting outlining the blueprint. To the literacy research community in general, it was another brick in the wall of the division of teaching methods. Open Court was used by Elena for two years from 1992 to 1994, and it is a program focused on explicit phonics instruction with limited attention to other modes of instruction. Foorman's comments illustrate her philosophical stance on reading instruction, specifically reading instruction for "poor children." This attitude toward "poor children" is also indicative of a deficit view of families and children of color and the application of the "at-risk" label to those families. As Valencia and Solorzano (1997) state, "The idea of at risk blames the victim, as does the notion of deficit thinking" (p. 196). Foorman is politically aligned with the Center and has created the Texas Primary Reading Inventory (TPRI), an assessment used by AISD mentioned in Chapter 2.

The meshing of the figured worlds of schools, districts, universities, and policy is tied together quite clearly through the critical view of the school district's statements in the blueprint. Yet despite the oppressiveness of a test-driven system, Elena's scores have not changed dramatically even with the recent move to "recognized" status in 2002. All of the accountability measures placed on Elena by the state demonstrated no significant changes in student achievement as measured by TAAS. Coles (2000) critiques the simplistic guarantees of the scientific research community that they have found the one answer to any child's reading difficulty:

> If the research were simply cloistered within professional journals and conferences—if it were solely "pure" research seeking to determine causal influences in learning to read—it could be considered work poorly done but without injurious consequences. Unfortunately, not only has it been used to justify policy and legislation that narrow alternatives for teachers and other school personnel but it has also been harmful because it falsely holds out the promise of a simple, "magic bullet" solution to the literacy failure of millions of children, especially those who are poor, while at the same time discouraging social policy attention to forces both in and out of schools that influence literacy outcomes. The research has also defined literacy success in thin, rigid terms that ignore countless matters about the purposes of education. (Coles, 2000, p. xvii)

Coles's (2000) comments are aligned with the ideas in Guerra's (1998) "Literacy as institution" and are contrasted with the Elena teachers' views of "literacy as practice." The teachers at Elena had previously sought out trainings on their own and attempted to diversify their knowledge as much as possible. The research positions Coles (2000) discusses created a set view of literacy teaching through a single view of research. With the increasing emphasis on TAAS and the schools district's blueprint plan, teachers were teaching in an environment with specific reading goals and teaching methods that left out research by literacy scholars and slowly narrowed the methods available to teachers.

Coles's (2000) analysis also rings true to the nature of how the larger policy of the state influenced the local school district's policy toward the blueprint schools. The school district's plan was highly connected to the state's philosophy, and the superintendent went as far as to call for a "culture shift." But this particular culture shift was directed at schools of color, schools that were unable to pass the TAAS test.

As part of this culture shift, we will also ask parents to sign a compact with the school, in which the school defines its responsibilities and expectations and the parent agrees to be a full partner in this process, including making sure their children take part in opportunities for extra help beyond the regular school day. Part of the compact will also guarantee that the schools will be courteous and responsive to students and their families. We are also asking the Austin Interfaith to work with these schools to teach them the Alliance school model for increasing parent involvement. I'm not asking them to become Alliance Schools. That's their choice. But I do want these schools to learn the best practices for parent involvement because that's so important. I have asked all our schools to make sure a Spanish speaker is in the front office to assist Spanish-speaking families in our schools.[1]

Street's (1995) notion of the colonization of literacy is clearly projected here. The "culture shift" mirrors what teachers at Elena felt the families should also do. The families of children attending these failing schools should be required to sign a form that will explicitly state their responsibilities with no indication of what or how this will be enforced or measured. The idea that Austin Interfaith would control the parental involvement through its "best practices" grade by the superintendent implies that schools and communities have no skills to engage effectively in such a relationship. There is no language here that supports any idea that the school will develop partnerships or overtures to the communities other than to dictate behaviors and expectations and to place a bilingual person in the office.

This colonization of the children, the families, and the teachers is clear and not embraced by many outside of the administrative realm. Penny, one of our special education teachers, spoke of how she viewed her experiences at the university and how open the discussions were and contrasted those same experiences with her experiences in schools. She understood that there was a difference and was afraid that over time she would succumb to the views of those in power.

> [Penny:] You are under an authority. You have your beliefs but the dominant belief of who you're under, the authority figure you're under is going to permeate your being. It's going to permeate you to where you start taking it on and that's what my fear is.

The teachers at Elena did struggle with the literacy expectations of the state, and they felt they were beneath what literacy assessment should be, but they shared the national, state, and district view that the children of color at Elena were in need of literacy and that functional literacy (Scribner, 1984) was adequate and was what could be expected. The children only needed to pass the test and be able to function in society. Such positions illustrate Guerra's

(1998) idea of "literacy as entity," the notion "that literacy is positivistically constructed as an object that exists apart from and beyond any social or individual constraints . . . [L]iteracy has magical qualities that can transform an individual or culture and bestow upon it special powers not available to illiterate others" (p. 51). Having all children reading was not the same as believing that all children could learn; between high-stakes testing and the blueprint of the district, it was clear that the notion of colonizing the literacy of the children of Elena was violent and validated as a means to ensure their success. Yet Valencia and Solorzano (1997) proposes that schools are not going to improve through the high pressure of high-stakes testing or "state-mandated strategies founded on the premise (un-validated) that schooling outcomes such as reading performance and graduation from high school can be improved through built-in sanctions" (p. 5).

Teachers' Loss of Power

Teachers' voices in the school district were silenced or ignored, and this was clear as (1) the programs in place were pulled without negotiation, and (2) the superintendent refused to discuss the issues when approached by members of the community.

> Austin school Superintendent Pat Forgione's blueprint to revamp underperforming schools would interfere with the popular dual-language program at Harris elementary . . ."The idea of having it non-negotiable that the teachers, parent, and principals have to sign contracts to abide by what you want to do, it bothers me," [a parent] said. (*Austin American-Statesman*, April 30, 2002)

The silence from teachers was deafening. Site-based decision making was long gone, and teachers had become used to the dictation of this top-down model of policing. The school district's blueprint is emblematic of the lack of discourse that now characterizes Elena's figured world. Teachers at Elena spoke frequently about their lack of power. When Penny attempted to engage in debate, she was marked down on her final evaluation.

> [Penny:] I am told I am argumentative or I'm not able to communicate effectively. Let's look at my Professional Development Assessment Survey [laughs] and that's what I get—not able to communicate effectively with other team members or faculty members. Why, because I tell you what I think and no one else does. I'm tired of going to [special education meetings] where teachers are like, "I'm just so glad you said that in that meeting. "Well, why didn't you, why didn't you back it up?"

Penny also spoke of being in special education meetings with teachers who were silent when discussions about children came up, but who approached Penny later to tell her they agreed with her. There was no longer a culture of "speaking up" at Elena. If some teachers made their dissenting opinions known, they were reprimanded. Bob, a veteran teacher, was marked down as unprofessional on his final evaluation for making public his questions about the overuse of pull-out programs on campus. Devin, a second-grade teacher, explained her thoughts about how administrators viewed those who spoke up: "We are more opinionated; she doesn't like that. You're kind of rocking the · boat. It changes. There are different people that are in favor now . . . There are a couple of people like that in favor. They've never ever spoken up." Devin felt that the teachers "in favor" now were the quiet ones who did not question the principal. Where there used to be dialogue and room for exploration and negotiation, there was now an emphasis on doing what you were told. It was important for all to row the boat in the same direction.

This also illustrates how the particular group of teachers who chose to participate in the study were very interested, educated, and willing to put themselves out there without fear. Yet many teachers were simply leaving. "Texas has about 700,000 certified teachers but needs only about 288,000 to fill its classrooms . . . after five years in the classroom, nearly 60 percent of all teachers in Texas quit instead of staying to face the students, the parents, and the administrators" (*Austin American-Statesman*, May 28, 2002). One year after this study, Bob had retired, Penny had transferred to another school, and Illeana, our Language Proficiency Assessment Committee chair, was transferred.

Fear is a strong word to use, but when the language used not only by the district but the national policy has threatening tones, it evokes powerful reactions. The colonization of literacy as it applied to Elena was driven by TAAS and the threatening rhetoric of policy messages. I would argue that the pressure of TAAS and the increased lack of attention to local literacies in favor of mastering "TAAS reading" as described by the teachers led to the state and the teachers actually seeking the same goal.

An historical view of Elena in relation to TAAS showed how the increased attention to TAAS did improve the children's scores by one rating step. The school maintained an "acceptable" rating for years, and most recently received its highest rating yet, reaching the status of "recognized" based on 2002 test scores. It remains to be seen if this increase can be attributed to TAAS practice, higher referrals to special education, or teachers' familiarity with the TAAS format. This positive reinforcement for TAAS success, as Elena teachers and administrators cheered the day the scores came in, meant everything had changed in the figured world of Elena. The state and the school agreed on a definition of literacy. Penny articulated how most teachers at Elena described what they called their "realistic goals for the children":

> Literacy is functional especially at the level that I'm working with kids here; it's functional. Many of these children I hope one day will attain the level we have, but I don't really see that as a valid goal right now . . . [O]ne of my students, the other day, we went on a field trip and he's like, "Can I eat in the bus?" and I'm like, "Read number 4." And then he looked up and read number 4 that said, "Do not eat and drink on the bus." That's what I want my kids to be able to do, at least the bare minimum and not that I always strive to reach higher and higher and higher for them but at the bare minimum I want them to be able to read menus and signs and fill out a job application. So literacy is functional for me.

Functional Literacy as the Goal of Colonial Literacy

The teachers' definition of literacy conformed to Scribner's (1984) definition of literacy as functional. Functional literacy could be categorized under Guerra's (1998) "literacy as institution" metaphor, the idea that individuals or groups are educated enough to meet the specific standards of an institution, which in this case was the public schools. If the idea of literacy as a functional tool for students to use in their everyday lives is defined by the institution in a position of power over the population "receiving" the literacy, then the role of culture in the interpretation of that literacy should be taken into account.

Street (1995) defines colonial literacy by the nature of power encased within a cultural ideology. At Elena, teachers were subjected to the view of literacy as it was described by the state and felt it was a more functional definition that did not encourage or assess high-level thinking skills. If race and culture are also recognized as factors in the transmission of literacy, then the institution dispensing literacy through the teachers should be examined critically.

Cultural transmission (Spindler, 2000) refers to the idea that culture is transmitted through education to those receiving the education whereby the "skills" are not only taught, but they are laden with the values of the dominant culture bestowing the instruction. Since the teachers were teaching the children in order for them to survive in the world outside of school, then a large part of the role of Elena teachers was to educate the children to read well enough to pass the TAAS test. That minimum expectation was the priority for the school and kept students at Elena subject to the state's test. The idea of cultural transmission of literacy as described by Macedo (1994) is relevant to this discussion because of the cultural identities of the children, the teachers, and the policies of the district, state, and nation. Macedo describes literacy as a source for cultural transmission. In his view, literacy can be used as a tool for those in power to educate those oppressed just enough to be of use. He borrows from Chomsky to illustrate the notion that most literate people would be classified as semiliterate.

Chomsky's ideas as embraced by Macedo (1994) typify some of the most educated people in the highest level of Chomsky's semiliterate classification as those individuals possessing the ability to read the word but not the world around them. They are the professionals at the top of their fields, so immersed in their topics of choice that they fail in their ability to comprehend the world outside of their areas and those people around them. They may have knowledge of their area but do not possess an understanding of others. The less-educated level of semiliterates are those individuals able to read text at the basic skills level, making them servants only to survival, not to questioning or to participating in the world they inhabit. Teachers at Elena, along with the state, fell into the semiliterate, more functional view of literacy, as they spoke about the expectations they held for the children.

The semiliterate definition can be referenced by Guerra's (1998) "literacy as entity" that described literacy as one-dimensional, measurable, and ignorant of issues related to power. If literacy should be expanded to include critical thinking in a political, influential sense such as espoused by "literacy as practice" (Guerra, 1998), and literacy is seen as an agent of true change and a vehicle for learning, then "literacy as entity and institution" should be unacceptable in the education system. Katia, a Latina teacher, defined functional literacy in this way: "Literacy to me is being able to interpret what you read. Reading is information. Reading is survival; it's survival because if you can't read, you can't read street signs; you can't read any important documents and so forth." The TAAS test served to narrow the path to literacy acquisition, and as schools and teachers followed suit under great pressure, the ideas of literacy became well defined, deceptively simple, and reinforced by the idea that the children were better off for their achievement of reading for survival. In other words, the children were safe from illiteracy and would be able to survive in the world.

Giroux (1997) equates this attitude of educating only for the ability to "get by" as the absence of true literacy, which in turn becomes an absence of democracy. Although literacy has been claimed to be the key to democracy, its true meaning depends upon the participants being able to fully comprehend and affect their governing institutions (Giroux, 1997). This type of literacy requires escaping the boundaries of being adept at reading words off a page; it requires an historical, cultural knowledge base with which to interpret the word and the world it is borne of. Only then can a person be truly literate and possess the full power of literacy. The oppressive views of functional literacy, within the colonization definition, serve to maintain the positioning of those subjected to the philosophies of the institutions in power.

Functional Literacy Is Delivered to the Illiterate

Another aspect of Street's (1995) definition of colonial literacy is the idea that those ideological, monolithic definitions of literacy are then refined and brought—by outsiders—to a community classified as illiterate. Throughout my interviews, the teachers expressed the feeling that the children and their families were not literate. Repeated references to the students' requiring basic instruction and the families' needing to learn more about the school indicated a strong feeling that these children and families were not literate as the school measured literacy. Colonial literacy, however, as defined by Street (1995), can be used to describe how the idea of literacy was presented to Elena as it supplanted any more complex ideas about broader definitions of literacy. I do believe that every teacher, administrator, policy maker, and parent did wish for only the best for each child. This desperate need to have every child reading can be illustrated by Guerra's (1998) metaphor of "literacy as institution," a double-sided view, and shows its weaving through society at large and how it is interpreted:

> The more capitalist-oriented approaches recommend literacy as a currency that makes it possible for members of the society to buy their way to success. The more literate one is, the richer one is and the more material goods one can acquire . . . [T]he second set actually posits literacy's opposite, illiteracy, as the disease or the enemy that we as a society must fight against using the institutional means available to us. If illiteracy is seen as a disease that leads to poverty, ignorance, and injustice, then literacy is seen as the cure for these particular elements. If, on the other hand, illiteracy is conceived of as an enemy against which all of society must be mobilized, then it becomes necessary for everyone from the neighborhood community organizer to the President of the United States to rally the troops and send them into the war zone. (p. 55)

Virtually no knowledge of community past the cursory attention to conferences was required of teachers at Elena or in the district. This distance created and perpetuated the views the teachers shared in Chapter 4. Although they cared deeply for the children, they were clear in their views that the families did not read to their children or have high expectations for them. No one I spoke to, formally or informally, mentioned any notions of reversing the expectations back onto the school to seek knowledge from the community. The community was expected, as Natalie (the campus literacy specialist) stated, to "change its culture." Valenzuela (1999) states: "As long as those in charge are neither themselves bilingual nor educated on the needs of either Spanish-dominant or culturally marginal Mexican American youth, schooling will continue to subtract resources from them" (p. 256).

Teachers and administrators at Elena took great care to set up expectations regarding parent-teacher communication, but little attention was paid to searching for strengths of the children or community. This deficit view crept into every conversation (Valencia & Solorzano, 1997). This state of affairs was the result of the discourses that had displaced those that valued the children and their culture and histories. There was a lack of initiative on the part of the school to connect with the community as it had in the past.

Research and practice is available to support a more balanced relationship between children's homes and schools, and many scholars advocate encouraging teachers to seek out the literacies and knowledge present within the community and build from there (cf. Ashton-Warner, 1963; Guerra, 1998; Gutierrez, 1994; Heath, 1983; Ladson-Billings, 1994; Ladson-Billings, 1995; Moll, Amanti, Neff, & Gonzales, 1992; Nieto, 1999; Schaafsma, 1993; Trueba, 1993). Yet in the new era of accountability, there was little room for exploring these ideas as the policies pressed for achievement as measured through standardized tests.

Although there is hope for opening up the definition of literacies and a push for teachers to understand what the children bring, there will continue to be boundaries for teachers to work within, boundaries consisting of a complicated matrix of state expectations, school resources, and high-stakes testing. But if there is no perceived need or pressure to recognize and value the literacies the families bring, I do not believe it will happen in the atmosphere currently permeating Texas. The state would have to make it a priority of the same significance and power of TAAS to ensure that research on "culturally relevant teaching" (Ladson-Billings, 1994) or "funds of knowledge" (Moll et al., 1992) reached schools and teachers.

Literacy as a State of Grace

Michael Apple (2001) states that "issues of Whiteness lie at the very core of educational policy and practice and we ignore them at our own risk" (p. 211). Critical race theory posits that the dominant culture is unaware of the effects Whiteness and race have in setting the standards and norms for institutions. Institutional racism characterizes the tendency of powerful institutions to overlook race, specifically Whiteness, as a factor in their epistemology and, therefore, passively create and support racist practices (Scheurich & Young, 1997).

The policies directed at the children of color at Elena were clear and admirable to a degree. If the logical arguments of the statistics are that Latina children are not successful as compared to White children, then of course the obligation for the policy makers to address those children is clearly understood.

- Hispanic children often don't attend school until they reach mandatory school age.
- They have the highest dropout rates of any group in the country—more than 30 percent of Hispanic students drop out.
- On the 2000 National Assessment of Educational Progress reading assessment, 40 percent of White fourth graders scored at or above proficient, compared to only 16 percent of their Hispanic counterparts.
- The racial achievement gap is real, and it is not shrinking.
- Just 10 percent of Hispanic students get a college education. (No Child Left Behind Website)

This information and the focus of the No Child Left Behind Act set up the argument and rationale for an all-out assault on solving this achievement crisis of Latina children, an assault conducted with an underlying message of saving the children of color who cannot read, the most persuasive, romantic, and justifiable view of White culture's need to institute swift, forceful measures in order to rescue the children. This line of reasoning is the most enduring and reactionary foundation of the accountability system and can be understood within Scribner & Cole's (1984) metaphor of literacy as a state of grace as it applies to Street's (1995) notion of colonization and explains the interconnectedness of White institutions saving children of color through the colonial view of literacy.

The metaphor of literacy as a state of grace or salvation is explained by Scribner (1984) as she chronicles the historical roots of literacy education. Possession of literacy was initially viewed as becoming enlightened. Once only belonging to the few, the ability to read began to be passed down, literally passed "down" to those economically "deprived," an echo of Street's (1995) colonization notion. Looking at the idea of "literacy as power" follows the premise that those possessing literacy move to educate those they perceive to need it. The "haves" educating the "have-nots" begs us to ask why? For what purpose? For whose purpose and finally how and how far to go? Again—do we want them to read? Or do we want them to read and think? What does this mean for those in power? Literacy as a state of grace is tied to the religious leaders of the ancient past granting literacy of their choosing to those who needed it (Scribner & Cole, 1984). Now literacy "giving" is connected to the more powerful perception that to be literate is to bestow the ultimate gift. But there are strings attached to the gift, or as Street (1995) explains in his definition, the recipients of literacy are also indoctrinated into the culture dispensing the gift. An underlying assumption when applying this idea to Elena is that not only was literacy given to the children who were so lacking, but it was supplanting literacies the students may already bring to school. Graff (1995) echoes Scribner & Cole (1984) and Street (1995) by placing the idea of literacy in a historical context:

> The Reformation, however, constituted the first great literacy campaign in the history of the West, with its social legacies of individual literacy as a powerful social and moral force and its pedagogical traditions of compulsory instruction in public institutions specially created for the purposes of the indoctrination of the young for explicitly social ends. (p. 17)

The language of this statement echoes the ideas of "literacy as institution" (Guerra, 1998) in that it admittedly advocates the power of the institution to dispense literacy as a means of individual "indoctrination into the young" with a specific cultural view. In 2001, the same state of affairs flourished at Elena. The authoritative combination of the state policy view was coupled with the strong identification of the children as deficient by teachers and the government in the righteous stance of saving the population or a culture judged to be in need, in this case, children of color. The "grace-filled" intention of ensuring that all children can read by the low-level expectation that passing one test has guaranteed illustrates the quality of the education system as an oversimplified, even racist notion. Although President Bush states that he seeks to abolish "the diminished hopes of our current system" and deplores "the soft bigotry of low expectation" (Hillocks, 2002, p. 9), the goal, as stated by the No Child Left Behind Act, is clearly speaking to those children who are expected to fail—the "poor" children—and the implied definition of those children as children of color.

> Improving the reading skills of children is a top national and state priority. The President, the First Lady, the Secretary of Education, governors, business leaders, elected officials, citizens, community organizations, parents, and teachers are deeply committed to doing whatever it takes to ensure that every child can read. In the past few years, science has provided tremendous insight into exactly how children learn to read, and related research has identified the most essential components of reading instruction. (No Child Left Behind Website, 2002)

Although the statement does not directly identify children of color as the target of such measures, it does fall in line with the ways in which the teachers avoided addressing the children and families in direct racial terms. In similar ways, the discourse of the policy of the state and the school district carefully place references regarding children of color in research data and then use broad goal statements encased in the "all children will . . ." framework. This rhetoric enables policy statements to appear equal and just and may allude to the implied theme of the ideals of democratic schooling as the savior of all children. Yet the "at-risk" designation listed in the No Child Left Behind tenets clearly mark the Latina children.

The targeting of children of color to meet the goal of passing the TAAS test was so evident and so very clearly enforced that all other programs at Elena, and many other schools, were beginning to fall away. Yet even with the improved scores of Elena and most Texas schools brought about largely by teachers' savvy understanding of how to teach to the test, there are still large numbers of children at risk of failing the test, which in 2003 means that by law they will not be promoted. This prompted the legislature to design a loophole to allow a committee to process and interpret the ability of the child to progress to the fourth grade if he or she fails TAAS.

> Estimates based on test results in recent years indicate that more than 37,000 third-graders won't pass the reading portion of the state's new assessment . . . [S]tudents who fail the TAKS [Texas Assessment of Knowledge and Skills] twice may choose another test from a list now being developed, or they can simply petition for promotion from a review committee made up of the student's parents, teacher and principal. (*Austin American-Statesman*, July 2, 2002)

The district is also purchasing a $1.6-million, commercially designed, computerized system capable of pre-testing students for the new TAAS, the Texas Assessment of Knowledge and Skills (TAKS). This program would give each teacher a report on specific test items not passed with an eye toward providing teachers with detailed data so they can assist the child in preparing for the actual test. This is a key component of Greene's (1988) look at how the product mentality of education can lend itself to technology dependency.

> At once, teachers and administrators are helped still to see themselves as functionaries in an instrumental system geared to turning out products, some (but not all) of which will meet standards of quality control. They still find schools infused with a management orientation, acceding to market measures; and they (seeing no alternatives) are wont to narrow and technicize the area of their concerns. (p. 13)

This computerized system may be viewed as helpful to teachers, which is how it was presented to the school board, but it highly encourages more attention to teaching to the test and measuring children solely by their ability to pass the test rather than evaluating their literacy acquisition. In the United States, schools are seen as the educators of democratic citizens (Dewey, 1990; Giroux, 1997; Macedo, 1994; Street, 1995). Not only is the road to success and freedom through the schools, but literacy is seen as the driving force (Berliner & Biddle, 1995; Finn, 1991). *The Manufactured Crisis* (Berliner & Biddle, 1995) outlines an argument that there really is no crisis in schools today. But the value of creating a crisis lies in the reform movements that can measure the "ailment" and then prescribe the "cure." Literacy has been the focus of the contemporary cycle of dismay over public schooling since 1983. Our country's children cannot read is the call, and the answers wait in the hand of those in power. The cries for literacy education ring loud and clear throughout history down to the present day. We are all justified in calling for literate children groomed to become literate adults. We save them by teaching them to read. We can ensure that they have jobs and can make it on their own. They can support our economic society's functioning. Being literate is culturally encased in our country, state, and community. What does literacy mean in schools? Literacy as a state of grace can be seen in schools as the gift we give to deficient children who come to the school's doors in need of education, in need of us. Realistically, however, literacy instruction in the United States is here to stay in its form of "teach, test, and keep moving." The current focus in the reading education of our children has persuaded the public to believe in explicit reading instruction and accountability through test scores. Schools, many times subject to top-down policy decisions, attempt to educate children by way of a one-way road to literacy from the school to the home. This is where these broader views of literacy become narrowed in the vises of hegemonic agendas.

Recommendations

The recommendations that follow are intended to broaden the existing literacy focus at Elena by a greater understanding that all of these suggestions are possible and reinforced by their prevalence in areas of research currently not embraced by the figured worlds of the district, the state, or the nation. At the time of this study, Elena—and schools in similar positions with comparable populations—were all subject to the tenets of the Texas accountability system. Rather than adhering exclusively to the TAAS test and dropout rates as indicators of success, the state should explore a middle ground between accountability and reality. Current legislation that provides a back door to the promotion of third graders, dependent on TAAS mastery, reveals the unrealistic enactment of high-stakes accountability. The never-ending cycle of setting high standards and then altering the passing criteria is evidence in support of how the pragmatic implementation of accountability is still subject to the human trait of individual interpretation. For as the decision to pass a child onto the next grade was originally set to be determined by the TAAS test, the closer the reality loomed the more the laws allowed for site-based decisions based upon teachers, parents, and principals.

Teachers Should Be Educated, Not Trained

If Title I schools are going to continue to be the focus of high-stakes accountability measures, teachers will need to rely on more than test scores and a deeper understanding that high scores are not the only indicators of successful literacy instruction. Shepard (2000) calls for assessment inside classrooms filled with multiple avenues for information gathering, co-constructed tasks between teachers and children that reflect an overall picture of learning—a model executed in many classrooms already but delivering data in unfamiliar formats for those in policy positions seeking either/or classifications. The swift, high-volume need to measure reading and writing has driven policy, which in turn has driven the curriculum and ultimately the classroom practices of teachers. Dolores, a third-grade teacher, describes how she felt the push and pull of being subjected to the trends of school reforms that disempowered teachers and negated their knowledge. She mentions her belief that teachers need to stick to what they know works and build on their knowledge, rather than being told what to do through policy. She ends her statement with her frustration that it all boils down to placing obstacles in front of children:

[Dolores:] I would agree with that idea [that teachers are oppressed]. It's kind of interesting because I have a niece who was a first-year teacher . . . But she asked, "Why is it that there are so many teachers that just aren't willing to try?" and I smiled. I said, "Well, after 13 years of people telling you this is what you need to do. No, no this is what you need to do . . . no no no, this is what you really need to do. You start to lose faith, even with some of the things that are quality suggestions." You no longer know. How long is this going to be part of my instructional day? Or one more thing I need to do . . . but I can understand why individuals wouldn't just leap on board and say, "Yeah, this is the answer," because it seems that the question remains the same. How to best meet our students' needs, but the answers are always changing and there's not really a right one. The best practice is, you've got to stick to what you know works and then build on that. And as far as the legislators are concerned, when I read the newspaper article, comparing different districts and how different students are doing and how with the new TAAS test that one-third of our third graders would fail, I'm going, "Well . . . okay, how is this serving our students? What is it that they are trying to get our students to do?" Because I'm puzzled now, I don't get it. Do they want them to fail? I don't know how they're trying to build them to be successful citizens. Sometimes it seems like they are placing obstacles in front of them rather than supporting their learning. A test doesn't teach.

Dolores is a highly educated teacher who sought out information and managed to be incredibly successful with her students. She was consistently able to balance TAAS instruction with "real literacy" education, yet she criticized the whole premise of the state threatening to fail her third graders for not passing TAAS. Her line of reasoning within this story about her niece shows how teachers realize that reform efforts construct training models and assessment measures to satisfy needs outside and independent of benefiting the children they propose to "help." Teachers should continue to be educated, but they do not need training. There is an environment gaining strength that is not conducive to truly educating teachers and maintaining a high level of professional knowledge based on a wide variety of resources. Teachers are on the verge of being force-fed the state-supported "scientific research" training.

There are two main avenues to acquiring teacher knowledge once a teacher is certified: (1) the staff development provided by the state and/or the district; and (2) continuing education through university coursework. The staff development model in Texas is now the reading academies mentioned in Chapter 3. These hold rigidly to the specific view of reading as seen through the eyes of the National Reading Panel and the National Institute for Child Health and Development (NICHD), which embrace a skills-based approach to reading not espoused by most literacy scholars. There is a precedent that Texas has reason to fear: "The fear is that Texas will become California. A 1997 education bill in California (AB 1086) included funds for professional development programs for teachers of reading that had to be conducted by 'approved providers' who met criteria established by the state Board of Education" (Coles, 2000, p. xiii). The situation in California has taken all decisions about teaching philosophies and methodologies out of the hands of the schools and teachers and placed them into the hands of policy makers who may not completely comprehend the complexity of research and may therefore make misinformed decisions. This situation can be compared to the healthcare system, which now places medical professionals at the mercy of large health maintenance organizations. Everyone is guaranteed some sort of healthcare, but the quality of that care is debatable, and the freedom of physicians to provide the best of care is hobbled by the policy mandates they must follow. Policy makers and often administrators are not well versed in the professional literature and thus may make inappropriate choices.

Teachers can also elect to continue their education through university courses, but they can find themselves unsupported. For example, each teacher received $600 when they attended the reading academies for four days. Reading academies pay, in contrast to Penny's graduate education, was not financially supported by the district or state. In addition, certification areas could be obtained simply by passing the state test with no required coursework. This simplified idea that teacher training or certification was simple and easily validated by a state test was becoming more common. Graduate-level coursework was not supported to the same degree as teacher trainings. Penny had one of her graduate classes overlap with her teaching time, and instead of taking personal days, she was docked for each day she was out, even though she still managed to show up for important meetings dealing with her special education students.

> [Penny:] I've been very, very disillusioned . . . [A]s much as Austin talks about raising the standards of teachers and things like that I'm not getting paid at all. I'm getting docked in pay because I'm going to graduate school . . . Why is that not something that's valued here?

Penny's frustration was also felt by teachers who used to have book clubs where they read and discussed research. But the atmosphere had changed to a very large degree. Katia described the district and state's view of teachers: "I think we are semi-literate. That's what they want us to be."

Functional literacy was not only a goal for the students; it had become a goal for the teachers. In order to guarantee uniformity, by which the district and state imply quality, teachers were being directed how to teach literacy and pressured to place priority on the TAAS test. The powerful force the state of Texas had in the classroom of every teacher I spoke to is mirrored in Apple's (2001) portrayal of the sobering tendencies regarding teachers under a strong state: "There has been a steadily growing change from 'licensed autonomy' to 'regulated autonomy' as teachers' work is more highly standardized, rationalized, and 'policed'" (p. 51). Devin describes how Elena once operated under a "licensed autonomy": "[Mr. Soza][2] was pretty innovative . . . for the time period. He let teachers bring in things and he let you buy things. He would give you money if you went and talked to him." Elena was ahead of its time until the accountability system began to erode the bilingual program, the focus on teacher education, the commitment to the community, and the contributions of its culture. It was becoming more difficult for teachers to seek out knowledge other than that advocated by the state. Apple (2001) also prophetically describes the road Texas appears to taking to educate its children and control its teachers:

> Under the growing conditions of regulated autonomy, teachers' actions are now subject to much greater scrutiny in terms of process and outcomes. Indeed, some states in the United States not only have specified the content that teachers are to teach, but also have regulated the only appropriate methods of teaching . . . Such a regime of control is based not on trust, but on a deep suspicion of the motives and competence of teachers . . . And this will be policed by statewide and national tests of both students and teachers. (p. 51)

Literacy scholars, who provide university education for teachers, were described by the Center for Reading and Language Arts as "reading experts [who] tended to pick their favorite theories and told teachers to teach in a manner that conformed to those theories. This has led to teachers receiving confusing and mixed messages" (3TRA, 2002, p. 10). This implies that literacy education provided to teachers was biased and one-sided, which is precisely the stance taken by the Reading Center in charge of facilitating the academy information. This either/or positioning of theories that could instead be used hand-in-hand is unfortunate and only serves to limit both teachers and children. The political nature of the research stances has affected the information that trickles down to teachers and assumes that teachers are unable to process vast amounts of information and make their own decisions. The result is disheartening for those who realize that the more knowledge a teacher has, the more methods they are privy to, and the more they are able to adjust to the needs of individual children. There is no one way to teach reading any more than there is one way to travel to work. Caroline was an active teacher and described her thoughts about the lack of power for teachers to make choices:

> I mean we're all professionals aren't we? We all are striving to achieve the same goal and we should all be able to put our own input in. I don't think it's ever been considered that teachers are intellectual giants. I don't think that that's the outlook that we have in the United States. Elsewhere, I think that's completely different. My sister lived in Germany, but here it's, "Oh she couldn't do anything so she's a teacher. She couldn't do all the hard classes, so she's a teacher." That's the attitude . . . our society doesn't necessarily value children either. They really don't. They may say it because it sounds good . . . if they wanted us to have a voice then we would be able to act collectively and strike and bargain that way but we can't. We don't have any way of coming together.

Caroline's feelings that teachers were not valued for their input mirrors the idea of the "danger of conscientizacao" (Freire, 1970). Freire describes the "danger of conscientizacao" or "the fear of freedom" (p. 28). Freire's efforts to educate the adults within his community beyond the technical skills of reading and writing were fraught with fear and led eventually to the suppression of his ideas. He advocated a "problem-posing" model of education where education was critical and unbounded. This was diametrically opposed to what he termed a "banking-education" model where information was simply deposited and was to be accepted without question. He realized that his problem-posing education model did not fit the oppressor's view of what was expected of the members of that community. In the view of the oppressors, the educated person was one who was able to function within the society without questioning. This is similar to the position the teachers of Elena were placed in: they were viewed by the state and some administrators as being dangerous. The knowledge of the teachers was more comfortable for those in power if that knowledge accepted the values of the oppressors. The school district's blueprint plan of having teachers sign a commitment to teach a particular curriculum at a specific time of day illustrates the amount of control the district felt was necessary to ensure conformity, but only conformity for those schools deemed unsuccessful on TAAS. Rather than encourage "problem-posing" (Freire, 1970) education in the face of questions, the state relied on the "banking-education" ideas of simply telling teachers what and how to teach.

If the problem at Elena was teaching children to read, then in order best to find solutions, teachers used to seek out multiple resources and make informed decisions. Now their resources are tied to the TAAS test and its accountability system. Bob described the differences between teachers' philosophies in the past, which were concentrated on the children's needs, with the teachers' now attempting to follow ideas and methods simplified and therefore easier for teachers:

> The problem we are having in this building is: [the new teachers are] following the easiest path for the teachers but we're not doing the easiest path for the kids. That's gone. The child-centered business is gone. It's not here, and I think that's the biggest difference right now. The child-centered [teacher] doesn't worry about who it's easy for, they worry about what's best for the kids. We'll do it, whatever it takes to do it, we'll have to do that and that's disappeared. The strong group of teachers? They're gone because they were unable to make any changes and now that they're gone, everything is just sliding downhill.

Just as Bob criticized the absence of a formidable staff of teachers at Elena who fought for the best interests of the children through questioning and educating themselves, Penny mirrored the same sentiments when she lamented the lack of teachers interested in furthering their education through advanced degrees:

> I think my fear about graduating UR is that I'm losing the conversation and losing the learning . . . I feel sometimes ashamed to mention in front of some people

that I'm getting my master's. It's not looked at as, "Wow, that's wonderful. I wish I could do that." Its either, "Oh," or "Oh God, you sure have more strength than I do. I'll never go back to school," and I'm like, "What? You should be forced to."

Penny felt empowered and stimulated by her continuing education and spoke many times of how she began to question and think more because of her coursework. In fact, at the conclusion of his study of high-stakes writing assessment, Hillocks (2002) confessed: "In my most cynical moments, I wonder if the master plan is to train people not to think" (p. 204). Both students and teachers are the victims of such plans, students as they were taught to pass a basic skills test and teachers who were under pressure to ensure the passage of that test. Both groups were subjected to the accountability of lowered expectations at the price of higher-level, more creative teaching.

Penny ran into negative evaluations for speaking her mind and soon realized that the status quo required acquiescence of teachers. As Hillocks (2002) also states: "When the urge to do well on the tests is high and the students are deemed unlikely to perform at satisfactory levels, the knowledge base becomes even more restricted by administrative directives indicating what should be taught, how long, and in what order" (p. 102). Penny's comparison of how two upper-middle-class school districts required advanced degrees contrasted with the Elena school district's lack of response and support for university advancement:

> If you look at these [two] districts, Moreland Forest and Stevenson, two of my friends work there. You have to get your master's within the first three years of teaching. You have to. Then once you get it and you show them a bill for it they'll pay you a stipend for going and you get an increase in salary. You have to get it or else you're fired, you better be looking for another job. Look at those districts. They are affluent districts that have teachers who know what they are doing, who are educated, who are questioning the schools. They work more as a partnership rather than a dictatorship. It's only going to get worse with the TAAS thing going where the referrals are going to go and go and go.

Another recommendation is that teachers should be continuously educated with an emphasis on choice, creativity, and culture. As the state of Texas became more aligned with a skills-based model of teaching reading, the risk increased of newer teachers not being exposed to alternative methods and veteran teachers giving up on other methods under pressure of continual reform. The newer teachers at Elena were seen as more traditional, not allowing the needs of the child to drive the curriculum, but rather as taking the curriculum and allowing it to drive the child. As Devin noted:

I think a lot of times [assessment drives instruction]. I think the newer the teacher, the more likely they are going to fall into a certain hole. A lot of times new teachers are not real sure about everything. [They] haven't formed all of [their] opinions yet and [they] haven't really tried out anything so [they] have to stick with what's safe.

During the fourteen years I was at Elena, literacy instruction methods were not completely mandated by the administration. Therefore, teachers were left to their own interpretations at times. In the past, the vast amount of training and teacher interest in the training offered encouraged most teachers to attend. By 2001, there was a separation between groups of teachers. The teachers I interviewed were alike in that they did hold similar views on literacy education. They all used guided reading, word study, literature circles, and some form of writer's workshop. They all had been to similar trainings and implemented new ideas in their classrooms. It was not the case with all the teachers. Changes were afoot. The emphasis and power structures were moving in different directions toward more conformity to the accountability measures of the state reading initiative. Coles (2000) reinforces how the state leaned toward the one research view of skills-based instruction in the reading initiative:

> Accusations of lowered reading test results are one-half of the arsenal used by supporters of conventional reading education, who also claim that their views are not mere opinion but are based on research that leaves no doubt about the need to scrap the newest reform, whole language, and to institute skills-emphasis teaching. (p. xiii)

Literacy within a Socio-Cultural Definition

Culture must be looked at as a set of powerful resources for students and teachers. The language of the state and the district mirrors how the teachers at Elena continually avoided naming race. If Title I schools are known—if not clearly named—targets of the high-stakes accountability design, then the discourse fails to acknowledge the culture of the children it is attempting to "save" through the literacy measures and the culture indoctrinating the illiterate. Both cultures, the White culture invoking the literacy model and measure, and the Latino culture of Elena, must be named and recognized without fear. The Open Court reading program is being brought to the Austin Independent School District to save failing schools and to supplant the Dual Language program at one school. To not understand the colonization paradigm Street (1995) defined is to attempt to be colorblind and is inherently racist by

Frankenburg's (1993) definition. Critical race theorists would characterize these policies as being colorblind, also a part of Guerra's (1998) "literacy as institution" metaphor. He writes: "In such an idealized state, of course, issues of poverty and injustice do not exist or are simply ignored. Because of the objectified nature of this construct, equality of opportunity and outcome is also assumed" (p. 52). The refusal to recognize differences is a part of the colorblind construct that many Whites and institutions hold onto in order to remain in what they believe to be race-neutral positions. But just as the teachers avoided race and believed it not to be relevant, literacy policy's refusal to name race and address cultural literacy serves only to promote monolithic literacy definitions simplified to minimum standards.

Although I believe that all of the entities involved wanted to provide the best for all children, I credit the new rhetoric with an admission of the lack of attention that the literacy of children of color has received in the past. Based on the data collected at Elena, I recognized the point where it is possible that more harm than good is done. Good intentions do not always make for good decisions, and the simplistic definition of literacy betrayed the richness and complexity of the culture of the children and their families. Without revisiting in great detail the greater implications of the White-dominant culture's role in the design and implementation of the accountability system, the attitudes of disdain and the deficit views toward the culture and the capabilities of the children were very much based on racial factors. The teachers' expectations for the children reinforced their ultimate goal of ensuring that the children reached a minimal functional grasp of literacy, rather than a powerful, critical, high level of democratic literacy.

Research has uncovered methods, models, and ways of interacting with respect to both cultures. According to Ladson-Billings (1995), "The common feature [the teachers who were successful with students of color] shared was a classroom practice grounded in what they believed about the educability of the students" (p. 484). Her propositions of what she termed "culturally relevant pedagogy" emerged from her study of a group of teachers where the teachers "(1) believed that all the students were capable of academic success, (2) saw their pedagogy as art—unpredictable, always in the process of becoming, (3) saw themselves as members of the community, (4) saw teaching as a way to give back to the community, and (5) believed in a Freirean notion of pulling knowledge out" (p. 478). This notion of culturally relevant teaching valued the culture of the students and focused on high expectations for children and teachers. Giving teachers a heightened awareness of culture, both White and Latina culture, would increase the possibility for greater understanding of children. Spindler's (1998) definition of cultural therapy, "the process of getting to know one's cultural biases, particularly as they influence one's perceptions of others representing cultures different from one's own" (p. 38), is one way of opening up the dialogue pertaining to culture.

Administrators Should Be Educated in Literacy Theory

[Caroline:] [Administrators] have no idea what goes on in a classroom and they think that they can make a difference with the TAAS scores or with whatever they want to and they don't step into the classroom or they don't even come into their area that they are supervising . . . [The superintendent] has no idea about the shack that this little girl has to live in.

The traditional role of principals was to manage and evaluate schools. Every teacher at Elena lamented the fact that the former principal's knowledge was not up to par. Although she was preferred over the new principal (hired in 2001) because of her willingness to attend as many trainings as she could, the year she retired, TAAS had altered her focus, too. The pressure on principals to perform was immense and was difficult to challenge. There was a distinct distance between all levels of educators and administrators. Katia debated the definitions of guided reading in her classroom, while some teachers saw the struggles of trying to connect with the new area superintendent. Caroline was present at a PTA meeting when a parent asked the area superintendent why she was not visiting Elena more often. This was during a highly stressful time when the school began to search for a new principal with the promise of the district's central office that the staff and parents would play a large role in the process. Many teachers, including Caroline, were upset that the area superintendent expressed surprise that she would have to conduct most of the meeting in Spanish. The distance and lack of knowledge about the school's neighborhood combined with the lack of interaction between the area superintendent and the staff was frustrating to teachers who remembered when administrators were more visible and responsive to the school's needs. Caroline showed her frustration as she related a story involving the area superintendent's lack of presence at Elena:

The PTA president asked [the area superintendent] why she didn't come to Elena. Why she didn't know our community. Why she wasn't out there visiting. Her response was she'd never been invited. She's our area superintendent. That's her job. I don't know what she thinks her job is, but you know, [the principal] doesn't wait for me to invite her into my room. [laughs]

The school district desired to enhance parental communication through increasing parental conformity to the school. The blueprint plan designed by the superintendent was a top-down method of requiring parents to be held accountable to the school's notions of proper literacy behaviors in their homes. Purcell-Gates (2000) found in her review of literature regarding family literacy that

> Real ideological differences emerge in the field, with some taking issue with the stance of family literacy programs that strive to change the behaviors of parents and family members and calling instead for (a) programs that place children's educational achievements in the context of restricted economic and political opportunities, and (b) collaborative approaches to working with parents, teachers, and schools to improve the academic performance of children, operating out of a posture of mutual respect of other's cultures and cultural practices. (Auerbach, 1995; Cairney, 1997; Taylor, 1997 cited in Purcell-Gates, 2000, p. 858)

Where Elena once had a community connection unique and adaptable to the families, the district now stressed the opposite and enlisted parents of children of color to sign papers promising to use school literacy practices at home. Uniform literacy assessment is the one thing in which every teacher must participate. Scribner & Cole (1978) suggest "that ideal literacy is simultaneously adaptive, socially empowering, and self-enhancing . . . Recognition of the multiple meanings and varieties of literacy also argues for a diversity of educational approaches, informal and community-based as well as formal and school-based" (p. 81). Graff (1995) adds that "the measurement of the distribution of literacy in a population may in fact reveal relatively little about the uses to which such skills could be put and the degree to which different demands on personal literacy could be satisfied with the skills commonly held" (p. 24). Cultural values are ever present in the transmission of language and literacy to any group by another group. As literacy was brought to the students of Elena, it was not critically examined in cultural ways other than to use the dominant culture's ways of knowing how to evaluate the community's responses. Lima & Lima (1998) explain the importance of understating literacy within a socio-cultural framework:

> The first is that an opening to cultural diversity in school does not mean the reproduction of a Latino and Latina environment as such, not only because of the sociological and psychological impossibility of such a task, but because the Latino and Latina experience in the United States is necessarily that of biculturalism. Perhaps even more than the difficulties of dealing with another culture, the American school has difficulty in dealing with the emotional and cognitive particularity of people who grew up through the mediation of more than one culture and one language. The symbolic systems developed by bicultural/bilingual individuals (or by multicultural/multilingual individuals) are necessarily diverse

from those who grow up with just one. Since language is a tool for thinking, to be fluent in more than one language also means that the individual may have different approaches to a new situation or a new problem to solve because his or her symbolic tools have been developed in more than one particular way. (p. 337)

The simplistic ideas of literacy as a trouble-free, "scientifically measured" set of skills that will magically secure the fate of the schoolchildren of Texas fails to understand the tools of learning that various cultures bring to schools. If the Latino/a children of Elena could bring their diverse cultural literacies into the schools to promote the richness of all cultures taught, the school and the teachers would be able to enhance and expand—rather than narrow—the literacy abilities of the children and the teachers.

·7·

WHAT WOULD HAPPEN IF THE WHOLE WORLD BECAME LITERATE?

The button said, "All children can learn." That was the clearly articulated philosophy of Elena when I arrived in 1987. Every teacher wore that button daily, and we knew what was expected of us as teachers at Elena. To be a teacher at Elena meant that we had a responsibility to be knowledgeable about the children in our classrooms and to tailor instruction to their needs. We were expected to be up to date on current teaching practices, bilingual, and ESL program requirements, and to maintain close contacts with the parents through home visits. Valenzuela's (1999) notion of educators as "honorary members" of the communities they serve describes the atmosphere at Elena in the late 1980s and early 1990s. These expectations were not only made verbally explicit by the principal, but they were constantly active in the daily lives of the teachers. Every decision was based on the idea that all children could learn and that they could learn in the classroom, not in the special education room, or the Reading Recovery room; they were the classroom teacher's responsibility. Over the years, administrators moved on, teachers transferred, policy changed, and the figured world of Elena responded to these changes in many ways. The idea of teachers as "honorary members" of the community could now be reversed—it was the parents of Elena who were to become members of the school community, and the teachers who were to become members of the state policy's community.

Through the policy language of the school superintendent, the state, and the nation, there was an overwhelming need to change the world of the families and schools. Natalie, the campus literacy specialist, expressed it as "changing a culture," while policy presented change in the form of uniform literacy. Therefore, schools as institutions viewed their role as one of modification: modification through the dispensing of literacy, but only to a degree comfortable to those in power. The idea of a group in control reordering the structure and focus of a population deemed to be "at-risk" is aligned with the idea of colonizing a community. "Traditional colonialism was grounded on the deviation of those colonized from the norm of rationality; thus colonization became a rational response to inequality" (Kincheloe & Steinberg, 1998, p. 7).

Policy rhetoric avoids using race unless it is framed within Feagin's (1998) notion of coding. The primary code here is one of rescuing. As long as the dominant culture maintains that all efforts to bring literacy to the at-risk child are framed within the savior framework of leaving no child behind, every measure is justified. The missionary idea that a population is in need and that the savior can save them—from themselves in some cases—speaks to the idea that all families and children need and want the same thing. In this environment, families and teachers were powerless to advocate their own ideas of how prevalent literacy was in the community or the means through which that literacy could be attained or measured.

One narrow definition of literacy became the means for controlling instruction and the futures of the children of Elena. Absent the time and freedom to explore alternative conceptions of literacy, Elena became ruled by an accountability system that allowed and encouraged a false literacy production. Test scores rose, and the school was rewarded by a government system set up to reinforce its own agenda, but teachers were not convinced that literacy had improved. Altering the accountability system set up by high-stakes testing and replicated by the No Child Left Behind Act (PL 107–110) would require a revolution, an upheaval of the entire systemic structure in Texas education. The Texas Reading Initiative and the No Child Left Behind Act are working in the sense that as of Spring 2003, reading scores on the national reading tests are rising. The false notion that the literacy development of children is improving is lost in the push for higher scores. Therefore, altering the new system of accountability will be difficult and requires asking again: What is a literate child? What is a literate teacher? And what might happen if the whole world of education changed? Change can be heard in the voices of Macedo (1994), Street (1995), and Freire (1987) and can be summed up in Graff's (1995) citation of Galtung:

> What would happen if the whole world became literate? Answer: not so very much, for the world is by and large structured in such a way that it is capable of absorbing the impact. But if the world consisted of literate, autonomous, critical, constructive people, capable of translating ideas into action, individually or collectively—the world would change. (p. 93)

The world should change. If the story of Elena illustrates anything, it should be that literacy is culturally formed and nurtured and will flourish only if its complexity is understood and respected. Suppression of the potential for all children to become literate, independent, active participants in the multiple worlds in which they live should not be the primary educational aim of a democratic nation.

Leaving No Child Behind: The Incantation of Low Expectations

> Democracy is the word with which you must lead them by the nose . . . Nor of course must they ever be allowed to raise Aristotle's question: whether "democratic behaviour" means the behaviour that democracies like or the behaviour that will preserve a democracy . . . You are to use the word purely as an incantation; if you like, purely for its selling power. It is a name they venerate. And of course it is connected with the political ideal that all men should be equally treated . . . they've no business to be different. It's undemocratic . . . Under the influence of this incantation those who are in any or every way inferior can labour more wholeheartedly and successfully than ever before to pull down everyone else to their own level. But that is not all. Under the same influence, those who come, or could come, nearer to a full humanity, actually draw back from it for fear of being undemocratic. (Lewis, 1961, pp. 162–64)

"Pulling everyone else to their own level" is not the more common interpretation of what democracy might mean for schools. Equality in Lewis's (1961) interpretation troubles the very idea of what equality might mean for literacy. Many times the United States' user-friendly version of democracy survives on the implied notion that equal opportunity will actually lift everyone up to elevated levels in their quest for "The American Dream." To mention any other interpretation of the meaning of the word democracy, especially by those in education, is to be quite "undemocratic." The juxtaposition of mediocrity within a meritocracy may appear too contradictory to coexist at first, yet within the realm of reading standards in Texas, they survived and worked together to create a colonial model of literacy education that began in 1996.

> In 1996 then-Governor George W. Bush and the 75th Texas legislature directed the Texas Education Agency to implement a plan that would ensure that all students to be [sic] able to read on grade level or higher by the end of the third grade and continue to read on grade level or higher throughout their schooling. (http://www.tea.state.tx.us/reading/model/histexrea.html)

This political call for ensuring that every child read by the end of third grade embedded itself deeply in the rhetoric for equal opportunity and success for all in Texas and continues today through the mission of the No Child Left Behind Act. Connecting the notion of a democratic nation educating its young for the glory of success and guaranteeing that all schools place an emphasis on reading standards leaves little room for critical deconstruction in educational circles. How do educators argue against teaching all children to read without seeming undemocratic?

> In his Foreword to the "No Child Left Behind" national education program, President Bush stresses "bipartisan education reform as the cornerstone of his administration. The quality of our public schools directly affects us all—as parents, as students, and as citizens. Yet too many children in America are segregated by low expectations, illiteracy, and self-doubt. In a constantly changing world that is demanding increasingly complex skills from its workforce, children are literally being left behind." (http://www.ed.gov/inits/nclb/part1.html)

The idea that all children will be reading by third grade at or above grade level is problematic, because the reality for many struggling readers is the minimum goal that high-stakes accountability testing emphasized. The incantation of leaving no child behind rests on the notions of institutional literacy (Guerra, 1998) and literacy as a state of grace (Scribner & Cole, 1978). For educators even to suggest that they have concerns with the No Child Left Behind Act is to be undemocratic and interrupts those who are saving the previously left-behind children. Adding in the factor of the predominately white community involved in making the policy a reality, and the ways in which literacy is constructed as a saving mechanism, serves to increase the level of concern of colonial literacy (Street, 1995). Teachers and administrators are now living in a world where literacy is defined and delivered by the government. There is no room for inquiries related to community literacies, language differences, or broader interpretations for the idea of a literate world within schools for teachers, parents, or children. Taylor (1998) describes the atmosphere within which educators in Texas lived: "This is the immediacy of the situation of which I write. Teachers have been silenced and speak of intimidation, educational researchers have had their work blacklisted, and some have been personally vilified" (Taylor, 1998, p. xxiii). Texas was a state where high expectations were an "incantation" used to bring reading achievement to schools by way of one monolithic definition of literacy, and the nation is following quickly along the same path.

Literacy and Democracy

"The era of low expectations is ending; a time of great hopes and proven results is arriving," President Bush said. "And together, we are keeping a pledge: Every child in America will learn, and no child will be left behind."

The development of these plans involved a lot of hard work. Governors stepped up to the line, along with their education chiefs. I also want to thank the principals and teachers and parents on the frontlines who are working so hard to improve our public schools. Instead of throwing up your hands in despair, you decided to challenge the status quo and to help each child. On behalf of the nation, I want to thank all who are involved in America's public schools, all who demand excellence, for your service to our country.

"Never before has a president of the United States invested so much in the education of our children," Secretary Paige said. "And never before has our nation responded with such enthusiasm. Just as we as a nation have always pulled together to ensure our freedom, we are now pulling together to ensure our children are educated. Americans have heard President Bush's call for meaningful education reform so that no child is left behind, and they are joining forces with him to see that the mission is accomplished. (Paige, 2003, http://www.ed. gov/ PressReleases/06-2003/06102003.html)

The marriage of literacy and democracy has a long history, and unpacking the underlying meanings and assumptions requires an analysis of the definitions, purposes, and political uses of the term democracy as it applies to reading standards. The reading standards espoused by the Texas Reading Initiative (1996), the Reading Excellence Act (1997), and the No Child Left Behind Act (2002) state that all children must be reading at or above grade level by third grade. The enactment of this mantra relies on states' setting specific reading measures and goals that force teachers to adhere to minimum standards.

Teachers of children within school populations where students do not struggle when meeting reading goals do not concern themselves with the ramifications of testing for literacy. Therefore, as the policy invocations target the struggling readers, they also sentence them to mediocrity. The additional transgression, as in the case of Elena Elementary, was the fact that most of the struggling readers were children of color. When placed within a desire for equality for all, this argument intensifies. The No Child Left Behind Act is indirectly supporting the notion that measuring literacy for all children need only require passing a test.

If democracy is to be a part of schooling in America, then literacy should not be exempt from that vision, and all students should have the opportunity to become highly literate. Giroux (1997) elaborates on his construction of democracy and schooling:

> The purpose of schooling now becomes fashioned around two central questions: What kind of society do educators want to live in and what kind of teacher and pedagogy can be both informed and legitimated by a view of authority that takes democracy and citizenship seriously? Such a view of authority points to a theory of democracy that includes the principles of representative democracy, worker's democracy, and civil and human rights. It is, in Benjamin Barber's terms, a view of authority rooted in "strong democracy," and is characterized by a citizenry capable of genuine public thinking, political judgment, and social action. (pp. 101–02)

Giroux (1997) and Lewis (1961) illustrate the complexity of investigating the ways in which legislation aimed at creating standards for the schools of a democratic nation interfere with the idea of actively participating in the democratic process. Framing the concept of democracy within the idea that it is replete with various understandings while holding the great power of patriotic vision is a nod to Lewis's (1961) reference to raising "Aristotle's question: whether 'democratic behaviour' means the behaviour that democracies like or the behaviour that will preserve a democracy" (p. 162). In order to become an active, engaged democracy, citizens must go beyond the concept that equality is a goal and recognize that there is a variety of experiences within the nation that require diversity rather than conformity.

When applied to literacy in schools, democratic behavior can become an elusive, utopian world that teachers, children, and families are not able to acquire. Taylor (1998) asks, "We do believe, don't we, that American society is built on the ideals of equality and opportunity? Regardless of where we come from, however poor our families, whatever our ethnicity, if we work hard, everybody gets a chance" (p. 127).

Changing the World

The goal of having every child reading by third grade takes an existing standard in schools and transforms it into a mantra that assumes there has been an absence of reading instruction. Some scholars argue that prior to the Texas accountability system, children of color and other struggling readers were not receiving any instruction Scheurich & Young (1997). The legislation of literacy in Texas, and now the nation, is viewed as a saving mechanism for inadequate teachers and suffering children. Yet in many cases, prior to the literacy legislation, teachers and children were free to pursue literacy. By Giroux's

(1997) definition, the teachers of Elena were highly literate. They were critical thinkers who sought out the best ways to teach the children of the community they served. Elena's history of challenging the school board's definitions of the children as at-risk, being advocates for the parents, and designing educational programs on their merit as they related to the literacy needs of the school, was unique and rare. The teachers of Elena were capable of transforming ideas into action, and they did exert power alongside those who would govern them and their students. The uncomfortable, messy world of critical thought and endless information challenges the figured world of policy makers who desire clear-cut objectives and simple answers.

As legislation and institutions streamline and promote the incantation of leaving no child behind, there is an absence of focus on the possibilities for educating children. Multiple literacies should be possible, along with the idea that all voices can truly be heard. The idea of deregulating government sanctions on literacy achievement might keep researchers and teachers open to new ideas relevant to the education of children. Diversification of methods, resources, and cultural influences might empower schools and communities to govern themselves in ways that benefit the development of truly literate citizens. Yet this empowerment of many requires a release from the government's hold on the definitions and measurements of literacy. While other fields of research are encouraged to search for ways to heal and grow, literacy research and teaching is narrowed and simplified. Chester Finn, more than ten years prior to the No Child Left Behind Act, asserted that:

> For better and for worse, the education revolution is not wholly within the orbit of public policy anyway. Radical change in this domain is quite beyond the capacity of government to make. The tendency of government will be—always is—to amend the status quo just enough to ease an immediate crisis, to squirt a little oil on the parts that squeak. Government, when pressed, can produce perestroika, but only the will of the people can make a revolution. (1991, p. 241)

Change requires a restructuring of existing policy; repeating the incantation of leaving no child behind is not enough. A full-scale liberation of literacy in order to discontinue the colonizing form of one literacy for all is required. Maybe understanding what a literate, democratic community actually is requires losing it. Over time, the ideals behind the policy of uniform reading instruction for all children will crumble under the weight of mediocrity, and citizens will be allowed the "undemocratic" behavior of questioning how a government entity finds the courage to lower expectations for all children in one fell swoop. The institutionalized (Guerra, 1998) and colonizing (Street, 1995) version of literacy will fall away, and children will not only learn to read but will learn to flourish within a world they have a hand in creating. Educational legislation should encourage and support such a world. If the cries for "leaving no child behind" are transformed into truly promoting literacy, and the dream that every child will become an engaged citizen is realized to the highest degree, then a revolution will ensue, the world will change, and the mediocrity of democracy that Lewis (1961) portrays will not survive.

> . . . a shared decision making process in which power, not just the opportunity to participate, is equitably distributed. If school reform is to become a truly democratic enterprise which affords equal opportunities that benefit all student groups and community constituencies, the pluralism advocated by the culturalists must become a critical pluralism, one that is highly attentive to the significant differences in knowledge, power, and resources of various community constituencies . . . in a democracy, constituency committee-based reforms are superior to expert-driven reforms, but the participation on constituency committees must equitably represent the community. (Scheurich & Imber, 1997, p. 25)

The teachers at Elena were among the most dedicated and loving teachers I have ever witnessed. That they opened themselves up to this exploration of their views and practices regarding the children to whom they have dedicated their careers only serves to reinforce my belief that they will continue to provide only the best for the children of Elena in spite of the rhetoric swirling around the four walls in which they teach. Their eroding power and the limits placed on their professional knowledge is disconcerting to them and should be to others. Illeana, our Language Proficiency Assessment Committee chair, shared her thoughts with me the last time we spoke: "To me, literacy is the way that the children get to communicate through reading, writing and language. It encompasses everything, speaking and being able to be good communicators. As far as being able to read and write, I think the majority of [the kids we graduate] can do that." The children of Elena could read and write; they were functionally literate by the state's, the administrators', and the teachers' definition. But is that enough?

·APPENDIX ONE·

RESEARCH METHODOLOGY

Elena: Contextualizing the Research and the Researcher:
"A Room of One's Own"

Virginia Woolf (1929) wrote of having a "room of one's own." She was referring to women needing a place to contemplate, to write down their thoughts, a place of luxury that few women or teachers can afford. I write of a room of one's own for teachers and researchers, for they also live in rooms. How they make them their own depends upon the luxury of time, of being able to sit in the room to have ". . . pondered [things], and made [them] work out of daily life" (Woolf, 1929, p. 4). One room, one place. I have journeyed through the labyrinth of knowledge within academia, all the while remaining in a room at the elementary school where I first learned to teach. I spent fourteen years on a journey in one room/one place—Elena Elementary. Maxine Greene (1988) describes the labyrinth of walls, rooms, and halls I traversed as I consciously and unconsciously "studied" my home school:

> The growing, changing individual (no matter how reflective and autonomous he/she appears to be) always has to confront a certain weight in lived situations, if only the weight of memory and the past. There are ambiguities of various kinds, layers of determinateness. Freedom, like autonomy, is in many ways dependent on understanding these ambiguities, developing a kind of critical distance with respect to them. Even when understood, however, even when analyzed, they still exist as factors (more or less repressed) in a human career. (p. 9)

My room was assigned to me by the University of Texas fourteen years ago, and my history there shaped my interpretations of this study. I was sent to Elena to learn to teach. I arrived a nervous student teacher. I then became a classroom teacher, a cooperating teacher with my own student teachers, a master's student, and now an unsure doctoral candidate learning to become a researcher—always in my room at Elena. At times the room was an enchanting place, a refuge, a home, and a source of great joy and learning as theory explained familiar phenomena with new language and depth. At other times it was dark and stifling as the real life of school laughed in the face of abstract ideals. I found myself torn between what I read and what I actually did. I was not getting the answers I thought I would from academia. Instead I was getting more questions: questions about my teaching practices, my beliefs, and my culture. At the same time, I was on the receiving end of vast amounts of information delivered especially for teachers from the school system through district workshops, state guidelines, and federal mandates. Where I was encouraged to question ideas at the university and think critically, I found my questioning within the school system unwanted. The question "Why?" was not appreciated. I quickly learned to keep my newfound knowledge to myself; I learned to talk the talk of two communities according to the venue I was participating in at the time. My "theory sharing" at Elena was not always welcomed, and my "reality sharing" at the university was often met with disenchanted faces.

Therefore, the education I received at the university both enhanced and conflicted with the learning that took place at Elena. The room became my borderland between academia and school, the theories my interpreters, and the teachers strangers as I wandered back and forth through the halls. As I took the time to reflect in this "room of my own," I was prepared to find ways to reconcile my experiences at Elena with my experiences at the university. For four years, I avoided conversations with my fellow teachers, having found myself unable to express my novel, theoretical language without exposing my status as "the graduate student." Once the study began, I opened the door to my room through my research and began to learn from and share with the teachers who taught beside me. My basic questions were simple: How do we construct the children we teach? When our eyes scan the classroom's sea of faces, what do we see? Do we all see the same children? How does what we see affect our teaching? How does our teaching affect children's lives?

These were my questions for myself and teachers throughout my teaching career. My interest in how teachers construct children began in ways I cannot recall, and I now realize the questions have only gained strength over the years, fueled by experiences and theories I have recognized along my journey. Two years ago, I pursued these questions with preservice teachers assigned to Elena. I inquired about their views of the children they taught. I found that they loved all the children immensely. I also found that, like myself, they did not realize the impact their own personal beliefs, knowledge, and identity had on their teaching decisions. My pilot study was conducted at the school where I teach. Because of all I learned about myself during the course of the study, I became a participant in the study. Delgado-Gaitan (1986) wrote of how research during her study of family literacy moved her to change her stance from the neutral observer to an involved participant. For my dissertation, I moved to the in-service teachers at Elena—my colleagues, teachers with whom I made decisions everyday, teachers whom I had known for years. I asked the same questions, but I pushed further.

Purpose of Study

The purpose of this study was to explore the teachers' thoughts about the children, parents, and literacy at Elena, situated in the broader theoretical and political contexts these constituencies inhabit. I hoped to discover what the underlying beliefs and tensions behind the teachers' attitudes and decisions regarding the children were. I began with these general questions. As the study developed, I opened up the dialogue in ways I could not have predicted, and I allowed the teachers' own questions to mesh with my own.

Research Questions

Initially, I presented three basic areas of questioning:

Literacy
- What do the teachers believe about literacy and why?
- How do the teachers define literacy?
- How do the teachers define literacy instruction?
- How do the teachers talk about the literacy of the children?
- How do the teachers evaluate the literacy of the children?
- What type of training in literacy have the teachers received?
- Have the teachers' views of literacy changed in any way?

Children/Parents/Community
- How do the teachers talk/feel about the children they teach?
- How do the teachers feel about teaching at Elena?
- What do the teachers believe about local families' literacy practices and why?
- How do teachers talk about the families and communities of the children?
- What are their perceptions of other schools' literacy experiences?

Teaching Beliefs/Knowledge
- What do the teachers believe about how children learn and why?
- Who do the teachers rely on for information?
- Who do the teachers rely on for advice?

Literacy

My personal history at Elena guided my theoretical frame decisions. I found my knowledge of literacy and my cultural identity to be a factor in how I viewed the children and families I taught. Therefore, I chose to place literacy and culture in the forefront of my study structure. My views of Elena provided a map of roads I traveled during the study. My positioning at Elena was complex. My participation in various figured worlds related to literacy may have created an inescapable, circuitous path for my interpretation of seemingly simple events. The veteran teachers knew me as a graduate student and former first-grade teacher who moved into a reading specialist position. The newer teachers had never seen me in a classroom. Nevertheless, I spoke to teachers at Elena in the capacity of a person knowledgeable about literacy. Most conversations I was involved in were related to the reading difficulties of emergent readers in the school. The genesis for my research questions came from my interactions over the years with the teachers, administrators, and parents in the school, community, district, and the university. In my role as a reading teacher, I had been a part of the literacy history at Elena. As I aspired to explore the classroom teachers' views of literacy and its relationship to the children and teaching, I realized that it was crucial to attend to the policies influencing teachers at Elena. The state of Texas had become subject to the 1996 Reading Initiative designed under the Bush administration. In 2001, the ideology embraced by the state had moved to the national level and given literacy education a higher profile.

Methodology

Although I did not collect data over long periods of time as per most ethnographies, I did use ethnographic methods to gather data over the spring, summer, and fall of 2001. My positioning within Elena lent itself to the reflexive stance of critical autoethnography (Behar, 1993; Foley, 1995; Reed-Danahay, 1997; Trueba, 1999). Autoethnography is defined by Reed-Danahay (1997) as

> a form of self-narrative that places the self within a social context. It is both a
> method and a text, as in the case of ethnography . . . It can be done by an autobi-

ographer who places the story of his or her life within a story of the social context in which it occurs. (p. 9)

The descriptive and interpretivist nature of ethnography guided this journey through my school. Ethnography's purpose is to provide a source of material for analysis by recording what is seen and heard. Spindler (2000) and Glesne & Peshkin (1992) define ethnography as an anthropological tradition of long-term immersion in the field, supplemented by interviewing and, at times, participant observation. Because of my fourteen years at Elena, I had a historical view of events at the school. Three of my participants were present as long or longer than myself, and their historical perspective was used in many cases to provide a check and balance of my own revisionist historical view. Since the research area was literacy, I maintained two principles of qualitative research on literacy espoused by Trueba (1990). I continually worked to "link literacy to broader sociohistorical, linguistic, cultural, and cognitive contexts . . . and [focus] interpretations established through linkages between macro- and micro-analytical levels of data collected, as well as on cross-cultural comparisons" (p. 240). Throughout the study I also attempted to heed Trueba's (1990) warnings of isolating literacy research: he lists four areas to monitor during literacy research. Entreating literacy scholars to study literacy in the context of schools with respect to the cultural aspects of teaching and studying literacy in depth, he recommends that literacy studies be conducted

1. *Not* only in the study of isolated, fragmented literacy events.
2. *Not* in literacy events with exclusive focus on the technical aspects of reading and writing.
3. *Not* in the performance of culturally different children in teacher-controlled activities that are meaningless to these children.
4. *Not* in the narrow context of cognitive processes assessed by standardized instruments normed in mainstream populations. (p. 240)

My Stance as a Researcher

I was known at Elena; I could not conceal my identity as it was true to me or to the other teachers. My many identities overlapped and bumped into what I was there (Blumenthal, 1999). I did use my complex positioning as a researcher, a teacher on campus, a graduate student, and a reading specialist as I collected and interpreted data. The undefined lines between what I was and what I was studying are embraced by Blumenthal (1999) as she depicts the postmodern influences within research: "they interrupt and fracture the totality of the narrative by revealing its contradictions, embeddedness in local contexts, and possibly even its roots in the author's will to power" (p. 377). My beliefs as a teacher, as a graduate student, as a researcher, and as an individual could not be avoided. I did not attempt to escape or objectify my identity. In fact, I attempted to make my positions even more clear. I depended on the new knowledge I gathered to challenge assumptions about myself, Elena, and the teachers who lived there. I did my best to understand and expose my beliefs prior to my data gathering, and I continued that most difficult part of the journey throughout my data collection and interpretation.

My basic beliefs regarding teaching reading were transparent to the participants. Educators I interviewed were familiar with my teaching philosophy in that I was a reading specialist who favored teaching methods geared to a balanced literacy model of instruction. I was not a teacher of children subject to standardized tests, and I had been virtually absent from participating in many campus decision-making bodies. The last five years of my tenure at Elena were spent observing meetings and teaching only in a half-time tutoring program.

True to ethnographic writing styles, my writing is descriptive (Van Maanen, 1988; Wolcott, 1994) and vacillates between impressionist and confessional modes (Van Maanen, 1988). My feelings as a researcher and teacher were revealed to the participants and will be exposed to readers of the study. I adhere to the critical hermeneutic idea of Habermas and Apel (as cited in Moss, 1994; and Skinner, 1985) wherein the interpretation of meaning takes the social context into account and meshes into a shared meaning. In order to allow readers to draw their own conclusions and measure my interpretations as much as possible, I included as much raw data as I could, keeping quotes intact as much as possible and only removing extraneous or repeated words. I edited for grammar more than content when quotes were selected to illustrate points. Each participant chose their own pseudonym for the final paper.

I shared my thoughts and the interview transcripts continuously throughout the data collection period. I hoped to create and recreate meanings from the text of our interviews and the context of the school that I have known so long. My hermeneutic circle revolved around and through daily conversations and revisiting of transcripts and events.

> For qualitative methodologists, it is imperative that the assumption of a rationally ordered integral identity be deconstructed and reconceptualized in order to open up a space where contradiction, ambivalence, and fragmentation can be usefully interpreted. Should we choose to explore the multiplicity and variations within and across human identities, the resulting texts would be compelling in their revelation of richer meanings than we—I—had ever dreamed of. (Blumenthal, 1991, p. 391)

Foley's (1995) and Scheper-Hughes's (2000) return to their communities served as examples of my return to Elena. Still an insider and yet outsider, I attempted to use both of my situated identities to create familiarity and novelty for those I enjoined to "study."

Data Collection

Approaching the Participants

Methodologically, I remained true to the data collection and writing techniques of ethnographic research. I relied on primary informants, secondary informants, fieldnotes, and artifacts to capture the literacy practices at the school. After clearance from human subjects, the district, and the school's administrators, I formally invited all of the teachers in the school to participate through an email message. By laying a foundation based on volunteering, I hoped to engage those teachers interested in viewing themselves and their teaching from a new perspective. Eleven teachers accepted the invitation. Because of difficulties in scheduling and other circumstances, I was only able to interview eight. These eight teachers became my primary informants. I scheduled four interviews with each teacher, one for each area of inquiry. Prior to the interviews, each participant received a copy of the interview questions. My intent was to make them as comfortable as possible. Two of the newer teachers expressed concerns that they did not "know enough." Once I explained my goal of wanting simply to explore the state of literacy at Elena because of my distance from the classroom, we began the interviews. All of the teachers were informed of their right to stop participation at any time, and they knew they would be given copies of all of their interview transcripts.

In order to understand the circumstances of the data collection, it is important for me to reiterate how close I was to many of the participants and reveal the layered roles that characterized our daily teaching lives at Elena. Table 4 provides a brief overview of the teaching experience, teaching role, and ethnicity of each participant, but in order to illustrate my relationship with them, I will describe how long I had known them and in what capacity. My presentation of each teacher will be structured around the Spindlers' (2000) concept of the "situated self" and the "enduring self."

Illeana was the assistant principal at Elena. Her "situated role" at Elena was viewed by the teachers in ways directly related to literacy. Unlike most administrators, she was well versed in literacy. She was a former bilingual teacher and a former Reading Recovery teacher who had been at Elena for six years in the role of assistant principal. Prior to the study, she and I spoke frequently

TABLE 4. Participants

Participant's Name	Total years in education	Total years at Elena	Grade level at time of study	Ethnicity
Illeana	20+	6	administrator	Latina
Penny	6	5	special education teacher	White
Natalie	18	15	campus literacy specialist	White
Devin	15	15	second-grade teacher	Latina
Dolores	15	7	third-grade teacher	Latina
Katia	2	2	fourth-grade teacher	Latina
Caroline	3	3	fifth-grade teacher	White
Bob	24	15	sixth-grade teacher	White

about issues related to the Reading Recovery program, and for a few years she was my primary evaluator. During the time of the study she was attending graduate school and was curious about the issues related to the study. Illeana was an active supporter of literacy education, and her comments related to teachers and children were often positive and hopeful. She was reflective and proactive in her position at Elena yet also possessed a quiet strength which enabled her to move within the halls as a support person for the literacy development of teachers and families. Illeana's "enduring self" was not something she shared. She rarely referenced her thoughts about literacy at Elena with personal anecdotes. Illeana did not speak about her experiences as a Latina woman during the interviews. When I asked her specifically about how she thought race affected her teaching decisions, she indicated that she did not think it was a relevant part of how she viewed the world, and our conversations moved on to specific issues. Illeana's time with me as a colleague and a participant were bounded more by her "situated" identity as an administrator at Elena. She kept her language neutral during our interactions and did not mention culture or race even as she described the bilingual program.

Penny was a special education teacher for the primary grades at Elena, and her "situated self" as a Master Reading teacher placed her in a position of authority in some cases. She was a colleague at Elena, and I had one graduate course with her at the university before the study. Penny and I interacted very little at Elena prior to the study, because I had little contact with the special education program. (I was not a classroom teacher and not in a position to refer children to her program.) We usually spoke about our university courses and experiences. Penny was confident and open. She did not hesitate to express her views professionally or personally in her interactions during school hours or in her interviews with me. Penny was comfortable using her "enduring self" as a reference point for interpreting her views about literacy and race. Her honesty throughout the data collection was a testament to her reflective nature and her willingness to completely expose herself in order to understand and be understood. Penny was one of the most willing and open participants when the topic of race was brought to the fore. As a White teacher in a school of color, she had a reference point for discussing racial topics. In addition to her position at Elena, Penny's candidness was due to her being accustomed to discussing difficult issues in her university courses. She was extremely interested in discussing how race and culture affected her teaching, and she shared those views throughout the interviews.

Natalie's "situated self" was well developed at Elena. As the campus literacy specialist and a former third-grade teacher, she was viewed as a literacy expert on staff. She was expected to assist teachers in the classroom, share new literacy information, facilitate and interpret assessment measures, and train the staff. Natalie and I had worked together in several capacities. We wrote a grant for the school's bookroom together in 1993; we attended several literacy trainings together throughout our years as teachers; and in the later 1990s I supervised student teachers in her classroom and conversed with her about literacy issues in research and on campus on a regular basis. Natalie did utilize aspects of her "enduring self" to illustrate a few of her views regarding literacy and race as we spoke, but most of her contributions to the study were related to her vast knowledge of how the district and school used and organized the literacy trainings and assessments. She did feel that race and culture were relevant issues to literacy education at Elena, and she was comfortable explaining her point of view many times from her perspective as a White teacher and her past experiences as a college student. Natalie was adept at staying current on all of the district guidelines and how teachers on campus were using and integrating them into their daily practices.

Devin was a Latina teacher whom I had known since I began teaching at Elena. She taught pre-kindergarten, first grade, and was teaching second grade at the time of the study. Her "situated self" could be encased within her position as an experienced bilingual teacher with a master's degree in library science. Devin and I spoke less and less throughout the years as I moved away from my position as a classroom teacher, although I did consult with her about a few of her students I taught in Reading Recovery. She was an outspoken advocate for the bilingual program at Elena and served on many committees. Devin provided several historical references to past practices at Elena as they compared to the time of the study. She did not spend a great deal of time referring to how her "enduring self" influenced her teaching, but she did use a few personal examples of how her childhood affected her views of the community. Devin was often critical of the administration's lack of focus on the racial and cultural aspects of literacy instruction, yet she did use her "enduring self" in ways that kept her separated from the Latino/a community of Elena. Devin

did not represent her views as the views of an essentialized member of a generally defined Latino/a culture; she compared and contrasted her childhood
with the childhood of the Latina principal and the experiences of the children
she taught. Devin's "situated self" at Elena fluctuated during interviews as she
moved in and out of her own reference points for evaluating the students and
families. Her thoughts were adjusted to the specific event or person many
times, and she provided one of the most complicated examples of how identities are multifaceted and avoid being bounded by discrete definitions.
Devin's pseudonym, chosen by her, was a nod to a first grader she taught years
ago, a White student highly literate and considered quite gifted by Devin.

Dolores, a Latina teacher, taught third grade at Elena, and we had previously worked together as I supervised student teachers in her classroom. We
spoke informally in the hallways, but at the time of the study we had not been
in touch on a regular basis. Dolores's "situated self" at Elena was as a strong
teacher. Her interviews were tightly focused on how her experiences at Elena
compared to her experiences at other schools. She used her "enduring self,"
her positioning as a mother and aunt, several times to contrast how Elena was
different from the other schools she had taught in and how her teaching experiences at Elena were not the same as those of her son's teacher or her niece.
This use of her outside, more personal experiences allowed glimpses into the
way she then viewed Elena. Racial and cultural aspects of teaching were not
directly articulated by Dolores. She maintained a focus on the nuts and bolts
of teaching and applied her views to the students and community in ways not
explicitly marked by race. Her references to her life outside of school were encased within comparisons of Elena children to those children outside of Elena.
Dolores was a Spanish-speaking teacher who elected not to teach in a bilingual classroom.

Katia was a fairly new teacher at Elena, and another Latina teacher who
chose not to become bilingually certified. She had been a student teacher of
mine prior to her taking a position at Elena. Katia and I got to know each
other through her university experiences at Elena. She participated in a university tutoring program at Elena, observed in classrooms, and student taught
there, so she was familiar with the school, and we had a history of discussing
issues that continued into the study. Her "situated self" at Elena was very
closely connected to her "enduring self." Katia constantly referred to how her
experiences outside of the school formed and guided her beliefs inside the
school. Katia was a parent before she was a teacher and spent many years volunteering in her children's school. Her stories reflect the depth of her convictions as they were shaped prior to her own classroom experiences. Racial issues were not seen as an important part of literacy education by Katia. She was
adamant about her position and felt that it was her task, as a teacher at Elena,

to teach the children to read in English. Her use of her "enduring self" was limited to the support of that view.

Caroline was a teacher with whom I interacted frequently but had never worked with in any way other than consulting about the children in her classroom. Prior to teaching fifth grade, she was a first-grade teacher, and I served a few of her students in the Reading Recovery program. Regarding her "enduring" and her "situated" self at Elena, Caroline revealed both sides that she brought to her teaching interpretations. Many of her stories were related to her understanding of her mother's or her sister's teaching experiences, and at times she referred to her childhood experiences. Caroline was an outspoken teacher and was critical and aware of political issues beyond the classroom. She was one of the White teachers who vocally supported the bilingual program and who was willing to discuss race during the interviews. Caroline used her "enduring self" when she talked about the community and the effects of race on her perceptions about the children. Many times her experiences as a White woman guided her thoughts and provided a standard for her interpretations.

Bob was a close colleague of mine, and we talked almost weekly about school issues. Before I left the classroom, we both taught sixth grade in adjoining rooms and worked closely together. Bob depended on his "situated self" to inform his teaching reflections. Because of his many years of experience at Elena, he was helpful in placing an historical view on many of the current issues. Bob did not use his "enduring self" as it existed outside of the school, but he used his years of experience in the school as his "enduring self." His reference point many times was related to the political climate that influenced the school and how it had changed over the years.

Interviews

Since I had previous relationships with the participants, the interviews were extremely informal and conducted in ways aligned with our usual conversations. I asked questions of the teachers, but they also asked me questions. There was not a ritual pattern where I asked, they answered, and then I went to the next question. Reflexivity was an important component in my research design. The interviews were more akin to conversations. The only difference was that the focus on the topic of literacy was somewhat predetermined. Many researchers recognize their inability to be invisible or to affect the context they move within, and I was not exempt (Behar, 1993; Foley, 1995; Wolcott, 1994). Rather than attempt to erase my subjectivity and increase my distance, I attempted to embrace it and used my familiarity with the campus and the teachers to move discussions beyond simple answers. I began by stating very openly my beliefs about reading and children at Elena, as I was wont to do at faculty meetings and in conversations before the study. Aware that this would be a factor in how the participants responded to my queries, I felt it was vital that I be clear and maintain an openness that I hoped would be reciprocated. The adjustments made by the participants in relation to my stance on issues will never be fully known. But because of their familiarity with me and my views prior to the study, I believed that I should not present any new or contradictory views as I presumed to alter my role from peer to researcher. To do so would only serve to try to conceal my views and falsely construct a sense of objectivity that I believe to be impossible when studying educational issues. Honesty and straightforwardness were a continual goal, and many times I found that the participants corrected my views or added additional information if I asked questions with a leading slant. I was careful to follow the lead of the teachers. One teacher had read all of the questions carefully and written the answers down. Once we sat down to talk, I let her lead the discussion, and I only asked follow-up questions according to what she shared. Other interviews were less structured, and although I asked the same questions of all the participants, we often veered off onto other topics. Our storytelling became the main vehicle for gathering data.

"Interviewing" by Way of Storytelling

Pinar (1975) advocates the use of *currere* to unpack the reasoning behind teachers' conceptions of why they teach, what they teach, and how they teach. He goes to great lengths to explain the necessity of teachers exploring their self-understood reasons behind their practice. I hoped to open up the dialogue of not only how we teach, but who we are and how our identities shape our teaching. I openly shared my views as the interviews progressed, and we went through the different questions. We engaged in informal conversations, and I constantly tried to move away from my role as researcher and speak to the teachers as a peer. Every interview became an exchange of teaching stories. During my four years in graduate school, I had distanced myself from faculty meetings, committees, and grade-level team meetings. My exchanges were limited to my Reading Recovery team, and I had little interaction with classroom teachers about instruction. Revisiting the issues of literacy and school policy by sitting down individually with people I used to teach with was enlightening and refreshing. I asked them about teaching reading; they asked me about graduate school. In most cases we agreed on issues related to the literacy instruction, and in some cases we shared new information with each other. I gathered information from volunteers, so I realize that the sample of the teaching population at Elena was limited and not directly generalizable to any other population. But the themes I uncovered after data analysis mirror many ongoing conversations I had throughout the district in my interactions with teachers and student teachers. As we talked, we also shared our personal views and insights into what makes literacy instruction, and my familiarity with the teachers and the campus allowed for extended dialogues that many times lasted for hours.

Exploring the identities of teachers at Elena was crucial to pursuing the constructions they held of the children. In order to untangle the places where beliefs and knowledge intersected, I allowed space for teachers to articulate their identities as teachers in ways comfortable for them. Clandinin & Connelly (1995b) describe teachers' personal and practical knowledge as moving in and outside of classrooms. They state that teachers' knowledge is equivalent to convictions derived from their experiences, and these convictions (both conscious and unconscious) are expressed in their practices and their storytelling of themselves. Clandinin & Connelly (1995b) explain three desires teachers have to make sense of their teaching lives, through storytelling, as they relate to their personal lives: (1) the desire to tell stories as a form of meaning making; (2) the relationship of telling stories to others as an active construction of meaning which moves experiences into more educative areas; and (3) the reflective aspect of storytelling which alters past experiences into new interpretations. I used the act of storytelling to allow the teachers and myself to explore our own identities. It was similar to the way I had previously interacted with them daily, and I wished to preserve our relationships as much as possible.

I interacted with my secondary informants in ways consistent with our previous roles as well. My secondary informants were graduate students working at the university reading center, fellow teachers at Elena, and teachers in the middle schools where I supervised student interns. Once I opened up the invitation to participate to the teachers at Elena, I began to share my research questions informally with other colleagues and friends. I never divulged the identities of my official participants, but I did bring up the general ideas of literacy; literacy assessment; and the current state of local, state, and federal positions on the topic. This informal gathering of data served as a way for me to check and balance my findings at Elena with teachers' experiences around the district. My university contacts, as well as my position as an employee of the district, gave me insight into how information and notions about literacy flowed and was directed to teachers, to university academics, and to the new state reading designers.

Fieldnotes supplied me with a record of my thoughts not only about my own growth through this process, but of events that unfolded and interactions that occurred. I recorded and collected artifacts from school newsletters, took notes at faculty meetings, and made general observations about conversations

I continued to have with colleagues. In alignment with ethnographic methods, all individuals and the site will remain confidential. In cases where I used data from non-consenting sources, I did not identify them in order to protect their identities. I was familiar with similar research by many scholars (Foley, 1995; Scheper-Hughes, 2000) who had elected to study environments close to home, and I was aware of the possibility that the end result of my research may result in the very teachers I studied and worked with becoming angry because of my constructions of them. All of the participants were generous in their comments and extremely forthright; their honesty with me made the study richer, and it was crucial that I allowed them the chance to have final say in the transcripts. None of the teachers I interviewed altered or deleted any parts of their interviews. In order to keep the process as open as possible, I shared all interviews and drafts with my primary informants and many of my secondary informants. After the preliminary findings and themes were organized, I conducted review interviews with all of the participants, except Illeana, who had moved to another school and did not respond to emails. During the review interviews, I shared the overall results of the study and asked the participants' opinions. Many expressed an interest in reading the final study, and they will all receive copies of the final draft.

Data Analysis and Presentation

As I worked through the stories of teachers at Elena, I attempted to keep awake the notion that we all brought multiple identities to our teaching experiences. My identities as a teacher at Elena, a university student, and a literacy specialist played a large part in how I viewed the data. Many times I found myself perplexed and frustrated by the complexity of my perceptions and the teachers' views. In order to analyze and present the data in ways organized around specific themes, I relied on Blumenthal's (1999) idea of "multiple identities per consciousness":

> Leaving aside the notion that informants and interviewers co-create stories for the moment, and assuring that informants have separate and distinct narratives of their own to share, we can make sense of interviews differently if we assume multiple identities per consciousness. Rather than making sense of contradiction by "resolving" it into a linear story, we can construct a kind of "hypertext" narrative in which the informant's experience can be told completely differently dependent on which identity is pursued at any given moment . . . we can ask how they "story" life differently depending on which identity is placed at the fore. (p. 380)

Appendix 1: Research Methodology | 191

This study provides no specific "linear story." There are overriding themes which did emerge over several reviews of the data, but within each theme there are references to other themes and contradictions of previous ideas. Interview transcriptions and field notes were analyzed in several ways many times over. My first reading of the interviews came as I transcribed every tape myself. Once the transcripts were completed, I reread the interviews and categorized the responses according to my *a priori* questions. Gaining an overall record of how the teachers and administrators answered the general questions, I then began to revisit each interview and regroup individual quotes by topic. This opened up the themes to additional areas not previously focused on during the study. Topics such as high-stakes testing, home visits, the bilingual and special education program, and teachers' thoughts about the administration became clear.

The complexity of the responses required a multi-level data analysis, and representing the data in all of its intricacy required searching for a writing style that would illustrate a natural flow of information similar to the storytelling style of the participants. Rather than break up the quotes to serve each area of data, I left them intact during analysis and in the final piece. This forced me to revisit the teachers' stories in ways that remained more true to their initial thoughts and kept my perceptions as far as possible from the interpretation. I felt this choice was necessary to create balance and to provide some distance from my proximity to the setting and participants.

Although I realize there is no way to divorce myself from my positioning as a long-term teacher at Elena, it was vital to attempt some semblance of distance. I felt that I had a responsibility not only to share my stories with the participants of my study, but to "analyze" and organize the pieces of themselves they shared with me in ways befitting the identities I shared with them through methods comparable to studies executed by Frankenburg (1993) and Behar (1993). Frankenburg (1993) interviewed women for her study of Whiteness and found herself sharing stories of her own struggles with race, while Behar (1993) found herself intertwined with the woman whose story she "translated." At Elena, I was a White teacher in a school of color attempting to teach children to read under great pressure from the state. To position myself during data collection or data analysis as anyone other than a White reading teacher would also have placed me in the precarious position of assuming I knew more than the teachers did, and I sincerely believed that was not the case. My experiences as a researcher had given me the opportunity to read theories and make connections. My ambition with this study was to share the theories and let the teachers' theories and voices shine.

Limitations

This study has many limitations. I did not interview any students or parents. I did not pursue many of the areas addressed in detail because of the broad focus of the original questions I sought to answer. Due to the ethnographic nature of the design, I purposefully included lengthy quotes by teachers to show the complex and often contradictory relationship between their love for the children and their knowledge and beliefs about their capabilities. These elaborate stories were difficult to categorize into discrete themes and were a constant reminder of the challenge of representing the often contradictory data in all of its complexity.

Further study focused on the contradictory nature of the teachers' statements made regarding the children is necessary. The teachers' complex and shifting notions of their roles, their constructions of their own identities as teachers, and their responsive constructions of the children as students are evident, yet relatively unexamined here. Holland et al.'s (1998) conception of identities as figurative and positional could be further used to illustrate how the teachers placed varying expectations and definitions on the literacy abilities of the community and the children depending on the defining circumstances they used. These notions were evident when teachers discussed their ideal child versus the children at Elena.

These teachers were knowledgeable about literacy, and their positioning was multifaceted. They brought in beliefs from their experiences outside of schools and used it to enhance and redefine their conceptions of literacy. Asking a teacher to define literacy in a theoretical sense and then in a practical sense is a difficult task and required the participants to change their positioning in each instance. This changing of positioning resulted in the teachers contradicting themselves many times. Some teachers used their experiences as parents, some used their childhood experiences, and others compared Elena to other schools. The contradictions may be unsettling for those seeking definitive "results," and it may appear that the teachers were unsure.

Yet the critical nature of literacy, as defined by Giroux (1997), Freire (1970), and Macedo (1994) would embrace the teachers' struggles and inability to simplify such a complicated issue as literacy and leave it as a testament to their high degree of knowledge. The more that is known, the more questions arise, and teachers who possess unequivocal, definitive answers are teachers who are unaware of the myriad variables enacted when literacy is presented to children.

A more systematic investigation of this area would be beneficial for research purposes and for the teachers by returning the study back to the site of the school. A substantial part of the limitations of this area of the study lies in how the process stopped short of what would move the contradictions into a more helpful dialogue for the teachers. The next step would be to bring the data back to the staff and allow more in-depth debate around the greater shared ideas across the group and the individual contradictions so prevalent within each teacher's interviews. The idea of colonial literacy was not shared with the teachers, as this part of the data analysis came after the completion of the study.

My own positioning limits the study in that it would be difficult to "replicate" in any more traditional notion of "research." Those audiences requiring "research-based" data would not find this exploration appealing and would tend to discount the subjective nature of the design itself. My long-standing residence at Elena was layered with various experiences, and my tendency to measure the present by the past provided a perspective slanted toward a clearly specified agenda. Greene (1988) explains the role of my initial views of Elena and later as a fourteen-year teacher and researcher at Elena: "The effects of early experience survive, along with the sedimentations of meaning left by encounters with a changing world" (p. 8). I am a creation of my earliest experiences at Elena. As a beginning teacher, I was greatly influenced both by the strong Latina teachers and the principal's commitment to the community. I was also explicitly taught that culture was valuable and that my culture was a dominating force to be critically examined.

·APPENDIX TWO·

(2001) 77TH LEGISLATURE

Again, the Texas Legislature clarified its message to Texas educators that all Texas children have the right to learn to read. They maintained a clear focus to end social promotion. Legislators expanded the teacher reading academy training into grades 3 and 4. In addition, they expanded the Accelerated Reading Intervention funding into grades 2 and 3, but at a lower dollar amount than in previous years.

After each legislative session, Texas lawmakers have made it clear that their top priority is high quality teaching and research-based instructional practice. Diagnostic assessment will drive instruction in the classroom. Superintendents, principals, and teachers will be held accountable for student performance. Immediate intervention will be provided for students struggling to learn to read in a variety of instructional formats. Texas children deserve nothing less.

The Texas Legislative Budget Board has set a performance measure for the Texas Education Agency. Ninety-five percent of the 3rd graders in 2003 must pass the newly designed reading portion of the Texas Assessment of Knowledge and Skills (TAKS), which will replace the Texas Assessment of Academic Skills (TAAS).

In 2001 86% of the Texas 3rd graders passed the reading portion of the TAAS. The "bar of excellence" has been raised. Now, not only must 95% of the 2003 third graders pass the reading portion of the TAKS, but also the test will have an increased level of difficulty.

Test designers for the TAKS have emphasized assessment of good instruction, not assessment of the TAAS test preparation materials. Test makers state that students who perform well in daily classroom instruction will perform well on the TAKS. (http://www.tea.state.tx.us/reading/model/legifound.html)

NOTES

Chapter 1

1. To view a table of all of the participants and their years of experience, see Appendix One.
2. The 2001 legislation for the Texas Reading Initiative can be found in Appendix Two.
3. For more information on the organization and development of the research used in the Texas Reading Initiative, see Denny Taylor (1998) and Richard L. Allington (2002).

Chapter 2

1. The Iowa Test of Basic Skills was given to grades 1–6 at Elena for years. The PALM replaced it briefly, but the ITBS has since returned.

Chapter 3

1. In the summer of 2002, I was trained by the Reading Academy to train third-grade teachers. Some principals required their teachers to attend the reading academies, but by definition they were voluntary and open to any teacher teaching the specific grade addressed by each section of training. The academy training lasted four days, and teachers were required to attend all four days in order to receive compensation. There were no accountability tools in place to ensure that teachers returned to their classrooms to teach according to the information and methods recommended by the academy.
2. This research stance originates from The Committee on the Prevention of Reading Difficulties in Young Children. Their report, *Preventing Reading Difficulties in Young Children*, adhered to these definitions of research. "These principles derive

from our commitment to the scientific method (1) science aims for knowledge that is publicly verifiable, (2) science seeks testable theories—not unquestioned edicts, (3) science employs methods of systematic empiricism." (National Research Council, 1998, p. 33)

3. The National Reading Panel was the result of the 1997 inquiry by Congress and the National Institute of Child Health and Human Development (NICHD) to commission "a national panel to assess the status of research-based knowledge, including the effectiveness of various approaches to teaching children to read" (National Reading Panel, 1999, p. 1).

Chapter 4

1. The state provided Texas teachers with the opportunity to receive training through a university course or a state region center course to acquire a Master Reading Teacher Certification. The certification allowed teachers to become literacy advisors on their campus and to receive additional stipends for their work, which was conducted in addition to their regular responsibilities in the classroom.

2. Project READ was a programmed training model for teachers geared toward special education that emphasized a systematic, phonics-based approach to teaching struggling readers to decode words. Elena had argued against using the program several times in order to pursue other alternatives for struggling readers.

Chapter 6

1. Text posted on the Austin Independent School District's Website. Submitted by Pascal D. Forgione, Jr., Ph.D., Superintendent as "A Letter to the Austin Community: The Austin Blueprint to Leave No Child Behind" on April 1, 2002.

2. Mr. Soza was the principal in residence from 1987 to 1992. He was extremely proactive and empowered teachers to seek out research and programs to best fit the needs of the community and the school.

BIBLIOGRAPHY

A Nation at Risk (1983). http://www.ncrel.org/sdrs/areas/issues/content/cntareas/science/sc3risk.htm

Adams, M. J. (1990). *Beginning to read: Thinking and learning about print*. Cambridge, MA: The MIT Press.

Allington, R. L. (2002). *Big brother and the national reading curriculum: How ideology trumped evidence*. Portsmouth, NH: Heinemann.

Apple, M. W. (1986). *Teachers and texts: A Political economy of class and gender relations in education*. New York: Routledge and Kegan Paul.

Apple, M. W. (2001). *Educating the "right way": Markets, standards, god, and inequality*. New York: Routledge Falmer.

Ashton-Warner, S. (1963). *Teacher*. New York: Simon & Schuster.

Au, Kathryn H. (2000). "A Multicultural Perspective on Policies for Improving Literacy Achievement; Equity and Excellence," in Kamil, Michael L.; Mosenthal, Peter B.; Pearson, P. David; and Barr, Rebecca, eds., *Handbook of Reading Research*, Vol. III. (pp. 835–852). Mahwah: New Jersey: Lawrence Erlbaum Associates.

Auerbach, E. (1995). Deconstructing the discourse of strengths in family literacy. *Journal of Reading Behavior, 27*, 643–660.

Austin Independent School District website (2002). http://www.austin.isd.tenet.edu/

Baker, C. (1996). (2nd ed). *Foundations of bilingual education and bilingualism*. Philadelphia, PA: Multilingual Matters.

Behar, R. (1993). *Translated woman*. Boston, MA: Beacon Press.

Bell, D. (1992). *Faces at the bottom of the well: The permanence of racism*. New York: Basic Books.

Berliner, D. C., and Biddle, B. J. (1995). *The manufactured crisis*. New York: Addison-Wesley Publishing Company.

Blanck, G. (1990). Vygotsky: The man and his cause. In L. C. Moll (Ed.), *Vygotsky and education: Instructional implications of sociohistorical psychology* (pp. 31–58). Cambridge University Press.

Blumenthal, D. (1999). Representing the divided self. *Qualitative Inquiry*, 5, 377–392.

Bobbit, F. (1918). *The curriculum*. Boston: Houghton Mifflin.

Bruner, J. (1959). The process of education. Cambridge, MA: Harvard University Press.

Cairney, T. H. (1995). Developing parent partnerships in secondary literacy learning. *Journal of Reading*, 38 (7) pp. 520–526.

Chall, J. S. (1967). *Learning to read: The great debate*. New York: McGraw Hill.

Clandinin, D. J., and Connelly, F. M. (Eds.) (1995). *Teachers' Professional Knowledge Landscapes: Secret, Sacred, and Cover Stories. Advances in contemporary educational thought series*. Soltis, J. F. (Ed). (Vol. 15) (pp. 3–15). New York: Teachers College Press.

Clay, M. M. (1991). *Becoming literate: The construction of inner control*. Portsmouth, NH: Heinemann.

Cochran-Smith, M., and Lytle, S. L. (1993). *Inside/outside: Teacher research and knowledge*. New York: Teachers College Press.

Cole, M. (1985). Cognitive development and formal schooling: The evidence from cross-cultural research. In *Culture, communication and cognition: Vygotskian perspectives*. New York: Cambridge University Press.

Cole, M., and Engestrom, Y. (1993). "A Cultural-Historical Approach to Distributed Cognition," in Salomon, G., Ed., *Distributed Cognitions: Psychological and Educational Considerations* (pp. 1–46). Cambridge: Cambridge University Press.

Coles, G. (2000). *Misreading reading: The bad science that hurts children*. Portsmouth, NH: Heinemann.

Crawford, J. (1989). *Bilingual education: History, politics, theory and practice*. Trenton, N.J: Crane Publishing.

Delgado, R. (1997). Rodrigo's eleventh chronicle: Empathy and false empathy. Delgado, R., and Stefancic, J. (eds.) *Critical white studies: Looking behind the mirror* (pp. 614–618). Philadelphia, PA: Temple University Press.

Delgado-Gaitan, C. (1993). Researching change and changing the researcher. *Harvard Educational Review*, 63 (4), 389–411.

Delgado-Gaitan, C. (1986). Teacher attitudes on diversity affecting student socio-academic responses: An ethnographic view. *Journal of Adolescent Research*, 1, 103–14.

Delpit, L. (1995). *Other people's children: Cultural conflict in the classroom*. New York: The New Press.

Derman-Sparks (1997). Teaching and learning anti-racism: A developmental approach. New York: Teachers College Press.

Dewey, J. (1990). *The school and society/the child and the curriculum*. (Reissued 1990 ed.) Chicago, IL: University of Chicago Press.

Feagin, J. R., and Vera, H. (1995). *White racism: The basics*. New York: Routledge.

Feagin, J. R. (2000). *Racist America: Roots, current realities and future preparations*. New York: Routledge.

Finn, C. E. (1991). *We must take charge*. New York: The Free Press.

Flesch, R. (1955). *Why Johnny can't read and what you can do about it*. New York: Harper & Brothers.

Foley, D. E. (1995). *The heartland chronicles*. Philadelphia, PA: University of Pennsylvania Press.

Foley, D. E. (1997). Deficit thinking models based on culture: The anthropological protest. In R. R. Valencia (ed.), *The Evolution of deficit thinking: Educational thought and practice* (pp. 113–131). The Stanford Series on Education & Public Policy. Washington, DC: The Falmer Press.

Frankenburg, R. (1993). *White women, race matters*. Minneapolis, MN: University of Minnesota Press.

Frankenburg, R. (1997). *Displacing whiteness*. Durham, NC: Duke University Press.

Freire, P. (1970). *Pedagogy of the oppressed*. New York: The Continuum Publishing Company.

Freire, P. (1987). *Literacy: Reading the word and the world*. Hadleigh, MA: Bergin and Garvey Publishers, Inc.

Gandara, R. (2000). How we live: A Latino enclave in east Austin. *Austin American-Statesman*, July 30.

Giroux, H. A. (1997). *Pedagogy and the politics of hope*. Boulder, CO: Westview Press.

Glasser, W. (1992). *The quality school: managing students without coercion*. New York : Harper Perennial.

Glesne, C., and Peshkin, A. (1992). *Becoming qualitative researchers*. White Plains, NY: Longman.

Graff, H. J. (1995). *The labyrinths of literacy*. Pittsburgh, PA: University of Pittsburgh Press.

Greene, M. (1988). *The dialectic of freedom*. New York: Teachers College Press.

Guerra, J. C. (1998). *Close to home: Oral and literate practices in a transnational Mexicano community*. New York: Teachers College Press.

Gutierrez, K. D. (1994). How talk, context, and script shape contexts for learning: A cross-case comparison of journal sharing. *Linguistics and Education*, 5, 335–65.

Haladyna, T., Nolen, S. B., and Haas, N. S. (1991). Raising standardized achievement test scores and the origins of test pollution. *Educational Researcher*, 20 (5), 2–7.

Hamachek, D. (1999). Effective teachers: What they do, how they do it, and the importance of self-knowledge. In R. P. Lipka and T. M. Brinthaupt (eds.), *The role of self in teacher development*. (pp. 189–224). Albany, NY: State University of New York Press.

Heath, S. B. (1983). *Ways with words: Language, life, and work in communities and classrooms*. New York: Cambridge University Press.

Helms, J. E. (1984). Toward a theoretical explanation of the effects of race on counseling: A Black and White model. *The Counseling Psychologist*, 12 (4), 153–165.

Helms, J. E. (1990). *Black and White racial identity: Theory, research, and practice*. New York: Greenwood Press.

Hillocks, G. (2002).*The testing trap: How state writing assessments control learning*. New York: Teachers College Press.

Hoffman, J., Assaf, L. C., Paris, S. G. (2001). "High stakes testing in reading: Today in Texas, tomorrow? *The Reading Teacher*, 54 (5) 484–492.

Holland, D., Lachicotte, W., Skinner, D., and Cain, C. (1998). *Identity and agency in cultural worlds*. Cambridge, MA: Harvard University Press.

IDEA Proficiency Test (IPT). (2002). http://www.ncela.gwu.edu/miscpubs/eacwest/elptests.htm#IPT.

Kincheloe, J. L. and Steinberg, S. R. (1998). Addressing the crisis of Whiteness: Reconfiguring White identity in a pedagogy of Whiteness. *White Reign: Deploying Whiteness in America* (pp. 3–29). New York: St. Martin's Griffin.

King. J. E. (1997). Dysconscious racism: Ideology, identity, and miseducation. in Delgado, R., and Stefancic, J., Eds., *Critical White Studies: Looking Behind the Mirror*. Philadelphia: Temple University Press.

Kozol, J. (1991). *Savage inequalities*. New York: Harper Perennial.

Ladson-Billings, G. (1994). *The Dreamkeepers*. San Francisco, CA: Jossey-Bass Publishers.

Ladson-Billings, G. (1995). Toward a theory of culturally relevant pedagogy. *American Educational Research Journal, 32*, 465–91.

Lather, P. (1991). *Getting smart: Feminist research and pedagogy within the postmodern*. New York: Routledge.

Lewis, C. S. (1961). *The screwtape letters*. New York: Simon & Schuster.

Lima, E. S., and Lima, M. G. (1998). Identity, cultural diversity, and education. In E. T. Trueba & Y. Zou (eds.), *Ethnic identity and power: Cultural contexts of political action in school and society* (pp. 312–343). Albany, NY: State University of New York Press.

Lott, T. (1994a, February 8). "33,000 Austin Students 'at-risk,'" *Austin American Statesman*, pp. A1, A7.

Macedo, D. (1994). *Literacies of Power: What Americans Are Not Allowed to Know*. Boulder : Westview Press.

Madaus, G. F. (1988).The influence of testing on the curriculum. In L. N. Tanner (Ed.), *Critical issues in curriculum: 87th yearbook of the National Society for the Study of Education* (pp. 83–121). Chicago: University of Chicago Press.

Mahoney, M. (1997a). Racial construction and women as differentiated actors. In R. Delgado and J. Stefancic (eds.), *Critical white studies: Looking behind the mirror* (pp. 305–309) Philadelphia, PA: Temple University Press.

Mahoney, M. (1997b). The social construction of whiteness. In R. Delgado & J. Stefancic (eds.), *Critical white studies: Looking behind the mirror* (pp.330–333). Philadelphia, PA: Temple University Press.

Marty, D. (1998). White antiracist rhetoric as apologia: Wendell Berry's The Hidden Wound. In Nakayama, T. & Martin, J. (Eds.), *Whiteness: The communication of social identity* (pp. 51–68). Thousand Oaks, CA: Sage.

McIntosh, P. (1988). Working Paper 189. *White privilege and male privilege: A personal account of coming to see correspondences through work in women's studies*. Wellesley, MA: Wellesley College Center for Research on Women.

Moll, L. C., Amanti, C., Neff, D., and Gonzales, N. (1992). Funds of knowledge for teaching: Using a qualitative approach to connect homes and classrooms. *Theory into Practice, 31*, 132–41.

Moon, D. (1998).White enculturation and bourgeois ideology: The discursive production of "good (white) girls. In Nakayama, T. and Martin, J. (Eds.), *Whiteness: The communication of social identity* (pp. 177–197). Thousand Oaks, CA: Sage.

Moss, P. (1994). Can there be validity without reliability? *Educational Researcher*, 23, 5–12.

National Assessment of Educational Progress (2001). http://www.cde.ca.gov/statetests/naep/naep.html

Nespor, J. (1987). The role of beliefs in the practice of teaching. *Journal of Curriculum Studies*, 19, 317–328.

Nieto, S. (1999). *The light in their eyes: Creating multicultural learning communities.* New York: Teachers College Press.

No Child Left Behind Website (2002). http://www.ed.gov/nclb/landing.jhtml

Oakes, J. (1985). *Keeping track: How schools structure inequality.* New Haven, CT: Yale University Press.

Paige, R. (2003). http://www.ed.gov/PressReleases/06–2003/06 102003.html

Pajares, F. M. (1992). Teachers' beliefs and educational research: Cleaning up a messy construct. *Review of Educational Research*, 62, 307–32.

Pinar, W. F. (1975). Currere: Toward reconceptualization. In W. F. Pinar (ed.), *Curriculum theorizing: The reconceptualists.* (pp. 396–414). Berkeley, CA: McCutchan Publishing Corporation.

Polakow, V. (1993). *Lives on the edge: Single mothers and their children in the other America.* Chicago: University of Chicago Press.

Purcell-Gates, V. (2000). "Family literacy," in Kamil, Michael L.; Mosenthal, Peter B.; Pearson, P. David; and Barr, Rebecca, eds., *Handbook of reading research, Vol. III* (pp. 853–870). Mahwah: NJ: Lawrence Erlbaum Associates.

Reed-Danahay, D. E. (ed.) (1997). *Auto/ethnography: Rewriting the self and the social.* New York: Berg.

Rodriguez (1998). Rodrigo's eleventh chronicle: Empathy and false empathy. In R. Delgado and J. Stefancic (eds.), *Critical white studies: Looking behind the mirror* (pp. 614–618). Philadelphia, PA: Temple University Press.

Schaafsma, D. (1993). *Eating on the streets: Teaching literacy in a multicultural society.* Pittsburgh, PA: University of Pittsburgh Press.

Scheper-Hughes, N. (2000). Ire in Ireland. *Ethnography*, 1, 118–40.

Scheurich, J. J., and Imber, M. (1997).Educational reforms can reproduce societal inequalities: A case study. In J. J. Scheurich (ed.), *Research Method in the Postmodern* (pp. 8–28). Washington, DC: The Falmer Press.

Scheurich, J. J., and Young, M. D. (1997). Coloring epistemologies: Are our epistemologies racially biased? (An Example of an Archaeological Approach), In J. J. Scheurich (ed.), *Research Method in the Postmodern* (pp. 132–158). Washington, DC: The Falmer Press.

Scribner, S. (1984). Literacy in three metaphors. *American Journal of Education*, 93, 6–21.

Scribner, S., and Cole, M. (1978). Literacy without schooling: Testing for intellectual effects. *Harvard Educational Review*, 48, 448–461.

Shannon, P. (1996). Literacy and educational policy: part two. *Journal of Literacy Research*, 28 (3) 429–449.

Shepard, L. A. (2000). The role of assessment in a learning culture. *Educational Researcher*, 29, 4–13.

Skinner, Q. (ed.) (1985). *The return to grand theory*. New York: Cambridge University Press.

Smith, N. B. (1965). *American reading instruction*. Newark, DE: The International Reading Association.

Spindler, G. (ed.) (2000). *Fifty years of anthropology and education*. Mahwah, NJ: Lawrence Erlbaum Associates.

Spindler, G., and L. (1998). Cultural politics of the white ethni-class in the mid-nineties. In T. E. Trueba and Y. Zou (eds.), *Ethnic identity and power: Cultural contexts of political action in school and society* (pp. 27–47). Albany, NY: State University of New York Press.

Star Reading. (2004). http://www.renlearn.com/starreading/default.htm. Wisconsin Rapids, Wisconsin Renaissance Learning, Inc

Street, B. V. (1995). *Social literacies: Critical approaches to literacy in development, ethnography and education*. New York: Longman Group Limited.

Tatum, B. D. (1997). *Why are all the black kids sitting together in the cafeteria?* New York: Basic Books.

Taylor, D. (1998). *Beginning to read and the spin doctors of science: The political campaign to change America's mind about how children learn to read*. Urbana, IL: National Council of Teachers of English.

TEA Website. (2002). http://www.tea.state.tx.us/

Texas Education Agency Website, 2002.

Third Grade Teacher Reading Academy, 2002.

Trueba, H. T. (1988a). Culturally based explanations of minority students' academic achievement. *Anthropology and Education Quarterly*, 19, 270–87.

Trueba, H. T. (1988b). English literacy acquisition: From cultural trauma to learning disabilities in minority students. *Linguistics in Education*, 1, 125–152.

Trueba, H. T. (1990). The role of culture in literacy acquisition: An interdisciplinary approach to qualitative research. *International Journal of Qualitative Studies in Education*, 3 (1) 231–43.

Trueba, H. T. (1993). Culture and language: The ethnographic approach to the study of learning environments. In B. Merino, H. T. Trueba and F. Samanigo (eds.), *Language and culture in learning: Teaching Spanish to native speakers of Spanish* (pp. 26–44). London: Falmer Press.

Trueba, H. T. (1999). Critical ethnography and a Vygotskian pedagogy of hope: The empowerment of Mexican immigrant children. *Qualitative Studies in Education*, 12, 591–614.

U.S. Department of Education (1991). *America 2000: An education strategy, revised*. Washington, D.C.

Valdes, G. (1996). *Con respecto: Bridging the distances between culturally diverse families and schools*. New York: Teachers College Press.

Valencia, R. R., and Solorzano, D. G. (1997). Contemporary deficit thinking. In R. R. Valencia (ed.), *The evolution of deficit thinking: Educational thought and practice* (pp. 160–210). The Stanford Series on Education & Public Policy. Washington, DC: The Falmer Press.

Valenzuela, A. (1999). *Subtractive schooling.* Albany, NY: State University of New York Press.

Van Maanen, J. (1988). *Tales of the field: On writing ethnography.* Chicago, IL: University of Chicago Press.

Vygotsky, L. S. (ed.) (1978). *Mind in society.* Cambridge, MA: Harvard University Press.

Wertsch, J. (1985). The voice of rationality in a sociocultural approach to mind. In M. Cole (ed.), *Culture, communication and cognition: Vygotskian perspectives* (pp. 111–126). New York: Cambridge University Press.

Wildman, S. M. and Davis, A. D. (1998). Making systems of privilege visible. In R. Delgado and J. Stefancic (eds.), *Critical white studies: Looking behind the mirror* (pp. 314–319). Philadelphia, PA: Temple University Press.

Winfield, L. F. (1986). Teacher beliefs toward academically at risk students in inner urban schools. *The Urban Review,* 18, 253–68.

Wolcott, H. F. (1994). *Transforming qualitative data.* Thousand Oaks, CA: Sage Publications.

Woolf, V. (1929). *A room of one's own.* New York: Harcourt Brace & Company.

Studies in the Postmodern Theory of Education

General Editors
Joe L. Kincheloe & Shirley R. Steinberg

Counterpoints publishes the most compelling and imaginative books being written in education today. Grounded on the theoretical advances in criticalism, feminism, and postmodernism in the last two decades of the twentieth century, Counterpoints engages the meaning of these innovations in various forms of educational expression. Committed to the proposition that theoretical literature should be accessible to a variety of audiences, the series insists that its authors avoid esoteric and jargonistic languages that transform educational scholarship into an elite discourse for the initiated. Scholarly work matters only to the degree it affects consciousness and practice at multiple sites. Counterpoints' editorial policy is based on these principles and the ability of scholars to break new ground, to open new conversations, to go where educators have never gone before.

For additional information about this series or for the submission of manuscripts, please contact:
Joe L. Kincheloe & Shirley R. Steinberg
c/o Peter Lang Publishing, Inc.
275 Seventh Avenue, 28th floor
New York, New York 10001

To order other books in this series, please contact our Customer Service Department:
(800) 770-LANG (within the U.S.)
(212) 647-7706 (outside the U.S.)
(212) 647-7707 FAX

Or browse online by series:
www.peterlangusa.com